Business Management and Enterprise

A Resource for Year 11 General

Elizabeth Criddle
Jason Hinton
Rumeena Nizam

Business Management and Enterprise: A Resource for Year 11 General
1st Edition
Elizabeth Criddle
Jason Hinton
Rumeena Nizam

Cover design: Leanne Quince, GraphicsAbove

Any URLs contained in this publication were checked for currency during the production process. Note, however, that the publisher cannot vouch for the ongoing currency of URLs.

First published by Impact Publishing in 2014

For product information and technology assistance,
in Australia call **1300 790 853**;
in New Zealand call **0800 449 725**

For permission to use material from this text or product, please email **aust.permissions@cengage.com**

ISBN 978 1 92 196579 1

Cengage Learning Australia
Level 7, 80 Dorcas Street
South Melbourne, Victoria Australia 3205

Cengage Learning New Zealand
Unit 4B Rosedale Office Park
331 Rosedale Road, Albany, North Shore 0632, NZ

For learning solutions, visit **cengage.com.au**

Printed in China by 1010 Printing International Limited
4 5 6 7 8 9 24

Acknowledgements

The authors would like to gratefully acknowledge family and friends for their feedback on particular sections of the text.

Contents

Contents

INTRODUCTION

OVERVIEW

The authors of Business Management and Enterprise believe strongly in the importance of business knowledge to the everyday lives of Australians. In this text, students will be encouraged to be innovative and creative in their approach to the world of opportunity offered by business. They will explore the perspectives of both employees and managers. The Year 11 General Course will provide students with the enthusiasm to commence their own small, local business. Students studying this subject should gain a better understanding of their role and rights as an employee, as well as the responsibilities of employers.

The study of Business Management and Enterprise will provide the knowledge and resources required to support entrepreneurial students to turn an idea, skill or service into a business and gain self employment. It will give them the creative skills and understandings to adapt ideas innovatively. We believe all students should be able to pursue and realise opportunities for innovation.

This subject encourages the development of entrepreneurship, shows how it can be done and give sources of support and advice. An ability to be entrepreneurial is vital in many areas of life, and will support students beyond the business world.

Business Management and Enterprise will also provide important career and life skills to assist students with understanding the world around them, and their impact on this world as a consumer, business operator, employee and citizen.

USING THE TEXT

LEARNING CONTEXTS	
Unit 1: Establishing a small business	Unit 2: Operating a small business
• Micro business	• Small local business
• Deli	• Home based business
• Greengrocer	• Franchises
• Fast food store	• Single service or good
• Newsagency	
• Restaurant	

UNIT CONTENT		
Environments	**Strategies and processes**	**People**
• Political and legal • Economic • Socio-cultural • Technological	• Management • Marketing • Operations	• Intrapersonal and interpersonal • Consumers and competitors • Human resources

ACTIVITIES
Check understanding, Business research, Response, Group projects (contained in this text) Slide presentations, Interactive quizzes (contained on the support Download)

COURSE OUTCOMES		
Outcome 1: Business concepts	**Outcome 2: Business in society**	**Outcome 3: Innovation and Operations**
Students understand the concepts, structures and factors underpinning business performance.	Students understand the interrelationships between business and society.	Students demonstrate knowledge, skills and processes required to manage business operations.

Each of these is explained below.

Learning contexts

The learning contexts for each unit are representative examples, and other contexts may be chosen. Programming can occur within a particular learning context. After the context or contexts are selected, relevant unit content is used from within the text.

Unit content

The content for each unit of Business Management and Enterprise is split into three main sections. These main sections form the structure of the text and are as follows.

- **Environments:** political and legal, economic, socio-cultural and technological (PEST)
- **Strategies and processes:** management, marketing and operations
- **People**

Alongside the unit content in the text, there is a coloured column containing supporting information:

1. **Real world examples:** these are examples of scenarios from real life, applying the theory from the text content. They give sample situations illustrating course theory.

2. **Definition:** important terms are clarified right next to the information where they are found, so that terminology is explained within a context.

BUSINESS CONCEPTS
A real world example is provided here.

Definition: the meaning of the highlighted word is given here.

The unit content outlined in the text is studied in conjunction with a range of relevant activities.

Activities

Activities are found at the end of each chapter or on the support Download. They have been split up as follows.

Check understanding

These are aimed at checking basic comprehension of the unit content in the previous chapter. They require the student to be able to define and explain terms and theories.

Business research

These are activities and worksheets available on the internet, or a question that must be researched using web resources. All directly relate to the content of the particular chapter and allow for interactive application of skills and knowledge.

Response

These are higher level questions which require the student to apply knowledge from the chapter to a variety of situations, or require higher order thinking such as analysis and justification.

Group projects

These are activities that suggest ways for students to work in groups to allow for interactive application of learnings.

Slide presentations

The slide presentations contained on the Download summarise concepts from the text in an illustrative way, and provide the opportunity for students to present information to one another, or for the teacher to present new concepts to the class in a visual manner.

Interactive quizzes

Contained on the Download, these are interactive multiple choice questions for students to complete, either as an individual or as part of a group. They are told immediately if their answer is correct, and are allowed to have another attempt if they are incorrect.

All activities prepare students to tackle the more complex tasks that form part of the assessment of the course.

Course outcomes

Outcome 1: Business concepts

Students understand the concepts, structures and factors underpinning business performance.

In achieving this outcome, students:

- understand marketing
- understand how leadership and management function
- understand how organisational practices, procedures and structures function.

Outcome 2: Business in society

Students understand the interrelationships between business and society.

In achieving this outcome, students:

- understand the impact of beliefs and values on business activity
- understand the impact of economic environments, government policies and legal requirements on business activity
- understand the impact of technologies on business activity.

Outcome 3: Innovation and operations

Students demonstrate knowledge, skills and processes required to manage business operations.

In achieving this outcome, students:

- apply business skills, tools and processes
- process and translate information required for effective business operations
- demonstrate interpersonal skills required for effective business operations
- investigate and evaluate innovative and enterprising opportunities.

USING THE DOWNLOAD

Student resources

The student resources on the support Download include interactive quizzes and slide presentations. These short presentations can be completed by students in a collaborative manner. The slide presentations relate to a specific section of the content of the course, indicated in the name of the presentation. Each quiz contains ten multiple choice questions pertaining to an entire section of the course content.

Teacher resources

The teacher resource section of the support Download includes a sample program for both units. This program contains suggested themes, outcomes, unit content, assessments and learning contexts.

A Marking Guide for the 'Check Your Understanding' Activities in the text book is provided in the Download. These are suggested responses only and should form the basis for further classroom discussion.

UNIT 1
SECTION A: ENVIRONMENTS
CHAPTER 1
Business Opportunities

'Sometimes when you innovate, you make mistakes. It is best to admit them quickly, and get on with improving your other innovations.'

– Steve Jobs –

A business operates within a community. This community has many levels; local, state, national and international. A business must manage relationships and the impacts of not just their customers and suppliers but also governments, citizens, businesses and technologies at all these levels. Businesses do not operate in isolation and to build ongoing success it is vital to monitor, understand and respond to the environment.

It is about identifying opportunities and threats, anticipating change and risk, identifying stakeholders and managing compliance with government and industry regulations. By doing this a business can be proactive in its fight for survival in a competitive environment.

Important aspects of the business environment are:

- social, cultural and economic
- political and legal
- technological.

The topics in this chapter are:

- Reasons for starting a business
- Identifying business opportunities
- Innovation and entrepreneurship
- Innovation and growth

INNOVATION AND ENTERPRISE

In a national online survey Mortgage Choice[1] reports the two main reasons why Australians want to buy a franchise are the potential to earn higher income and the chance to improve their lifestyle. Other reasons include being able to have more control over balancing work and life, looking for stimulation, challenge and personal achievement and being able to use life experiences.

REASONS FOR STARTING A BUSINESS

An enterprising person is someone who has original and creative ideas and is able to take business concepts into action. They have the ability to recognise business opportunities and are able to motivate and lead others to achieve business goals. It is a big step for an individual to take these ideas and abilities and start their own business.

---

1   Mortgage Choice, www.mortgagechoice.com.au, accessed 10 January 2008.

Business is a part of the community. Small business owners have a significant role in the community. Through their business they have working relationships with and contribute to the standard of living of customers, employees and suppliers. The families of all these people benefit from the business activity and all rely on business success for their quality of life.

Some reasons for wanting to start a business are included in Figure 1.1.

Wealth creation

Generating revenue and maximising profits are the main goals of a business. Business owners benefit by receiving income and business profit. A business owner also increases their wealth through investments in capital such as buildings, vehicles, inventory and equipment.

Figure 1.1: Reasons for starting a business

Business ownership and growth is often financed through debt. Although there may be an increase in assets on paper the true indicator of wealth is net assets or the amount of equity in the business. Wealth may also be created from the reputation and goodwill of a business. The value of the brand and the potential for future success will increase the sale price if an owner decides to sell their business.

Employment options

Continuing employment is dependent on the decisions and success of the employer. Business owners have more control over employment opportunities and choices. Small business owners make decisions about how and where to work. That might be from home, part time, school hours or online and adapting as needed. This flexibility may not be available to an employee.

You may have a skill that is not being used as an employee or a dream of running a business. Starting your own business will create the freedom to pursue personal goals and vision, rather than working to achieve someone else's goals.

BUSINESS IN SOCIETY

There are 211,203 small businesses in WA, representing about 96% of all businesses. Australia wide, small business employs more than 45% of private sector employees.

Financial security

A business creates wealth and earns income for the benefit of the owners. An employee is paid a salary but the majority of the wealth is retained in the business and distributed to owners. An owner of a successful small business will receive the benefit of wealth and profit earned. The amount that is possible to be earned as a business owner can be significantly larger than as an employee.

Small businesses are expensive to run and must be managed well to ensure they are profitable. As a sole trader, business and personal financial security are at risk.

Innovation

Through business an owner can be an **entrepreneur** and pursue an interest, develop ideas and create an enterprise.

Starting a business gives people the chance to develop an **innovation**, to turn new ideas and new ways of doing things into business success. Creating a new product or a new service is risky and an established employer may not be interested in taking on the challenge and financial risk. The only option may be to start a small business and try to turn the innovative idea into a successful business.

INNOVATION AND OPERATIONS

A survey by the ABS in 2005 found that business is responsible for 88% of all innovation in Australia. This refers to the transition from an idea in a laboratory or research centre to a successful business. Another contribution is through the education system. Innovation and research in Australia creates world leading tertiary institutions, scientists, engineers and technologists.

BUSINESS IN SOCIETY

In 2013 Australia ranked second with a score of 8.12 out of 10 on a Quality of Life Index list. Switzerland was first with an index of 8.22. The index is calculated based on a survey of factors including availability of consumer goods, economic conditions, shopping convenience, health services and housing. A strong business sector providing these goods and services will lead to a higher index.

Entrepreneur: a person who organizes and operates a business or businesses, taking on financial risks and providing leadership to get the business going.

Innovation: to make changes in something established, to introduce new methods, ideas or products.

Community

By starting a business the owner can have greater participation in and impact on the community. The new business will create employment that has an impact on individuals and their families, provide economic growth for the local community and provide goods and services that contribute to the quality of life.

Activities small business owners could do to contribute to the community include:

- **Sponsorship of community events:** sporting clubs, high school awards, art awards, fairs, Variety Club Bash, Shave for a cure, Movember

- **Donations of equipment, products and materials:** donating products to non-profit groups and schools, donating sausages and bread for a charity sausage sizzle

- **Contributions of time and expertise:** legal or finance companies who offer their expertise to non-profit groups, companies who allow staff time off for voluntary and charity work

- **Community services:** pharmacies who pick up and deliver prescriptions free of charge to pensioners, businesses that give free information sessions or health clinics

- **Training and employment initiatives:** developing training and employment programs for young people, old people or local indigenous groups

- **Purchasing policies:** support of community businesses by purchasing locally produced products and services

- **Fundraising:** running charity drives to raise money or collecting items to donate to community welfare groups such as Good Samaritan Industries, Starlight Children's Foundation.

Goodwill: the established reputation of a business regarded as an asset and included in the dollar value of the business. A business may generate friendly, helpful, or cooperative feelings from others by the way they operate.

If a business makes a contribution to the local community around it, it will enhance **goodwill** towards the business and its public image. Employees may be more motivated because they know their employer is supporting the community in which they live.

BUSINESS IN SOCIETY

Tourism businesses in WA contribute to the community in a variety of ways including accommodation, cafés and restaurants and air and water transport. Sources of tax revenue tourism businesses pay to governments that benefit the whole community include fuel, alcohol, gambling, accommodation services and takeaway and restaurant meals.

IDENTIFYING BUSINESS OPPORTUNITIES

What are products or services that people often talk about, wishing they could get them? Look overseas or interstate for products or services that are emerging but not yet available locally.

Once a business opportunity has been identified as a business opportunity, evaluate it for profitability and potential for success and also in terms of personal ability and skills to make it happen. Anticipating customer demand and purchasing trends can also reveal a business opportunity. These may be short-term fads but they may also grow into ongoing trends.

Talk about the idea with friends who own businesses, are accountants or who work in retail or marketing.

Franchise

Look in the local community for successful franchise businesses and opportunities to buy a franchise in the region; for example,; *Hungry Jacks, Muzz Buzz, OPSM* or *VIP*. The Franchise Council of Australia has a website that lists franchises for sale. A franchise offers an established brand and operations and marketing support. The franchisee will have to pay a royalty to the franchisor and they don't have total control over operational decisions.

Established business

A small business owner may be selling their business. It could be a cafe, a deli, or service based such as a hairdresser, gardening or retail. Businesses for sale are listed online and in newspaper classifieds.

New business

Some business ideas come from looking at things that frustrate or irritate the new business owner. Not being able to find the right product, poor quality, not being able to access services out of hours or not being able to customise a product. Look at past experiences and abilities. What can you do better than anyone else? Do you have an idea that can be registered as intellectual property? Does the marketplace need and want what you can do and is it prepared to pay for it at a profitable price?

E-business

There are websites such as ebay and Gumtree that people use to sell unwanted items. These sites can be used to set up an online shop front. People can sell items they make, repair, restore or source from suppliers.

Online business operators often make mistakes that create a poor impression or make it difficult for customers to make purchases; for example, not including photos of the items, setting the start star price too high or wording descriptions poorly.

Online auctions provide the opportunity for people to start an easily accessible online business cheaply and without the cost of their own website. The names of items must be well written because they end up in search results if potential customers are looking for a product.

Low fee options to increase visibility of items, good item descriptions, communication with buyers and consistently quick deliveries can lead to online success.

An example of an online business is **dropshipping**. This is where a seller's page is set up to sell products from a supplier. When a sale is made the order goes to the supplier and they send the item to the buyer. The seller pays the supplier a wholesale price and keeps the profit and does not have to maintain stock or arrange delivery.

> **INNOVATION AND OPERATIONS**
>
> Emerging and growing trends include micro-transactions. The customer gets a product or service for free but have to spend very small amounts of money while using it. Facebook games and mobile apps use micro-transactions in this way. Online payments, digital wallets, cloud computing and the need for convenience have created an opportunity for mobile businesses such as food trucks, fashion trucks, shoe trucks and hair salon trucks to hit the road.

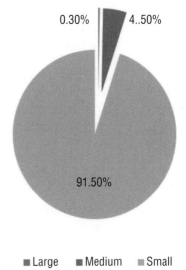

0.30%   4..50%

91.50%

■ Large   ■ Medium   ■ Small

Figure 1.2: Breakdown of businesses in WA by size

INNOVATION AND ENTREPRENEURSHIP

An entrepreneur is a leader, someone who sees a need or an opportunity and organises people and resources to exploit it. They have the vision and the creativity to develop new ideas and the courage to take on the risk of failure. Entrepreneurs build products and services from ideas and the systems (production, people, payments, delivery) needed to sell to people who will pay for them. Entrepreneurs lead people to make decisions about:

- setting goals
- targeting markets
- raising capital
- building teams
- adapting to change.

Entrepreneurs have the qualities outlined in Figure 1.3.

Traits of entrepreneurs are explored further in a later chapter.

Innovation is vital for long-term business success. Innovation is a response to new technologies, competition, changing business environments, changing lifestyles and economic conditions.

Figure 1.3: Entrepreneur qualities

Because innovations are new untested concepts it takes leadership, confidence and tolerance for risk to get the resources and support to make them real. These qualities are those associated with entrepreneurship. Entrepreneurs create jobs, help Australia compete in the world and provide goods and services that people need. It takes innovation and entrepreneurship to enter a market, to create a new market and to turn a business idea into success.

The Organisation for Economic Co-operation and Development sees entrepreneurs as essential to accelerate the generation, application and spread of innovative ideas; ensure the efficient use of resources; and expand the boundaries of economic activity.

Innovation and entrepreneurship is important on an individual basis for someone starting a new small business. It is also important for Australia. New ideas and businesses help it compete in a global market, so the nation's economy can grow and prosper, providing a good standard of living for most people.

Innovative entrepreneurs and businesses are more likely to:

- take advantage of changes in the macro environment
- continuously improve the business to maintain competitive advantage
- develop new ideas for efficiency and business growth.

BUSINESS IN SOCIETY

A survey conducted by the Australian Industry Group found that businesses who committed time and resources to innovation contributed to employment growth and increased revenue more than businesses who did not.

Innovation can be encouraged through the work environment. A successful business has a culture of openness and honesty. All contributions are valued and employees are encouraged to develop creative ideas thorough brainstorming, the provision of stimuli such as journals and media, and a work environment where ideas are valued. Ideas that are proposed need to be evaluated and tested, in order to determine if further development is required. Risk taking and experimentation need to be rewarded. The manager needs to be positive, and flexible in their response to suggestions.

Additionally, if employees are encouraged to not be negative when ideas are proven to be flawed in some way, they will be able to learn from unsuccessful ideas. A working environment where all contributions are valued and thinking 'outside the box' is encouraged, will assist with innovation.

Types of innovation

Innovation can build on established systems, goods and services or replace them with new methods and ideas.

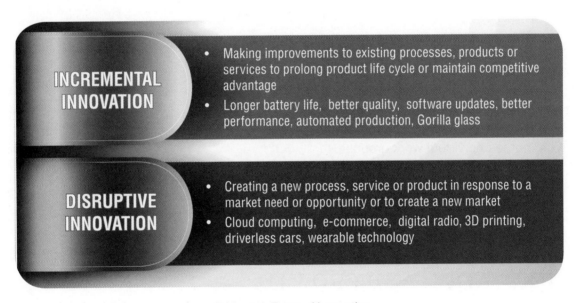

Figure 1.4: Types of innovation

The two types of innovation can be combined to create a new way to produce and manage an existing product, service or process; for example, developing a digital distribution system for concert tickets or self-service checkouts at the supermarket.

INNOVATION AND OPERATIONS

The Australian Bureau of Statistics defines innovation as introducing any new or significantly improved goods or services, operational processes, organisational/ managerial processes or marketing methods.

Table 1.1: Types of innovation in business

Type of innovation	Explanation	Example
Product	Development of a new or improved product	A kitchen vegetable peeler being made easier to use
Service	Development of a new or improved service	Customer service becoming more interactive at an information counter
Market	Development of improved marketing techniques	Product packaging becoming more environmentally friendly in response to consumer demand
Technological	Development of new or improved information technology	The use of self service checkouts
Process	Development of a new or improved manufacturing, delivery or operational process	An assembly line becoming automated

Innovation is more than just changes in technologies or systems. Marketing innovation includes new pricing strategies such as bundling. An example of bundling is when an insurance company gives an overall discount if a customer buys car, home and health insurance. Workplace innovations include changes to traditional arrangements such as working from home and virtual work groups.

Innovation is also about more than just cutting costs and increasing market share and profit. Innovation can be focused on environmental sustainability or **fair trade**.

> **Fair trade:** conducting international trade in an ethical way to ensure better prices, safe and decent working conditions, local sustainability and fair terms of trade for farmers and workers in the developing world.

INNOVATION AND GROWTH

Innovation can help your business adapt and evolve in response to changes in the business environment. Business agility means that you can maintain and create competitive advantage when there are changes.

Innovation can take advantage of emerging technologies to create new markets and new ways of selling existing products and services such as social media, mobile computing and analytics.

INNOVATION AND OPERATIONS

Tencent[2] is a technology company operating in Asia. It offers an instant messaging service and an SMS service. Neither are new but they have an innovative business model. They are not trying to make money by signing up as many people as possible and selling advertising. They are using micro-transactions to make money. They charge a small amount of money for things such as customers changing their avatar, themes, icons, virtual pets and for online games. These many small transactions have added up to grow the company to be worth over $100 billion.

---

2   http://t.qq.com

1. Social media

Companies are trying to turn Facebook profiles and Twitter posts into dollars. Social media provides access to millions of customers and their interests and opinions.

2. Mobile computing

People carry the Internet in their pockets and soon on their wrists. Mobile devices have make us more informed, more mobile, less private and more social.

3. Analytics

Data is collected about everything we do; what we buy, where we go, what websites we use, how we shop. This data is analysed to make decisions about how to produce, sell and distribute products and services.

Figure 1.5: Innovations for growth

Innovation helps businesses grow in the following ways:

1. Financial

Finding better and cheaper ways to produce, sell and deliver goods and services reduces costs. Businesses will have more money to spend on advertising, staff, stock, and product development. Innovation may cost money in the short term but it can lead to long-term profit.

2. New markets

If a business invents a new product or service they can create a new market. By using e-commerce and digital distribution they may be able to sell to customers in other states and overseas.

Protecting an innovation is important. Patenting an innovation can help a business prevent others from copying their product.

3. Longer product life

Products have a life cycle. They often get to a point where sales fall and customers move on to another product or brand. Innovations can keep customers interested and wanting your product or service. Increased quality, limited editions, personalised options, more features or added value will maintain sales.

Factors that have an impact on innovation

Each of the following factors can have an impact on the success of an innovation.

- **Timing:** if the innovation does not meet the customer need at the right time, the success of its eventual adoption by consumers is affected. Other innovations that come onto the market might help or hinder. If another innovation is more advanced this will diminish the marketability of the innovation. On the other hand, a competitor's innovation might support or enhance some feature and so boost promotional opportunities.

- **Available and emerging technologies:** a business must do more than make minor adjustments to products and relaunch them as something new. It is important to be aware of new and emerging technologies and to anticipate the effect these can have on the product range. New ideas, knowledge and skills will enable the development of unique products that directly address the needs created by changing technologies.

- **Marketing strategy:** targeted marketing campaigns will have much more success so it is vital to really know the consumer who is most likely to want to purchase a new and innovative product or service.

- **Demand:** instead of researching new innovations then developing a marketing campaign after final development has taken place, the business could consider how the consumer can have input into recognising problems, suggesting solutions and creating alternatives. Using consumer demand results in a much more responsive and ultimately more innovative result.

- **Product promotion:** advertising will affect consumer awareness and the take-up rate of any new innovation.

INNOVATION AND OPERATIONS

Household products such as detergents and cleaning products regularly relaunch their brands with new packaging and a 'new and improved' formula. This maintains customer awareness and creates the impression of better value. Apple are masters at this product innovation. They extend the life of their products by introducing a choice of colours, extending battery life or making a product thinner and lighter.

ACTIVITIES

A. CHECK YOUR UNDERSTANDING

Business opportunities

1. Outline three reasons for starting a small business.
2. What are some of the risks of starting a small business?
3. Explain why a business should make a contribution to the local community.
4. What are two ways by which a business can contribute to the community?
5. What is goodwill?
6. How does dropshipping work?
7. Why is dropshipping a good option to start a small business?

Innovation and growth

1. Define 'entrepreneurship'.
2. Explain four ways by which business can improve our standard of living?
3. Discuss the difference between the two types of innovation.
4. Describe three ways innovation can help a business grow.

B. BUSINESS RESEARCH

1. Research innovation in business. Describe two types of innovation that could be found in a business.

2. Research local businesses and their contribution to the community. List the business and the strategies they have implemented; for example, sponsoring sports teams, giving donations to charities or supporting community groups.

3. Consider two products and services that are locally available. Propose how technology could be used to improve the way they are delivered and the value customers can get from them.

C. RESPONSE

1. Think about the local community. Identify a business opportunity. It could be a franchise, an established business or a new business idea. Write down your business concept:

    *   What is the business opportunity?
    *   What are the products and services it will offer?
    *   Are there similar businesses in the community?

2. Compare working as an employee with owning your own business. Outline the advantages and disadvantages in terms of:

    *   financial security
    *   decision making and control
    *   lifestyle.

3. If someone is new to business ownership explain why a franchise would be a good option. List examples of franchises in the local area.

4. How entrepreneurial are you?

    Entrepreneurial people have certain traits. This quiz identifies if someone has entrepreneurial characteristics. This does not determine whether someone can be an entrepreneur but identifies traits they possess and other areas they will need to work on.

    Read each statement and tick the column that best describes you.

		Not yet	Sometimes	Often	Always
1.	I am passionate about my goals	❑	❑	❑	❑
2.	I have a spirit of adventure	❑	❑	❑	❑
3.	I have a strong need to achieve	❑	❑	❑	❑
4.	I am self confident and self reliant	❑	❑	❑	❑
5.	I am goal oriented	❑	❑	❑	❑
6.	I am innovative and creative	❑	❑	❑	❑
7.	I am persistent, I don't give up easily	❑	❑	❑	❑
8.	I am hard working and energetic	❑	❑	❑	❑
9.	I am a positive thinker	❑	❑	❑	❑
10.	I am willing to take the initiative	❑	❑	❑	❑
	SUBTOTAL:				
	TOTAL:				

Scoring

Total your score in each column. Give yourself one point for every tick under 'Sometimes', two points for every 'Often', three points for each 'Always'. Then add your column subtotals together for a total score.

- **If you scored 31-40:** You are a very entrepreneurial person, ready to take on the challenges and opportunities of a new business.

- **If you scored 21-30:** Your characteristics make you well suited to a career as an entrepreneur with a bit more experience.

- **If you scored 11-20:** You have entrepreneurial traits but there are areas that need improvement before taking on the challenge.

- **If you scored 0-10:** Your entrepreneurial skills can be developed through reading biographies, stepping up to new jobs and responsibilities in life and work and working with other people.

5. Discuss how timing can influence the success of commercialising a new or emerging technology.

D. GROUP WORK

Business opportunities and innovation

1. In pairs or small groups discuss the following question and write down key points.

   Would you rather start a new business or buy a franchise?

   Discuss it in terms of control of the business, financial risk and reward and likelihood of success.

2. Choose a product that you often use and are familiar with. Develop an innovation that could increase value and attract new customers. Describe how the innovation will benefit the business and consumers. Use a template such as the one shown below to record your product innovations.

Existing product
Describe your innovation
How will the business benefit from your innovation?
Sketch your new and improved product – use a new page for more space or create a prototype.

CHAPTER 2
The Business Environment

'I do not believe maximising profits for the investors is the only acceptable justification for all corporate actions. The investors are not the only people who matter. Corporations can exist for purposes other than simply maximising profits.'
– John Mackey –

A business operates within society but not in isolation. There are many influences that have an impact on how a business is run. To achieve long term success a business owner must be aware of what is in the environment and be able to respond to and manage these influences.

The topics in this chapter are:

- The business environment
- Business ethics

THE BUSINESS ENVIRONMENT

The business environment has three parts. A business has different levels of control and influence over each part of the environment.

The macro, operating and internal environments are examined here.

Macro environment

This is the big picture. The macro environment influences business but business has little control over it. Influences include laws and regulations, government policies, technologies that are new and changing, demographics, social and cultural trends, and economic issues such as consumer spending, growth, interest rates and inflation.

Internal
- culture
- employees
- management style
- business form

Operating
- competitors
- customers
- suppliers
- local community

Macro
- laws and regulations
- technology
- economy
- social trends

Figure 2.1: Three business environments

The natural environment is an important consideration. Businesses have long had seasonal fluctuations in trade and the climate influences what customers want to buy. Natural disasters such as flood or drought also affect how a business can run, what people buy and what they need. Natural resources such as water and land can determine whether a new business is viable or if an existing one can continue.

For a fast food store the macro environment will include youth wage policies, health and safety regulations, the health consciousness of customers and whether the people living in the local area like the food that the business is selling and how often they buy it.

UNDERSTANDING BUSINESS

PEST is a method used to analyse the macro environment of a business. Each of the factors identified in a PEST analysis are examined in terms of their impact on the business and the likelihood of it occurring. The analysis should be ongoing so change and trends can be identified and included when making decisions about the business. PEST is an acronym identifying the four elements of the macro environment.

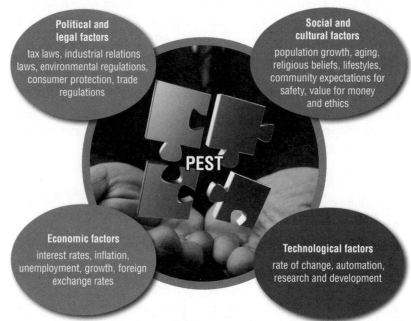

Political and legal factors
tax laws, industrial relations laws, environmental regulations, consumer protection, trade regulations

Social and cultural factors
population growth, aging, religious beliefs, lifestyles, community expectations for safety, value for money and ethics

PEST

Economic factors
interest rates, inflation, unemployment, growth, foreign exchange rates

Technological factors
rate of change, automation, research and development

Figure 2.2: PEST

Operating environment

In the operating environment are stakeholders that deal with the business directly on a daily basis. A business owner must negotiate and work with stakeholders to achieve business goals and to give stakeholders what they want so they will continue to support the business.

Stakeholders include people who have a direct relationship with the business such as the owners and shareholders, employees, customers and suppliers. Stakeholders can also include community groups, local councils, state and federal governments (the laws and regulations that have direct impact on a business) and local residents.

A supermarket may be asked to sponsor local sports teams. This may have benefits for the business but it is an added cost. Local residents may complain about parking arrangements or traffic congestion around the store and demand change to the parking area. The local council may fine the supermarket if their trolleys are found dumped in the neighbourhood. Suppliers may try to pressure the business owner to increase orders and there may be great difficulty in finding staff to fill positions in the supermarket. It is not just a matter of selling grocery items but also managing these varied concerns and impositions and to keep everyone supportive of what the business is doing.

Three criteria can be used to identify **stakeholders**:

1. They supply resources that are critical to the success of the business

2. They are directly affected by the success or failure of the business

3. They have sufficient power to affect the business favourably or unfavourably

Stakeholder: a person or group having an interest in and affected by the activities and performance of a business or project.

Internal environment

The business owner has the greatest level of control over this part of the environment. This is about what happens inside the business; the business culture, employees, management styles and business form.

When planning to start or expand a business an analysis of the internal environment is carried out to identify strengths and weaknesses. Strengths include skilled, motivated and loyal staff, new technologies and efficient processes. Weakness are when these are absent. Strengths can be used to start and grow a business and strategies must be used to overcome the weaknesses.

Culture: the beliefs, values and standards common to a group of people in a country, region or workplace.

A culture identifies similarities within a group and consists of values and beliefs, ways of life and accepted guidelines for behaviour. **Culture** means a people's customary way of life, including arts, values, beliefs, customs, inventions and technologies. Just as in a society a culture within a business can give people a sense of belonging and ways to decide what is right and wrong.

Internal culture has expectations and unwritten rules, learnt with experience, about the way things are done and what employees are expected to do. Internal culture grows out of the things people value, and the way employees relate to each other, share ideas and work together on a daily basis.

A culture within a business can be developed and managed. Businesses may have a formal statement of values, a code of conduct and methods for decisions and communication which encourage a culture that supports the goals of the business. A positive internal culture gives employees a sense of belonging, a shared view of the direction of the business, and can result in greater job satisfaction and loyalty to the business. The culture of a business will determine whether staff enjoy working for a company.

UNDERSTANDING BUSINESS

According to BHP Billiton, key stakeholders are identified as people who are adversely or positively affected by operations, those who have an interest in what the business does, or those who have an influence on what the business does. Some of the key stakeholders identified by BHP are: employees and contractors, local and Indigenous communities, shareholders, customers, investment community, business partners, community organisations, unions, suppliers, governments, media and industry associations. BHP identified these stakeholders using the following method.

'A regular review process is a central requirement of stakeholder identification, to ensure that all appropriate groups and individuals are part of an ongoing process of engagement. Aspects of the process of engagement are:

Trust and transparency – promote a commitment to acting with honesty, integrity and fairness in all our activities.

Our approach to dialogue – effective, transparent and open communication and consultation is maintained with stakeholders

Benefits of dialogue – information received from stakeholders helps refine the management of our activities and mitigate their potential impacts.

Stakeholder grievances and concerns – mechanisms to address grievances and concerns have also been established. The confidential Business Conduct Helpline and email address provide a further means for raising issues of actual or potential concern such as harassment, conflict of interest, fraud or bribery.[1]

---

1   BHP Billiton, www.bhpbilliton.com, accessed 20 July 2007.

An owner wants an internal culture that will keep people happy and will give them clear expectations so they work together to achieve business goals. Happy and motivated employees will provide better service to customers and give the business a competitive advantage.

Managers and leaders in a business can build and support a business culture by:

- being a role model for staff by behaving in the way that they want them to behave
- rewarding behaviour that demonstrates the norms of the culture (good decisions, good customer service, teamwork)
- communicating to staff what behaviour is desired in as many ways as possible
- providing training in order to support the culture.

Questions about the internal culture of a business[2]

1. **Structure:** how are decisions made, by managers alone or are workers involved? Are there unwritten rules about when to eat lunch or when to start and finish work each day?

2. **Communication:** how do people communicate about work, is it informal or only at organised meetings? If an employee has done a good job, how do they know? If they have done something wrong, do they receive constructive feedback?

3. **Workspace:** do workers eat at their desk? Are people allowed to have personal belongings such as photos and plants around the workspace?

4. **Social:** do workers keep work and personal lives separate? Does the company organise social functions for staff?

Figure 2.3: Establishing what internal culture is like

UNDERSTANDING BUSINESS

Research[2] on over 900 organisations in New Zealand and Australia found that too many organisations have cultures that promote conflict and competitiveness. While all employees from senior executives down said they wanted a culture that encouraged good relationships and cooperation, the research found that self interest, blame shifting and playing politics to gain influence was widespread.

Examples of business environments

Table 2.1: Examples of how environments can have an impact on a business

MACRO	OPERATING	INTERNAL
High interest rates and petrol prices can cut into spare money and customers may not spend as much on fast food and entertainment.	A shortage of people with the skills needed in an industry can stop new businesses starting. Businesses that have the demand may not be able to expand because of the lack of skilled workers.	Skills shortages mean that the workers a business does have may be overworked and stressed. This may lead to mistakes and bad customer service.

---

2   Human Synergisics, www.human-synergistics.com.au, accessed 20 July 2007.

MACRO	OPERATING	INTERNAL
A TV repair business operator will have to be trained in repairing LCD and plasma TVs or they may go out of business due to changes in technology.	A greengrocer will have to decide between supporting local fruit and vegetable growers or switch to cheaper imported suppliers.	A new technology may mean savings in time and money but before it can be used employees have to be trained and capable of using it.
A social and lifestyle change to people using home theatres instead of going to the cinema is occurring. In Perth a large multiscreen cinema complex recently closed.	A business operator may not want to work on Sundays or week nights but knows that their competitors will.	A supermarket owner may want to take advantage of Sunday trading but staff do not like the idea of working on Sundays. Will any increase in business cover the increased payroll costs of staying open?
The state government is changing laws to allow extended trading hours.	A café owner may not want to open every week night but the shopping centre management could make it compulsory.	A fast food owner wants to take some time off and have a break but because all staff are juniors there may not be a senior employee to take over day-to-day management.

BUSINESS ETHICS

Ethics requires people in business to think beyond their personal needs and the success of their business. It involves considering the effects a planned action can have on the wider community.

> **Ethics:** a system of conduct or behaviour, moral principles that govern the behaviour of a person or a group.

The expectation of the community is that small business owners consider the macro or external business environment when making decisions. Self-interest and profit should not be the only consideration for a business owner. What is good for the community and society should play a part in business decisions.

This includes being aware of community attitudes. Mass media and social media quickly expose the unethical conduct of a business. Ethical business is not only good for society but is an important part of building a positive public image, customer and employee loyalty and long term success.

Business ethics refers to the way business is conducted in order to operate in harmony with all stakeholders. The ethics of a business can be formalised in an ethics statement or code of conduct. If an employee is in a situation and they do not know what to do they can rely on the ethics of the business they work in to make their decision. The ethics of business are demonstrated in the way employees treat each other, deal with customers and suppliers and when business decisions are made. It is about doing the 'right' thing, not just what is best for the business.

**The Department of Education and Training
has a code of conduct for all staff**

The aims of the code are to:

- assist staff in dealing with ethical issues in ways that reflect the Department's values and standards
- promote professionalism and excellence
- express shared assumptions, beliefs and values
- provide staff with guidance in ethically ambiguous situations
- communicate the Department's standards
- detail the Department's social responsibilities
- motivate staff to do the right thing
- provide a statement on public accountability and corporate governance
- assist staff to meet the minimum standards of conduct and integrity described in the Code of Ethics[3]

BUSINESS OPERATIONS

Research[3] has found three actions by managers and leaders in a business that will result in a more ethical workplace. Being seen to do the right thing is more effective than formal ethics statements and training programs. Employees need to see their superiors and peers demonstrate ethical behaviour in the work they do and decisions they make every day. The three actions are:

1. Setting a good example
2. Keeping promises and commitments
3. Supporting others in adhering to ethics standards

Figure 2.4: Sample code of conduct

Ethical dilemmas in business

A business dilemma exists when a business operator faces a choice that will have impacts on profits and competitiveness and stakeholders. There are situations where business owners have to decide what is the right or best thing to do. It can be difficult when the right action will result in bad consequences such as a colleague getting fired, a project being delayed or a decrease in profits.

Some common ethical dilemmas in business – what would you do?

You uncover a friend's dishonest behaviour at work. You have a duty to your employer to report it but also loyalty to your friend.

You work for a very successful business making large profits from a product that has recently been proven to have toxic effects on users. What is your priority – consumer safety or continued business success?

You discover safety issues with equipment. If you report it the project will be delayed because of the time needed to fix the problem.

You devise a business scheme that would make you very rich but it requires you to withhold information about risks from investors.

3   Amber Levanon Seligson and Laurie Choi, ***Critical elements of an organisational ethical culture,*** Ethics Resource Center, Washington DC, 2006.

ACTIVITIES

A. CHECK YOUR UNDERSTANDING

Business environments

1. Explain how the internal culture can influence the success of a business.

2. What is your definition of a 'stakeholder'?

3. Why can it be said that a business only has real control over the internal environment and not over the external environment?

4. What is the internal environment?

5. What is the operating environment?

6. What is the macro environment?

7. How can the internal environment affects a business?

8. How can the operating environment affects a business?

9. How can the macro environment affects a business?

Business ethics

1. What are ethics?

2. Explain the purpose of a code of conduct.

3. How can business dilemmas affect business operations?

4. Choose from the list of words to complete the following sentences:

   conduct   laws   accepted

   Ethics is not a set of rules or _____ but a code of _____, a generally _____ way of behaving.

   stakeholders   courageous   fairly   honestly

   Business must aim to work _____ , _____, care for _____ and make _____ decisions.

   duty   self   environment   obligations   dilemmas   community

   Many businesses encounter _____ when deciding between their _____ interest, their _____ to shareholders and their _____ to the _____; for example, to employees, suppliers, local residents and the _____.

B. BUSINESS RESEARCH

I. Choose one franchise business in your local area. It could be a pizza business, carpet or tyre retailer, video shop or electrical store. Use the Internet to research the franchising system behind the store.

Write a brief report on the following:

A. Does the business have a code of ethics or values statement? If so what are the aims or main points?

B. Find out if they have a community support program, sponsorship arrangements with community groups or events or if they support any charities. In what ways do they make a direct contribution to the community?

C. What are examples of businesses that compete for the same customers?

D. Describe how lifestyles and attitudes in the community could affect the success of this franchise.

2. Go to ASIC's Money Smart website **www.moneysmart.gov.au** or **www.scamwatch.gov.au**. Explore the types of scams and how to avoid them.

Prepare a slideshow or report on the following:

A. Identify the common methods used in scams and rip-offs.

B. Describe two examples of non-investment scams.

C. How can consumers protect themselves from scams?

D. If scams and rip-offs have been around for a long time why do you think they still work?

3. Identify examples of small businesses contributing to your community.

4. Evaluating Codes of Conduct

Research the Codes of Conduct of two businesses. Once you have an understanding of the code of conduct, investigate what the business does. Compare the code of conduct for the two businesses. Note that the code of conduct may be called a statement of ethics or values.

Create a table summarising the following for each business:

A. What are the main points of the code of conduct?

B. List the stakeholders that are identified or those you think are involved with the business.

C. Do the business' products, services and activities reflect what their code says?

D. Does the impact of the business on the environment and community demonstrate what is in the code of conduct?

E. Describe examples of business conduct that support the code and any examples that undermine it.

C. RESPONSE

1. Identify the stakeholders in your school. Who are the people and groups that are involved in your school and are affected by it? List examples of concerns each stakeholder has.

2. Why would some businesses prefer to pay a fine for breaking the law rather than simply operating lawfully?

3. Write an ethics statement for students in a high school. What values should students have and what ethical behaviours should they demonstrate while at school?

4. Analyse the macro environment of a small local business of your choice, using a PEST analysis matrix such as the one below:

Political and legal factors	Social and cultural factors
Economic factors	Technological factors

5. On the diagram label each part of the business environment.

    Classify each item below according to the type of business environment into which it fits.

    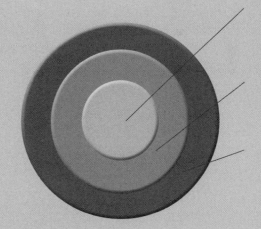

    *   Customers
    *   Health and safety regulations
    *   Competitors
    *   Interest rates
    *   Culture
    *   Employees

6. Case study: Ethics

    John Yamaha is the environmental compliance manager for a small manufacturing company. He is currently faced with the decision whether or not to spend money on new technology that will reduce the level of a particular chemical in the wastewater that flows out the back of the factory and into a river.

The factory's emission levels are within legal limits. However, John knows that environmental regulations for this particular chemical are not based on the latest scientific evidence about its dangers. Recently a scientist has been reported in the local newspaper saying that if the current level of the chemical flow into the river continued the fish in the lakes and rivers in the area will have to be declared unsafe for human consumption.

If manufacturing companies don't self regulate and reduce emission levels, the local and state governments will be forced by evidence and public opinion to legislate and make companies use the new technology. Monthly emission level testing and reports will be required which are both expensive and time consuming.

But the company's environmental budget is very small. Asking for the new technology to be installed would mean taking money away from production and marketing and could jeopardise the company's ability to show a profit this year.

Questions:

1. Why would the business want to install the new technology?

2. Why would the business want to delay installing the new technology?

3. Why might the manufacturing businesses in the local area want the government to impose new regulations?

D. GROUP WORK

1. Working in small groups use the questions from 'Figure 2.3: Establishing what internal culture is like' to describe the culture of your school. Identify the shared values, ceremonies, unwritten rules and the ways students and teachers communicate and work together. Compare your description with other groups.

    Explain why the culture within a business is often referred to as the 'glue' that is holding the business together.

2. Local business survey

    This project requires a small group of students to investigate a local business. You will investigate and report on the following aspects of the business:

    * Type of business
    * Industry sector
    * Role of the business in the local community
    * Recommendations for practices to contribute to the local community

    Your research can be based on observation, discussion with the manager and employees, and review of advertising and business literature such as the website, brochures, TV advertisements. A one-page questionnaire may be useful to collect information.

CHAPTER 3
The Legal Framework of Business

'If we could ever make red tape nutritional, we could feed the world.'
– Robert Schaeberle –

Operating a business involves managing legal requirements to ensure that regulators do not impose fines and penalties. There are legal requirements regarding the form of business an owner chooses. Each form has advantages and disadvantages which are considered when deciding which form is best for the business.

The topics in this chapter are:

- Forms of business
- Legal requirements of setting up a business
- Choice of legal structure

FORMS OF BUSINESS

The choice of the form of business organisation to use when starting a business is a major decision. It is a decision to be reviewed over time as the business grows and the business environment changes.

Aspects of a business to consider when making decisions about the form of organisation include:

- tax – which form will minimise the tax burden
- ownership – how best to share business ownership
- liability – how best to protect owners and investors from being personally liable for business debts
- succession – how best to set up the ownership and control of the business for the future (very important with family businesses)
- sources of finance – consider the capital needed to start the busines.

This section will examine the following forms of business:

- Sole trader
- Partnership
- Private company
- Not for profit organisation
- Franchise

Table 3.1: Forms of business

	Type	Definition	Liability	Taxation	Ownership
Sole trader: a business run and owned by an individual.	Sole trader	A single person operating a business under their own name	Unlimited liability. The owner is personally liable for all debts and damages owed by the business. All contracts and assets are in the owner's name.	Profits of the business are taxable income of the owner.	The business can be run in the name of the owner or a business name can be registered.
Partnership: an association of two or more people to carry on a business with a common view to profit.	Partnership	When 2 or more people go into business together with a view to make profit. Governed by the *Partnership Act 1895*. The Act can be overridden by a formal Partnership Agreement.	Unlimited liability. All contracts and assets are in the owner's name.	Profits of the business are distributed to the partners and considered part of their personal taxable income.	Contracts entered into by one partner are binding on all partners. New partners can enter with the consent of all partners. There is a maximum of 20 partners except for a limit of 400 for some professions, eg. accountants, lawyers
Private company: a company formed without the ability to raise money from the public.	Private company	A separate legal entity. It has Proprietary (Pty) and Limited (Ltd) in its name.	Liability of shareholders is limited to any unpaid shares.	The business completes a company tax return and pays a company rate.	It can have no more than 50 shareholders. Shares cannot be offered to the public.
	Not for profit organisation	A non-profit organisation is not operating for the profit or gain of its individual members. Any profit goes back into the operation of the organisation to carry out its purposes and is not distributed to any of its members.	An incorporated organisation provides financial protection by limiting personal liability of members to outstanding membership and subscription fees. Members of an unincorporated organisation can be liable for debts and legal claims.	If approved by the ATO non-profit organisations can be exempt from income tax.	Non-profit organisations are either; unincorporated or incorporated associations. An unincorporated association is not a separate legal entity to the members associated with it. An incorporated association is a legal entity separate from its individual members. An incorporated association can continue regardless of changes to membership.

Type	Definition	Liability	Taxation	Ownership
Franchise	Franchising is a business arrangement where the franchisor (the owner of the franchise concept) licences the business model to franchisees in return for ongoing fees or royalties.	Liability for debts depends upon the form of business that owns the franchise.	The taxation of a franchise depends upon the form of business that owns it, eg. private company, sole trader or partnership. Franchise costs such as franchisor fees and royalties are tax deductible.	The franchisee owns the franchise. They may sell it to another person but there may be conditions set by the franchisor.

BUSINESS IN SOCIETY

The non-profit sector's main sources of income are the sale of goods and services and government grants and contracts. There are as many as 700, 000 non-profit organisations in Australia, most of which are small and dependent on the voluntary commitment of members. There are approximately 380,000 non-profit organisations that are incorporated.

Unlimited liability: assets and debts are in the names of the owners and their personal assets may be used to repay business debts. Limited liability protects personal assets from business debts.

Table 3.2: Advantages and disadvantages of forms of business organisation

Type	Advantages	Disadvantages
Sole trader	• The owner has full control • The owner keeps all profits • Easy to set up	• Unlimited liability – if the business goes broke the owner could lose personal assets to pay off business debts • No-one to share the work load
Partnership	• Easy to establish • Partners can bring in money and skills • Work can be shared amongst partners	• Unlimited liability • There can be disagreements between partners over decisions • Rules must be set for partners leaving otherwise the partnership will end
Private company	• Limited liability – personal assets are not taken to cover business debts • A person can sell their shares if they want to leave the business	• Expensive to set up • Less say in the running of the business because there are so many owners • Profits are shared amongst more owners • Must operate within the Corporation Act

Type	Advantages	Disadvantages
Not for profit organisation	• Inexpensive to incorporate • Few formalities and a low compliance requirements • May be eligible for tax exemptions	• Limited to operating in the state of incorporation • Not closely monitored or regulated so no clear guidelines for operation and for resolving disputes
Franchise	• A well established brand and product or service • Franchisor offers management training and assistance • Established operating procedures, manuals and management systems • Obtaining finance may be easier due to established market presence	• Franchisees have to operate the business according to the franchisor's procedures • Less autonomy in business decisions • Restricted territory for operation and promotion of the business • Ongoing cost of payments to the franchisor • There may be restrictions on selling the business

BUSINESS CONCEPTS

A fast food chain selling pies wants to encourage existing franchisees to add stores and become multi-unit franchises. They are discounting their franchise fee. They will decrease the royalty percent the more stores you own:

- one store: 6%
- two stores: 5%
- three stores: 4%
- four or more stores: 3%

Choice of legal structure

There are factors to consider when deciding which legal structure to use when starting or expanding a business. Aspects of a business to consider when making decisions about the legal structure are shown here.

Size
The number of employees and owners

Tax
How to legally minimise income tax

LEGAL STRUCTURE

Ownership
How best to share business control

Liability
Protect the owners from personal liability for business debts

Choosing a legal structure is an important decision when starting a business and considering the best legal structure for a business is ongoing. A small business operator may be planning to increase sales and expand the business or changes in tax laws and other government regulations may mean that a change in structure is necessary. A death, retirement or business closure may also require a change to the legal structure.

In the table on the following page the factors to consider will be explained when deciding between the three most common legal structures for business.

Table 3.3: Factors to consider when choosing a legal structure

Factor	Sole trader	Partnership	Company
Size	If a business can be run by an individual with few employees a sole trader is suitable.	Suitable when expanding a sole trader. Up to 20 partners can be in a partnership. More partners means more leaders and managers to supervise a higher number of staff.	Used for a large business or one that is expanding nationally and globally.
Tax	Business profit will be taxed as personal income, good if the business is the sole source of income.	Business profits are divided amongst partners and taxed as personal income. Income splitting can be used in partnerships to minimise tax.	Business profits are taxed at the company rate. The company rate is lower than the top individual tax rate. Owners can then be paid a salary and taxed as an individual rather than on the full amount.
Ownership	Suitable if the operator wants to have ownership and control. If a sole trader dies or retires the business will end. Commonly used in a family business where a family member can take over the business.	The partnership structure and agreement make clear guidelines for ownership and decision making. Partners are motivated to act in the best interests of the business. If a partner dies or retires the partnership will end but arrangements can be made to keep the business going in the Partnership Agreement.	Because a company is a separate legal entity owners can leave the business but the business will continue. Suitable for owners who want the financial return from a business but without having to run it on a day to day basis.
Liability and risk	An owner must have high risk tolerance as personal assets can be taken to cover business debts.	Personal assets of partners can be taken to cover business debts. Less risk than a sole trader because losses and debts are shared amongst partners. Expertise that one partner does not have can be supplemented by other partners.	A business is still risky, it can fail, but owners' assets are protected by limited liability. Only business assets can be taken to cover business.
Finance	The business is funded through business profits and personal assets. A sole trader usually commences business with a large debt. It can be difficult to obtain finance for expansion until the start up debt is paid off. Enough revenue must be made to cover business expenses and for the owner to live.	Partners can bring in capital and assets to fund the business. The combined borrowing power of partners can make it easier to get loans from banks. If money is needed new partners (and their capital) can join the business.	Unlike a sole trader and partnership a company has the ability to issue shares and debentures to the public to raise large sums of money for sales growth and expansion.

UNDERSTANDING BUSINESS

A Family Business Australia survey found that 25 per cent of family businesses surveyed do not have a formal succession plan to organise what will happen if the sole trader of a family business dies or retires. Without a plan conflict can arise amongst family members arguing over business assets.

Income splitting: when a high level of business income is split up amongst family members. The overall tax bill will be less than the business owner paying tax on the whole amount. Each person will be able to use the tax free threshold. Often used in a situation where a business operator splits income with their spouse.

Legal requirements of setting up a business

Once a legal structure is chosen it must be set up correctly so the business can open a bank account, register a business name and comply with local and state government regulations. As the size of a business increases more complex legal structures are necessary to assist in the management of finances, tax obligations and ownership.

In this section we will explore the legal requirements for setting up sole traders and partnerships. Both forms of business are not separate legal entities. A sole trader and the partners in a partnership own assets and liabilities in their names.

Table 3.4: Legal requirements

Sole trader: the simplest form of business. A small business owner registers a business name to trade under but assets and debts are in the name of the owner.

Business name	Tax File Number (TFN)	Australian Business Number (ABN)	Goods and Services Tax (GST)
A sole trader can trade in their own name or register a business name. A bank account can be opened to accept and make payments in the name of the business – John Smith trading as On Time Electrical	A sole trader trades on their individual TFN.	An ABN is needed to avoid having amounts withheld from payments to the business. Some customers may have to withhold 46.5% of any payments if they don't have an ABN. An ABN is compulsory if the business collects GST. ABN applications should indicate if the business wants to register as a sole trader.	Register for GST if expected turnover is $75,000 or more.

Partnership: a partnership is formed when two or more people (up to 20) go into business together. Partnerships can either be general or limited.

Business name	Tax File Number (TFN)	Australian Business Number (ABN)	Goods and Services Tax (GST)
A partnership can trade under the partners' names or they can register a business name.	A partnership has its own TFN and lodges a partnership tax return. But it does not pay tax. The partnership's profits are divided among the partners and they pay personal income tax on their share.	A partnership must have an ABN.	Register for GST if expected turnover is $75,000 or more.

A **general partnership** is one where all partners are equally responsible for the management of the business and each has unlimited liability for partnership debts.

A **limited partnership** is one where the liability of one or more partners for partnership debts business is limited. The partnership will have one or more general partners with unlimited liability and one or more partners whose liability is limited. Limited partners are 'silent' partners. They invest in the partnership and share in the profits but are not involved in the running and decisions of the business.

Business names are registered with the Australian Securities and Investments Commission (ASIC). An ABN is required to register a business name. Apply for an ABN through the Australian Business Register website. The availability of a business name can be checked by searching the business names database in the ASIC website.

Limited partnership: some partners are involved in running the business with unlimited liability and some partners with limited liability are not involved in running the business.

BUSINESS CONCEPTS

When choosing a business name:

- Choose a name that will appeal to your target customers.
- Choose a name that gives an impression of how you will treat customers.
- Something that is short, sharp and memorable.
- Make sure you can use it to register a website domain name.

Partnership Act and Partnership Agreement

Partnerships are governed by the *Partnership Act 1895 (WA)*. The Act sets rules for setting up the partnership, conduct of partners, profit sharing and what happens if a partner wants to leave the business or if they die.

If partners want to have different rules they must write their own Partnership Agreement. A Partnership Agreement replaces the Act. It is a good idea for partners to write their own Agreement to take into account their situation. An important part of the Agreement is to set out a process for resolving disputes if the partners cannot agree on a business decision.

Domain name: is the main part of a website address and can be part of a business email address, eg. www.ontimelectrical.com.au and jsmith@ontimelectrical.com.au

Potential partners must agree on the following issues when setting up a partnership:

- the contribution by each partner of time, effort, money and assets
- how profits and losses are shared
- partnership salaries, if any
- how each partner will be involved in running the business.

Table 3.5: Other differences between the Act and an Agreement

Under the *Partnership Act 1895*	Under a Partnership Agreement
A partner cannot be expelled from the partnership by resolution of the other partners	Rules can be set about expelling partners based on conduct and work performance
Every partner may take part in the management of the partnership business	Rules can be set about how much involvement partners have in running the business
If one partner signs a contract it is binding on the partnership	Rules can be set about who and how many partners need to sign contracts
A partner cannot receive a salary, just a share of any profits	Includes an entitlement to receive a partner salary
A partnership is dissolved upon the death of a partner	A partnership can continue after the death or retirement of a partner
"All the partners are entitled to share equally in the capital and profits of the business, and must contribute equally towards the losses".	The share of partners can be set percentages or based on the size of their investment in the partnership

An extract from a partnership agreement template is presented on the following page.

Partnership Agreement

THIS PARTNERSHIP AGREEMENT is made this _____ day of _____ , 20 ___ , by and between the following individuals:

_____ Address: _____

_____

_____ Address: _____

_____

1. <u>Nature of Business</u>. The partners above hereby agree they shall be considered partner in business for the following purpose:

_____

_____

2. <u>Name</u>. The partnership shall be conducted under the name of _____ and shall maintain offices at _____

3. <u>Day-to-Day-Operation</u>. The partners shall provide their full-time services and best efforts on behalf of the partnership. No partner shall receive a salary for services rendered to the partnership. Each partner shall have equal rights to manage and control the partnership and its business. Should there be differences between the partners concerning ordinary business matters, a decision shall be made by unanimous vote. It is understood that the partners may elect one of the partners to conduct the day-to-day business of the partnership; however, no partner shall be able to bind the partnership by act or contract to any liability exceeding $ _____ without the prior written consent of each partner.

4. <u>Capital Contribution</u>. The capital contribution of each partner to the partnership shall consist of the following property, services, or cash which each partner agrees to contribute:

Name of partner	Capital contribution	Agree-upon cash	% share

The partnership shall maintain a capital account record for each partner; should any partner's capital account fall below the agreed to amount, then that partner shall (1) have his share of the partnership profits then due and payable applied to his capital account; and (2) pay any deficiency to the partnership of his share of partnership profits is not yet due and payable or, if it is, his share is insufficient to cancel the deficiency.

5. <u>Profits and Losses</u>. The profits and losses of the partnership shall be divided by the partners according to a mutually agreed schedule and at the end of each calendar year according to the proportions listed above.

6. <u>Term/Termination</u>. The term of the Agreement shall be for a period of _____ years, unless the partners mutually agree in writing to a shorter period. Should the partnership be terminated by unanimous vote, the assets and cash of the partnership shall be used to pay all creditors, with the remaining amount to be distributed to the partners according to their proportion share.

7. Disputes. This Partnership Agreement shall be governed by the laws of the State of   . any disputes arising between the partners as a result of this Agreement shall be settled by arbitration in accordance with the rules of the _____ and judgement upon the award rendered may be entered in any court

ACTIVITIES

A. CHECK YOUR UNDERSTANDING

The legal framework of business

1. Explain two aspects of business to consider when making decisions about the form or organisation to use.

2. What are some differences between a sole trader and a partnership?

3. What forms of business protect owners from personal liability for business debts?

4. Why is a sole trader risky for a business owner?

5. What are the advantages of a private company?

6. When should a business register for the GST?

7. How are rules set for how partnerships are run?

8. Discuss which business form is best for taxation purposes?

9. Why is a domain name important for a business?

10. What is a limited partnership?

B. BUSINESS RESEARCH

1. Explain what an invoice needs to include for it to be a 'tax invoice' for GST purposes. Design a tax invoice for a fictitious business.

2. Find or create a flowchart that explains how the GST works for small businesses in Australia. What is the current GST rate?

3. Devise three business names for businesses you would want to operate. Use the ASIC website to test whether each name is available for registration.

C. RESPONSE

1. Discuss the advantages and disadvantages of a sole trader and a partnership. Describe a situation where a sole trader would be the best option and when a partnership would be the best choice.

2. Discuss when a limited partnership would be a good choice for a business structure.

3. Why would potential partners decide to write their own partnership agreement? Draft proposed clauses covering the distribution of profits and the resolution of disputes.

4. Discuss why it would be a good idea for a partnership to form a private company. What are the pros and cons of the private company structure?

5. Explain the concept of limited liability. Which forms of business have limited liability?

D. GROUP WORK

1. In a small group discuss a potential business you could start or purchase in the local community. In your group make the following decisions and explain why you made your choices:

   - Select a business form – sole trader and employees, partnership or private company
   - Decide whether you would need to register for the GST.
   - Choose a business name and check for availability.
   - Describe the products and services you will offer.
   - Design a tax invoice for the business.

BUSINESS ENVIRONMENTS CROSSWORD

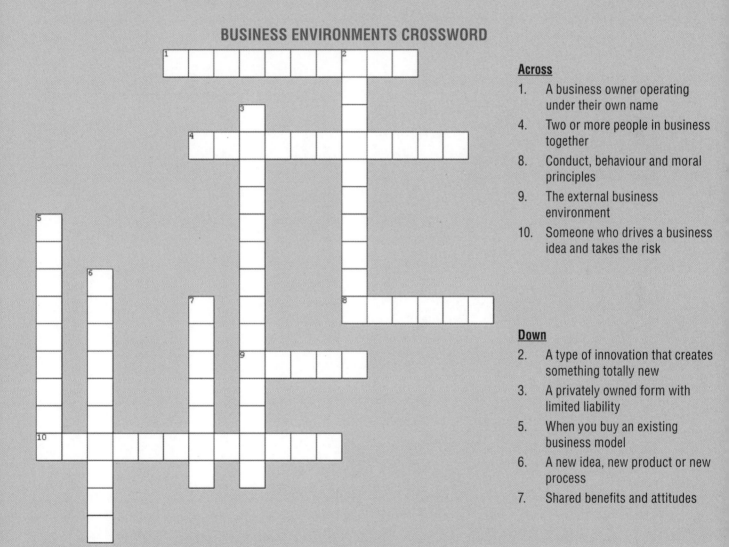

Across

1. A business owner operating under their own name
4. Two or more people in business together
8. Conduct, behaviour and moral principles
9. The external business environment
10. Someone who drives a business idea and takes the risk

Down

2. A type of innovation that creates something totally new
3. A privately owned form with limited liability
5. When you buy an existing business model
6. A new idea, new product or new process
7. Shared benefits and attitudes

SECTION B: MANAGEMENT

CHAPTER 4
The Marketing Mix

'A market is the combined behaviour of thousands of people responding to information, misinformation and whim.'

– Kenneth Chang –

This chapter will examine the importance of identifying potential customers and competitors. This is relevant to the owner of the small business, because they often have a relatively small market thus must focus their product carefully.

The main elements of the marketing mix will be outlined. The business owner should plan a targeted approach to product, price, place and promotion.

CUSTOMERS AND COMPETITORS

It is not enough for a small business to just have a great product, be it a good or a service. The business owner needs to identify who the **customers** of the business are. By selecting the appropriate target market, the business will be able to focus on customer needs.

Additionally, a business needs to identify and research potential **competitors** to ensure they remain aware of the market and the alternatives that consumers may have.

Having a customer focus

If staff are focused 'outwards', they prioritise the needs of customers, suppliers and other stakeholders. They do not become too focused internally on the business and should not end up losing sight of customer needs.

If a staff member is focused on stakeholders, they are always interested in finding out about the needs of that individual or customer. When those needs are identified, the staff member can move on to possible solutions. Ensuring that a 'win-win' solution is aimed for will result in both the business and the stakeholder coming out of the transaction happy.

By focusing on the needs of the customer (or supplier), the business does not get lost in marketing its product nor does it prioritise this over the actual wishes of the stakeholder. The business instead focuses on adapting its product to ensure the best possible benefit is delivered.

Customer service focuses on meeting the expectations of customers, so it is useful to have procedures in place for occasions where the business does not get it right. It is vital to have effective complaints procedures, because if it is too difficult for a customer to make a complaint they are not likely to bother with the business but are more likely to tell others of their negative experience, which is bad public relations for the business.

Complaint procedure

The business needs a clear procedure for employees to follow whenever there is a complaint from a client, customer, supplier or other stakeholder. Figure 4.1 suggests a simple process.

BUSINESS CONCEPTS

Lewis is meeting with a retailer who is considering stocking some of the products that his business sells – wristbands and jewellery for men. Instead of a generic "sales pitch" about his product, he needs to firstly determine what the retailer wants to fit the product mix in her shop, how frequently she will require restocking, her advertising budget, and customer type. It is only after Lewis understands these needs that he can explain the benefits of his product range. This will assist the retailer to meet their priorities.

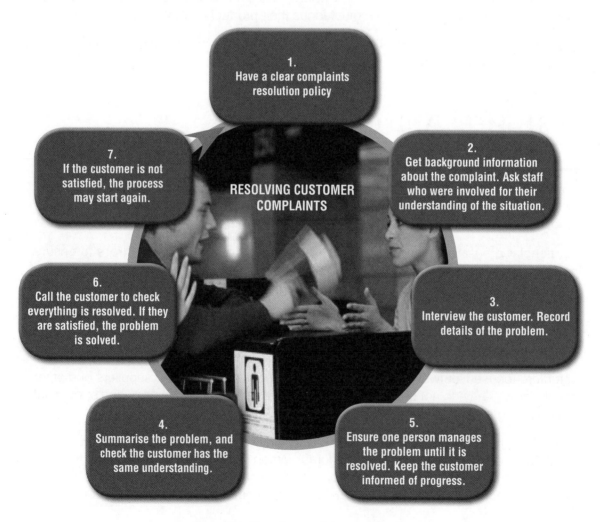

RESOLVING CUSTOMER COMPLAINTS

1. Have a clear complaints resolution policy

2. Get background information about the complaint. Ask staff who were involved for their understanding of the situation.

3. Interview the customer. Record details of the problem.

4. Summarise the problem, and check the customer has the same understanding.

5. Ensure one person manages the problem until it is resolved. Keep the customer informed of progress.

6. Call the customer to check everything is resolved. If they are satisfied, the problem is solved.

7. If the customer is not satisfied, the process may start again.

Figure 4.1: Steps in complaint resolution

It is important to interview the customer thoughtfully. They should be treated with patience and should have an understanding of how the complaint will be dealt with. Even when all care is taken, if the customer is being unreasonable the business may have to decide whether they are able to keep this customer. It is important to document all that has been done so that the person being assisted realises that they are being given special treatment.

IDENTIFYING POTENTIAL CUSTOMERS

In order to identify the customers of the business, the owner will need to conduct market research, and then group the market into segments. The focus of this chapter is the development of **market research**. Market research aims to assist the business owner in knowing who will purchase the good or service being produced by the business. The main focus is to identify the target audience for the business, and to ensure that the product meets the needs and wants of that group of people.

> **Market research:** gathering information about the marketplace, consumers and competition in order to identify the target market and their needs and wants.

Gathering market information

A business might have the most unique and innovative product or service. It may have many great qualities and excellent potential. However, if the owner and managers of the business do not know exactly what their potential customers want, the businesses will not be profitable. Marketing enables the business to focus on who their customers are, what their customers want, and how to deliver to customers.

The business needs to conduct market research in order to know the consumer, and to know the business competitors. This market information enables the business to identify the target market of potential customers for the business. Market information is also important because the business can develop a plan for the business, ensuring that the marketing mix is correct.

Sources of marketing data

Marketing information is generally collected from either a primary or a secondary source. **Primary data** is collected from the original source, usually from the customer. The organisation might conduct the collection of primary information itself. Usually it involves interacting directly with customers by interviewing, surveying, observation or test marketing.

Primary data can be collected through interviews, such as discussion with customers, or small focus groups.

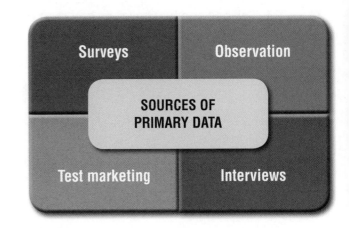

Survey questionnaires can be conducted either over the telephone, on the Internet, by post or face to face. Another method involves observing how an individual or a group of people behave when shopping, or collecting information about their purchasing habits. Finally, test marketing is an alternative whereby the customer is given the product and their response, use and reaction is observed.

Secondary data has already been collected by another organisation, such as the government or another market researcher. It is published in journals, government reports, industry association information and other publicly available locations.

Secondary data can also be generated within the business. There will be reports from other areas such as operations, finance, divisional offices and so on. This information can be analysed and interpreted by the marketing manager.

> **Primary data:** information collected directly from the consumer, usually for market research purposes.

> **Secondary data:** information collected indirectly from another organisation or within the business, usually for market research purposes.

> **BUSINESS CONCEPTS**
> Ashani is the owner of Games and Gadgets, a specialty toy store. She INTERVIEWS her customers to find out if they are likely to purchase new toys, by discussing their purchases with them in the store. She also OBSERVES their reaction to the sample toys that are made available in the store. These are both sources of primary data for Ashani.

INNOVATION AND OPERATIONS

The owner of Games and Gadgets wishes to research the age groupings of potential customers in her local area. In order to do this, she accesses the Australian Bureau of Statistics website to find out demographic information.

Target market

Every business organisation must identify their potential customers, and within this potential market aim to supply a specific **target market**. Some businesses do not focus on all possible customers, or the **mass market**. A small business is particularly likely to want to find a market segment or a small niche market. If the whole potential customer base is represented as an entire pie chart, smaller segments and niches can be shown as a portion of the pie chart.

> **Target market:** a particular section of the market, with customers at whom the product (good or service) is aimed.

> **Mass market:** the majority group of potential customers who might wish to purchase a good/service.

Figure 4.2: Mass market divided into three segments and one niche

The target market can be divided, or segmented, according to its main characteristics.

Table 4.1: Market segmentation

Geographic:	by region, post code, city or other location
Demographic:	by income, sex, age, ethnic background
Behavioral:	attitude, use of product
Lifestyle:	interests, beliefs, opinions

BUSINESS IN SOCIETY

A soft drink brand targeted teenagers from affluent demographic by producing a crowdsourcing marketing campaign that invited young adults to create new colours and names for its next variation of flavour. Television and web based advertising was aimed at this age group, using production and timing.

IDENTIFYING POTENTIAL COMPETITORS

When the business owner has made a decision about their target market, and identified their market segment, they are able to analyse potential competitors. Basically, competitors are businesses in the same market segment, offering comparable products at a comparable price.

> **Questions to ask about potential competitors**
> - Who are the top three direct competitors?
> - Are there any indirect competitors?
> - What are the strengths and weaknesses of each competitor?
> - What is the market's opinion of these competitors?
> - What are the goals of the competitors?

The business owner should obtain as much information as possible about competitors. When information is obtained, it is used to predict the behaviour of competitors.

Competitor outline

A **competitor outline** compares the proposed business with its main competitors along a range of elements. The following sample breakdown would be used for a small to medium business.

Competitor outline: a summary that compares the business with its main competitors.

Table 4.2: Sample competitor breakdown

ELEMENT	BUSINESS	COMPETITOR A	COMPETITOR B
Location			
Opening hours			
Interior			
Exterior			
Perceived quality			
Customer capacity			
Promotions			
Street advertising			
Product			
Prices			
Staffing			
Service			
Licenses required			

MARKETING MIX

When the business has identified potential customers and competitors, it is then time to create a marketing campaign. A marketing strategy is usually developed around the elements of the marketing mix. The strategy details how the four parts of the marketing mix can work together in order to achieve the marketing objectives that the business has set. The mix is also called the **Four P's**: Product, Price, Promotion and Place. For each element of the mix, the businesses product (good or service) is matched with the target market, with the aim of ensuring a competitive advantage.

Figure 4.3: The 'Four Ps' of the Marketing Mix

Product

The business organisation will decide on the goods and/or services it wishes to market. This product is designed to meet particular needs for the customer, and will be presented to consumers, using a variety of product strategies.

A consumer will purchase a product that meets their wants and their needs, and different consumers will be attracted to different product aspects. Less tangible aspects such as the name, packaging and branding will appeal to particular customers. The type of service and warranties provided will be important to other types of customer.

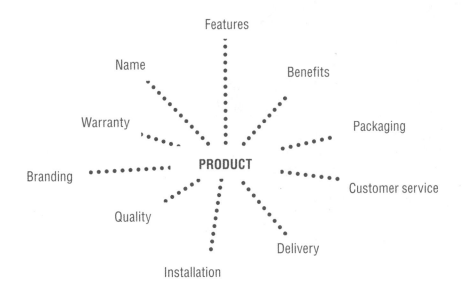

Figure 4.4: Elements of product

INNOVATION AND OPERATIONS

Fruit at Work delivers fresh fruit to workplaces around Australia. Their product strategy is to source the 'highest quality and freshest products ... mouth-watering fruit with incomparable fruit quality.'[1]

The small business owner will want to distinguish the business from competitors. One popular method is through the development of unique design, packaging and labelling for the good or service. This will ensure that it is easier for consumers to identify and remember the business, and can enable the business to focus specifically on market segmentation or the niche market.

Branding a product

A **brand** is a name, symbol or design that is used to identify a product and differentiate it from competitors' products. Brand identity is the business' belief in the meaning of the brand, which is reflected in the marketing and advertising of the business. The business organisation will undergo activities aimed at **branding** their product, to ensure consumers can identify the brand, feel confident about it, and remain connected in some way to it. Brands are often highly valued by the business, and their reputation is protected very carefully. This section focuses on branding from the business owner's point of view.

Brand: name, symbol or design used to identify a product or service.

Branding: creating a unique identity for a product or service, so that customers can identify with it.

---

1   www.fruitatwork.com.au/, accessed February 2007.

Figure 4.5: Product differentiation

Creating a brand design

A brand is created in order to make the product appear unique. There are several ways to distinguish a brand from others in the market, and often elements of a brand will be **copyright**.

Copyright: the exclusive right to use and limit access to an idea or creation.

Table 4.3: Elements of a brand

ELEMENT	EXPLANATION
Font	The brand name or an abbreviation can be shown using a unique font, created for the product.
Colour scheme	Some brands even attempt to have a specific colour copyrighted to them, in order to appear individual.
Sound	In the multimedia world of today, the business can have unique noise or music associated with the product.
Graphic	Attention-grabbing pictures or symbols will assist with the visual appeal of the brand.

In order to protect the brand from being copied, the business must register it and apply for a trademark. A trademark can be a word, phrase, letter, number, sound, smell, shape, logo, picture, aspect of packaging or a combination. A trademark is indicated with the symbol ™ at the end of the brand name. It is not compulsory to register a trademark, and some are difficult to register. It cannot describe the product, or mislead the consumer and it is difficult to register a geographic name or a common surname as a trademark.

---

2   www.confectionerynews.com/news/ng.asp?n=69360-cadbury-schweppes-darrell-lea, accessed February 2007.

Packaging a product

The Australian Packaging Council defines packaging as follows.

> all products made of any materials of any nature to be used for the containment, protection, handling, delivery and presentation of goods, from raw materials to processed goods, from the producer to the user or the consumer.[3]

Packaging can be used for one of the following three purposes:

1. **Primary packaging** is used for an item that is being sold to the consumer at the place of purchase; for example, the glass bottle to hold a drink or the blister pack used for tablets.

2. **Secondary packaging** is around a group of items, and is often used to place those items on the shelves at the place of purchase. It does not have to be included with the product for the product to work; for example, a cutaway box used to hold chocolate bars or small tins of fish on a supermarket shelf.

3. **Tertiary packaging** is used for the handling and transport of a number of items or grouped items in order to prevent damage. It does not include road, rail, ship and air containers; for example, plastic wrapping used to keep multipacks of soft drink together on a palette.

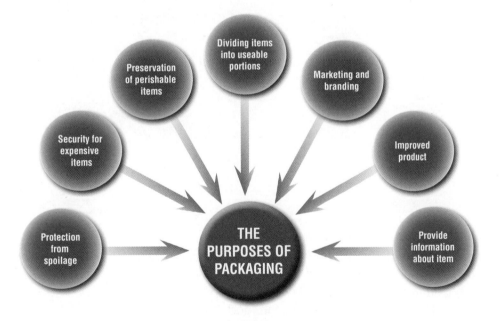

Figure 4.6: Purposes of packaging

BUSINESS CONCEPTS

Hardware stores use primary packaging such as plastic bottles for liquids and paper cartons for bulk purchases of small items like nuts and bolts. Secondary packaging is used to keep a number of items, such as boxes of nails, on the shelves. Larger boxes or plastic sheeting is used to transport wood and items to retail outlets.

Packaging can be important for the marketing of a product or even a service, because it can make it appealing to the consumer, and improve the appearance of quality. The package used can distinguish the items from other brands, make the product more easily identifiable for the customer, and be eye-catching and therefore more recognisable to consumers.

3   The Packaging Council of Australia Inc, www.packcoun.com.au/, accessed December 2006.

Packaging choices

The major packaging materials used in Australia are glass, metal (aluminium and steel), paper (cartons and corrugated), and plastics (PET, PVC, polypropylene and polystyrene). Paper is about 36% of the total Australian packaging market. Plastics is the second largest sector at 30%, a large increase from the early 1960s when plastics had less than 10% of the packaging market. Metal packaging has lost market share but still accounts for 20%, with glass at 10%. Other types of packaging make up the remainder.[4]

> **Packaging:** the wrapping used to protect, deliver and store products.

Packaging is used to help sell a product, and the choice of **packaging** used by business can be reflective of consumer decision making patterns. Consumers demand that their products are differentiated, and that they fit in with their lifestyle, and packaging can assist in achieving these requirements. The external package that a product is contained in must have high quality graphics and be strongly related to the advertising campaign that the business might use.

Customers are also demanding that packaging be tamper evident, environmentally friendly, and inexpensive. Some of these requirements compete with the cost effectiveness and financial goals of the business.

> ### PACKAGING STRATEGIES
> ☞ What is the cost per item?
> ☞ What does the target market want?
> ☞ How can the brand be included?
> ☞ Does the community want recycled or minimal packaging?

Labelling

Product labels are generally aimed to fulfil two main functions. One is the marketing of the brand and the other is to inform the consumer. In Australia, labelling laws are clear about the information that must be provided to consumers. Food labelling laws must follow the Food Standards Code. All food labels must identify the food, lot number, Australian address of the supplier, ingredients, the date, nutrition information, country of origin and any warnings. Foods are only exempt from labels if they are unpackaged, not for sale without an outer package, packaged in the presence of the purchaser, certain fruit and vegetables, ordered directly, or sold as a fundraiser.

BUSINESS CONCEPTS

The nutrition information panel found on Australian food products is required to state information about quantities within one serve of the product, and within 100 grams of the product. This is an attempt to make foods comparable.

---

4   The Packaging Council of Australia Inc, 2006.

PRICE

The business will need to determine the price required to cover costs and meet profit objectives. The business also needs to determine the price the customer is willing to pay, and remain competitive. There can be several negative effects of an incorrect price.

Table 4.4: Approaches to pricing

Competitor	A price is set in response to competitors' prices.
Market price	Increase price if demand is up and decrease if demand declines.
Discount	This is used to stimulate demand if sales are low.
Cost plus margin	Ensure the business makes a profit. The total cost of production is calculated then a **margin** for profit is added.

Margin: an amount by which the price is increased, to gain a profit from each sale.

BUSINESS IN SOCIETY

The Marvellous Moves 70's clothing store is experiencing a downturn in sales, due to the Christmas holiday. In order to stimulate some demand and move slow moving product out, they have decided to offer a DISCOUNT to customers of 10% for any purchase over $200.

Discount: an amount by which the price is reduced, in order to encourage a higher level of sales.

Pricing strategies

Financial calculations are used to determine the price required to cover costs and meet profit objectives. If the price is too high, the consumer may decide the product is not of high enough quality, or does not offer enough customer service, to justify the higher price. If the price is too low, the consumer may believe the product is too cheap and poor quality. The reputation of the business might be adversely affected. The main pricing strategies that a business can use are price skimming, penetration pricing and equivalent pricing. Price leadership is a more general strategy which could potentially be used.

Skim pricing: a high price is set for a product or service, which customers should pay because of the perception of quality, innovation or exclusivity.

1. Skim pricing

A high price is set because customers are happy to pay more. Generally this can occur when a new product is launched, because consumers who are early adopters of new products or new technology are unconcerned about paying a premium price in order to get hold of the product first. The business can build a particular image for the product if it is able to demand a relatively higher price, and this may flow on to being able to afford particular promotional methods. The business can segment itself into a particular section of the market.

BUSINESS CONCEPTS

High-end designer handbags demand a premium price due to PRICE SKIMMING, where the consumer is happy to pay more because they believe in the quality and exclusivity of the product.

2. Penetration pricing

A low price is set because customers will then respond by purchasing more and new customers will start to purchase the product or service. The product needs to be relatively popular. Alternatively this pricing strategy may be used because of competitors moving into the same market segment. A business might be able to afford low pricing when the accessories that come with the main item are sold for a higher mark-up. Caution is required, because competitors might potentially attempt the same pricing strategy, and because the image of the product could suffer at a relatively lower price.

BUSINESS CONCEPTS

Many personal electronic gadgets such as mobile phones and music devices are sold at low PENETRATION PRICES to attract consumers then their accessories, which fit only that product, are sold at a much higher mark-up to make up for the loss of income from the main device.

3. Equivalent pricing

Customers may have an expectation about the prices in the specific industry that the business is located. In this situation prices are set in accordance with the expectations and to be comparable with competitors.

> **Penetration pricing:** a low price is set for a product or service, which should attract a high number of customers.

4. Price leadership

This is a more general strategy and one which may be chosen by the business as part of its overall strategic plan. The owner may wish the business to be seen as the first to introduce any price changes, and in doing so would set the precedent in pricing for other business entities to follow. Usually only a large business can set prices for the rest of the entities in the industry to follow.

Prices can be set in relation to competitors, or the market price, or set at a discount to stimulate more demand. Generally break even analysis is used to determine the margin added to make a profit.

PRICING METHODS

TARGET: a price is set so that particular profit goals can be reached.

VALUE BASED: a price is set based on the value the consumer places on the product or service, compared to the competitors.

ABSORPTION: a price is set that covers all the variable costs, and a proportion of the fixed costs.

COST PLUS: the price covers all costs, plus a mark up amount above the costs.

Figure 4.7: Pricing methods

PROMOTION

Every small business needs to set up a strategy for promoting their good or service to the consumer. Promotion involves the communication of information about the product to the target market, while also attempting to influence the behaviour and attitudes of the consumer. Promotion methods can fall into a variety of different categories.

The main methods used to carry out promotional strategies are advertising, sales incentives, personal selling, and free publicity.

Public relations: management of the connections between a business and its customers and clients.

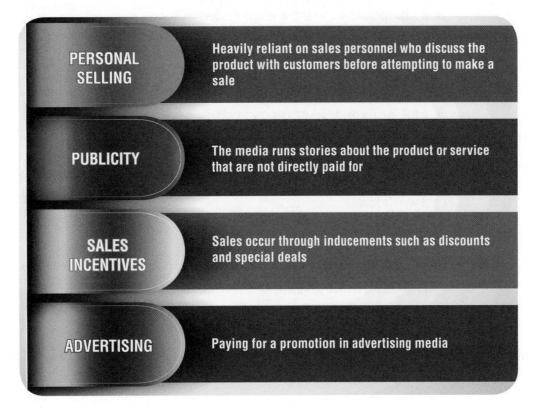

PERSONAL SELLING	Heavily reliant on sales personnel who discuss the product with customers before attempting to make a sale
PUBLICITY	The media runs stories about the product or service that are not directly paid for
SALES INCENTIVES	Sales occur through inducements such as discounts and special deals
ADVERTISING	Paying for a promotion in advertising media

Figure 4.8: Promotional methods

INNOVATION AND OPERATIONS

The business ModelCo[5] has developed a 'no advertising' method of marketing its make-up products. The organisation focuses on building the profile of the brand in cost-effective ways by using the press – through beauty editors in magazines and newspapers. The products are sent to stylists and make-up artists, who then use the products on celebrities, who then endorse the product.

---

5   www.modelco.com.au/, accessed February 2007.

Promotional strategies

Promotion involves ensuring that the consumer knows about the advantages and benefits of the business' product or service. There are two main promotional strategies that can be used as part of the four P's. These are 'push' and 'pull' promotional strategies.

Push promotion strategy: retailers promote a product to customers, creating demand.

A **'push' promotional strategy** attempts to create demand from customers for the product. Information about the product is disseminated through the distribution chain of wholesalers and retailers. Retailers are encouraged to know as much as possible about the product and to advocate its benefits. When a 'push' strategy is used, the customer is directly advertised to, and the distribution chain is flooded with the product.

Pull promotion strategy: customers demand a product from retailers.

A **'pull' promotional strategy** involves a lot of spending on advertising before the release of a product or service, to create demand from customers for the product or service. When it is released, consumers will request it from retailers and wholesalers.

BUSINESS CONCEPTS

In Australia, mobile phones are usually sold through PUSH strategies such as small retail outlets where the retailer is encouraged to sell high volumes of the product, and given incentives to personally promote the benefits. The retailer can be approached personally or through trade shows.

BUSINESS IN SOCIETY

In Australia, new children's toys are often heavily promoted through advertising and television shows before their actual release for sale as a type of PULL strategy.

BUSINESS CONCEPTS

Marko owns a pie shop and on Sundays offers a deal where customers can purchase three items and be given the fourth for free. This is an example of a SALES INCENTIVE.

There are several possible advertising methods which a business can use to send the message about their product to consumers.

Online shopping portal: a website that provides access to shopping sites and the ability to search for particular goods or services.

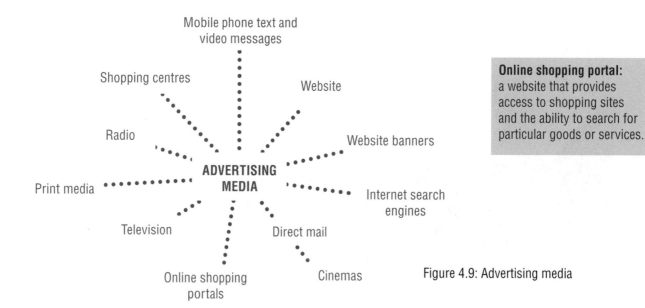

Figure 4.9: Advertising media

Branding strategies

Brands are valuable marketing tools, and an important part of the marketing strategy. The choices made about branding can be reflective of consumer decision making patterns. The consumer will associate particular levels of quality with a **brand**, and will have a specific image of the product or service provided by the brand. Brands can be registered as designs or trade marks.

A **design** is the 'the overall appearance of a product. The visual features that form the design include the shape, configuration, pattern and ornamentation which, when applied to the product, give it a unique appearance.' [6] A design registration means that the visual features are registered to the owner. It must be new and distinctive.

> **Design:** visual characteristics of a product or service.

A **trade mark** 'can be a word, phrase, letter, number, sound, smell, shape, logo, picture, aspect of packaging or a combination of these.' [7] The registration of a trade mark means that the owner has the legal right to use the trade mark within Australia.

> **Trade mark**: a unique identifier for a product or service.

BRANDING STRATEGIES

☞ **Brand creation:** What do customers like about the business? What are the strengths?

☞ **Customer values:** What priorities do customers have and how does the business meet these?

☞ **Brand establishment:** Are the strengths of the business reflected every where – such as in the product name, logo, jingle, website, shop signage, uniforms, customer service area, packaging, distribution, stationery?

☞ **Advertising budget:** What is most appropriate and likely to reach your customers?

☞ **Feedback:** What do customers and employees say about the brand? What do potential customers think?

PLACE

The term 'place' refers to the method of distributing the product or service to consumers. The method of transport from the **wholesaler** to the **retailer** is very important, as is the number of retailers who will then be used to sell the product directly to consumers. Additionally the management of inventory at all stages of the **distribution chain** is required.

The use of the internet has changed distribution networks significantly for small businesses, and manufacturers can often access consumers directly.

> **Wholesaler:** a business which redistributes, sorts and delivers goods to retailers for sale to the public.

> **Retailer:** a business which sells goods directly to the consumer.

> **Distribution chain:** the organisations required to move a product or service from the manufacturer through wholesalers to retailers or the customer.

---

6   IP Australia, http://www.ipaustralia.gov.au, accessed December 2006.
7   IP Australia, http://www.ipaustralia.gov.au, accessed December 2006.

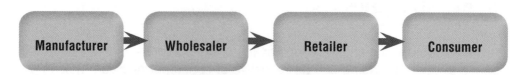

Figure 4.10: Simple distribution chain

BUSINESS CONCEPTS

Deals Direct is an online shopping website which provides a range of shipping options to customers. Items are sent with transit insurance, faulty items replaced, and consumers can purchase bulk wholesale products, resell them online and the business will ship the sold items on.[8]

---

8   www.dealsdirect.com.au/

ACTIVITIES

A. CHECK YOUR UNDERSTANDING

Potential customers and competitors

1. What does it mean for a business to have a 'customer focus'?

2. Summarise a simple process to follow when a customer makes a complaint.

3. Outline the purpose of market research.

4. Explain the difference between primary and secondary market research, using examples.

5. Give examples of each of the following forms of primary research:
   A. Interview
   B. Survey
   C. Observation
   D. Test marketing.

6. Why does a business define its target market?

7. Describe four ways for a business to segment the market.

8. What questions would be researched about potential business competitors?

9. Describe the purpose of a competitor breakdown.

10. Summarise the main headings found in a competitor breakdown.

The marketing mix

1. What are the five main areas of branding strategy?

2. What are the most popular types of packaging?

3. What is the purpose of product differentiation and how does it apply to branding?

4. What are the main purposes of a label?

5. What is a consumer likely to think if a price is too high or too low?

6. Compare and contrast 'skim pricing' and 'penetration pricing'.

7. What is price leadership and which type of business is likely to be able to use this?

8. Summarise four pricing methods that a business might choose between.

9. Summarise Figure 4.7: Pricing methods.

10. Why is packaging an important aspect of advertising?

11. Describe three different forms of advertising media.

12. Compare 'push' and 'pull' promotional strategies.

13. Summarise the following promotional methods, giving one example of each:
    A. Advertising
    B. Sales incentives
    C. Personal selling
    D. Publicity

14. List some possible distribution strategies.

15. Show a simple distribution network diagram, and define each part.

16. How does the distribution network change for a business that uses the internet as its main source of orders?

17. How can a business identify distribution opportunities?

B. BUSINESS RESEARCH

1. Choose a popular Australian business and access their website. What information does the site give you about their target market? What are the business' potential marketing objectives, and how do they appear to meet each objective?

2. Access the 'Marketing' section of the Small Business Development Corporation website at **www.smallbusiness.wa.gov.au** and outline why market research is important when identifying potential customers.

3. Go to the 'Lesson Store' in the Marketing Teacher site at **www.marketingteacher. com** and complete the activities for one of the following topics:
    A. eMarketing
    B. Internet marketing
    C. Marketing environment

4. Collect three different print advertisements from a newspaper. Create a table to analyse the pricing strategies being shown by each business: skim, penetration, equivalent or price leadership.

5. Collect four packages for four different products. Create a table to analyse how each product has been differentiated from the other, using the elements of product differentiation from Figure 4.5: Product differentiation.

6. Cut ten brand symbols/logos out of newspapers and magazines. Attach these to a piece of paper and see how many another class member can identify. Which businesses advertise with only their symbol and not their name? How do they reinforce the recognition of their logo?

7. Use catalogues from two different hardware shops to compare the availability of a list of standard items such as:

    - power tools
    - pot plants
    - outdoor furniture.

    How is place (or distribution networks) used to gain a competitive advantage for these businesses?

8. Use secondary data for your local area. Go to the Australian Bureau of Statistics website at **www.abs.gov.au** and click on the "Census Data" link. Complete the following:

    A. Search the census data by location for your local area and analyse the Community Profile (you will need to download the Profile). How does this broad information assist you in analysing the following aspects of your local area:

        - Total people aged 15 years and over, and 65 years and over
        - Australian citizens, and language spoken at home
        - Employment levels?

    B. Download a Census Table for a specific topic such as birthplace, education, income, internet usage, migration or occupation (you will need to download the selected Table). How can this more specific information assist in the formulation of market research for your area?

    C. Summarise what you have learnt about your local area from the statistics you have analysed.

C. RESPONSE

1. Create a business profile for a small local business. Select one of the competitors of this business. Use 'Table 4.2: Sample competitor breakdown' to summarise the main elements of this competitor.

2. Describe the target market for each of these products:

    A. Mobile phone with video messaging
    B. 'Big Day Out' concerts
    C. A fit ball and set of hand-held weights
    D. Shakespearean theatre
    E. Energy soft drinks
    F. Retirement planning

3. List four local businesses and illustrate their approach to marketing, as you have observed it as a consumer. What is the most effective aspect of each businesses' marketing? What one aspect could be improved and why?

4. Choose a board game that you are familiar with. Create a survey for an organisation that wants to research the response of primary school students to this board game.

5. Name a business that you are familiar with, that appears to have successful marketing strategies. Explain how this business has successfully implemented each of the four 'Ps' of marketing.

6. Explain how the following changes in the marketing environment would influence the marketing mix for a specific business.

    A. Change of Federal Government
    B. Changes in society's beliefs about marriage
    C. New laws about junk food advertising
    D. Higher interest rates decreasing consumer spending

7. Consider Figure 4.4: Elements of product. Create a table summarising these elements for your choice of a locally produced product. When you have finished, share your summary with another class members and record their product elements for another product.

8. Table 4.4: Approaches to pricing gives different methods of setting prices for a business. Explain how each would apply to a business that wants to determine their pricing policy.

9. Analyse how a local business has used at least one of the promotional methods listed in this chapter for 'branding strategies'.

10. What do consumers demand of packaging that might be environmentally friendly but not cost effective?

11. List the primary packaging, secondary packaging and tertiary packaging needs of a deli.

12. Your friend Gia really enjoys coffee – so much so that she has decided to start her own small business; a mobile coffee truck that is driven to workplaces to make coffees and teas for the workers at each business. She has purchased a vehicle and has had it fitted out with all her requirements. Using the product strategies outlined in this chapter create her business brand and packaging and design the vehicle logo for Gia's new business.

13. How do large electrical and whitegoods stores use both price skimming and penetration to undercut their competition? Use examples to illustrate your answer.

14. Use shopping catalogues from two different supermarkets to compare the prices of a list of standard food items such as:

    * Chocolate
    * Milk
    * Bread
    * Fruit
    * Meat

    How is price used to gain a competitive advantage for these businesses?

15. A local gymnasium and fitness centre wishes to establish their brand in the marketplace. Write a report explaining to the business how this can be achieved through the use of product name, logo, jingle, website, shop signage, uniforms, customer service area, packaging, distribution and stationery.

16. Choose three types of advertising media from Figure 4.9: Advertising media. Define each one, and explain how a small local business selling crockery and cutlery would use each one.

17. Describe a paid advertisement for children's cereal that you have seen in the media. Use Figure 4.8: Promotional methods and outline how this product could be further promoted using the three other methods.

18. As online businesses increase in number, are distribution strategies becoming less relevant? Why or why not?

19. Layla has just created an innovative new card game, aimed at students in Year 7-10, and designed to assist with learning health and physical education concepts. She has found a manufacturer who can produce 5000 decks of the game. Provide a report to Layla outlining the distribution network she would need to set up for her product.

20. Marketing case study.

    Carole is commencing her new business 'Card capers', which will sell high quality paper and cards which Carole has manufactured herself. She is considering holding lessons for customers on how to create their own cards and photo albums. Her main competitor is 'All occasions for less cost', a discount paper shop in the next suburb. Carole's opinion is that their product is likely to be slightly cheaper and of lower quality. Her shop front has an excellent amount of window display space, and the street itself is quite crowded containing about ten other local shops.

    Complete the following:

    A. Outline a detailed approach to the marketing mix for the business
    B. Design a promotional advertisement for the local newspaper
    C. Draw a design for the window display of the shop.

21. Target market case study.

    Erika owns a home based business, and has developed a number of accessories for the home office and for people to use in a workplace environment. She is developing items that people would give as gifts.

    One item that she has developed stores paper business cards in an easily accessible format, as well as having the option of a small hand-held scanner and software so that card information can be scanned into a computer and become easily searchable.

    This most recent innovation is a new product that she is yet to name and brand. She has shown the product at a Trade Fair and a major retail store has placed orders. It will need to be delivered to twenty shop locations within Western Australia.

A. What type of consumer should this product target?

B. Complete the following for this new product:

- Name
- Features
- Benefits
- Warranty

- Packaging
- Branding
- Quality
- Delivery

D. GROUP PROJECTS

1. Many business organisations market products to tweens and to teenagers, due to a belief in 'pester power', where children influence their parents' purchasing decisions. For example,; several food manufacturers aim their advertising at children, who do not have the funds to purchase groceries for the family, and children pester their parents to spend money on the groceries.

   Using a small local business, or a local franchise business, you are to choose an appropriate product that is not currently being marketed in this way – something that is not marketed to teenagers. For example you might choose a local butcher or a car servicing franchise. Research this product online, and compare their marketing strategies with other products in the same industry. Gather both primary and secondary research data. Design and conduct a target market survey to determine how this product can be marketed to a new target market – teenagers.

2. In pairs, choose a **local** product with a broad customer base, and collect at least ten print/television advertisements for this product.

   A. Define the current target market for the product.

   B. Redesign the product so that it is aimed at a specific niche market, different to the current target market and create a sample video or print advertisement.

   C. Design a slide presentation that summarises the branding, packaging and distribution methods required for the redesigned product.

CHAPTER 5
Business Planning

'Setting a goal is not the main thing.
It is deciding how you will go about achieving it and staying with that plan.'
– Tom Landry –

Business plans are important to the small business owner. They set the direction and enable the planning, coordination and control of the business. With the focus provided by a good business plan, the owner can set their strategy through a targeted mission statement. This enables them to specify their business profile and design the blueprint for the businesses future.

This chapter will cover:

- Planning business activities
- Features of a simple business plan

PLANNING BUSINESS ACTIVITIES

All business owners and managers want business to run smoothly and careful planning should enable this. Planning is one of the most important parts of the management function of a business. It ensures that there is some coordination and control as the business plan can be used to guide operations. If there is no planning, then the business will not have any direction and will not know how to prioritise activities.

A business plan is a proposal that aims to give direction for the achievement of the business owner's goals and objectives.

Types of goals

Strategic planning and the creation of a business plan is important to the business because it gives focus. Along the way, owners can review the business plan and see how well goals were achieved, then can change objectives as required in response to internal or external influences.

Figure 5.1: Business goals

Profit: the extra amount of income that a business makes over its expenses.

Cash flow: the amount of cash entering and leaving the business over a specified period of time.

Market share: the proportion of the entire market that the business is selling it product or service to.

Goals give the business owner information about required results or outcomes. They also provide the owner with measures to check that goals are being achieved.

BUSINESS CONCEPTS

The owner of a kitchen ware shop has set the profit goal of 'achieving a weekly profit of $2000 every week, with an increase to a profit of $3500 or more on weeks preceding Mother's Day, Father's Day and major public gift-giving holidays or events. This goals is to be achieved within the first two months of opening and must be sustained for the financial year'.

FEATURES OF A SIMPLE BUSINESS PLAN

When developing a business idea, the owner/s will need to: establish the goals of the business, find financing, and create a simple business plan for their new business idea.

Setting goals and objectives

The first aspect of strategic planning is the development of a **Mission Statement**. The business can use this to outline goals and objectives. Ongoing reflection and review will allow the small business owner to ensure that goals do not obscure the mission, or prevent the business enterprise from remaining innovative.

Mission statement: the main overarching purpose of the business.

To develop explicit goals, the Mission Statement is broken into its component parts, and different types of objectives that will assist with meeting the Mission Statement are listed. The owner should then analyse the present and future resources that will be available to meet the Mission Statement goals, as these will restrict the final decisions that are made.

The business owner might then allocate **goal setting** to people within the business (depending on the actual structure). If employees set their own objectives, keeping in mind the overall restrictions, then they are more likely to have **ownership** of the goals. Finally, it is important that objectives are relevant, achievable and reviewed on a regular basis. Otherwise they may become outdated and not be relied on. These steps are illustrated in Figure 5.2.

> **Goal setting:** deciding on the main objective or aim.

> **Goal ownership:** when an individual personally believes in the importance of a goal.

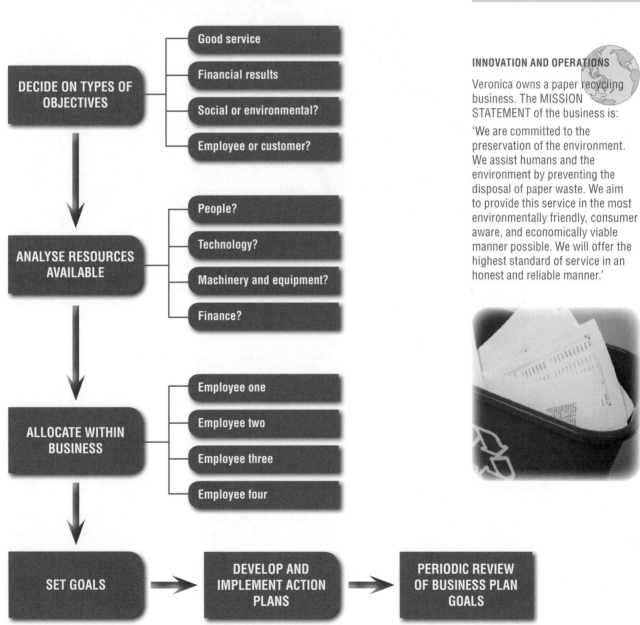

Figure 5.2: Steps in goal setting

INNOVATION AND OPERATIONS

Veronica owns a paper recycling business. The MISSION STATEMENT of the business is:

'We are committed to the preservation of the environment. We assist humans and the environment by preventing the disposal of paper waste. We aim to provide this service in the most environmentally friendly, consumer aware, and economically viable manner possible. We will offer the highest standard of service in an honest and reliable manner.'

BUSINESS PLANS

Abusiness plan is a detailed outline of goals and how future operations, financing, management and marketing will assist in achieving those aims. A business plan is often prepared when a new business is being set up. It might also be required when further finance is being sought, or if the business owners require detailed information about the future strategic direction of the business. This section will discuss simple business plans for small to medium businesses that are just starting up.

1. Purpose

The business plan should have an **overview** that contains the main sections in the plan, as well as a clear explanation of the purpose of the plan. The purpose of a business plan for a start up business is usually to obtain finance for the business or to describe the basics of the new business.

This summary can also include information on the *current position* of the business and the expected *future outlook* if the plan is implemented.

> **Overview:** summary of the business plan contents and purpose.

> **Mission statement and goals:** the aims to be achieved by carrying out the strategies contained within the business plan.

2. Mission statement and goals

The mission statement and business goals are the first section of the business plan. This is because of their importance in setting the scene for the rest of the information, and because they give a focus for all other elements of the plan.

The philosophy behind the proposed new start-up business should be clear in this section.

Goals should be **SMART Goals:** specific, measurable, attainable, realistic and time-bound.

3. Business profile

The business profile includes a description of the ownership, status, competitors, customers and advisors.

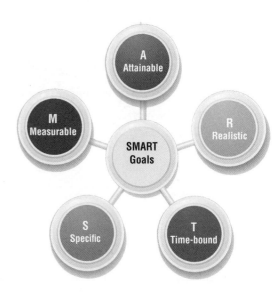

Business profile: an overview of the business, including ownership, status, competitors and clients.

Competitor outline: a comparison of the business with its main competitors.

BUSINESS OWNERSHIP	• profile of each owner, including their previous business experience and education
BUSINESS STATUS	• how the business will be set up and the amount of capital required • main activity of the business and the product (good or service) to be sold • the competitive advantage of this product
COMPETITOR ONLINE	• summary of the industry that the business is working within • location of the business • competitor breakdown
CUSTOMERS AND ADVISORS	• details of any major clients or advisors

Figure 5.3: Business profile

4. Marketing plan

The marketing plan outlines the target market as well as details of product, price, promotion and place.

> ### THE MARKETING PLAN
>
> 1. **Current market position**
> 2. **Any barriers to entry** and market research results
> 3. **The product** (good or service)
> 4. **Target market** and market segmentation
> 6. **Marketing strategy:** product, price, promotion and place

Marketing plan: a profile of the strategies that are to be used to achieve marketing goals.

Barriers to entry: Challenges such as low brand recognition, high production costs, poor training and other issues that make it difficult to establish a new business.

5. Operational plan

The **operational plan** is a summary of how the business will operate each day and how it will undergo the production process if required. There are a number of sub-sections, depending on the type of business.

All businesses would detail capital funds management, supply and distribution networks, location, pricing strategies, internal controls over assets, and risk management strategies.

A **trading/retailing business** would require a summary of inventory needs. This includes main suppliers, plans for the storage and display of stock, and any distribution needs. Decisions need to be made about **turnover** targets and reordering of stock.

A **manufacturing business** would require more specific information, such as production process requirements, process diagrams, production schedules, building capacity, inventory details for raw materials and finished goods, and details of manufacturing equipment required.

Operational plan: details of how the production process and daily operations of the business will be used to achieve production or operations goals.

Turnover: the total sales for a certain period of time.

6. Resources

Information about the personnel required needs to be detailed here as part of the **human resources** information. This section includes the main responsibilities of each employee, training, insurance, Occupational Health and Safety issues and new staff requirements.

Physical resources are the assets that the business requires. The main assets required in the shopfront, or for a virtual shopfront, must be priced and listed. A time plan for the purchase and replacement of assets that will have depreciated rapidly needs to be included.

Resources strategy: details of the physical and human resource requirements of the business.

7. Financial plan

The **financial plan** is often the most extensive part of the business plan, containing information on anticipated earnings. There are a number of forecasts that would be made in this section, all aimed at predicting the likelihood of success for the business. It is vital that all estimates are made as carefully as possible.

Financial plan: a detailed plan of the financial goals and earnings requirements of the business.

THE FINANCIAL PLAN

☞ Start up expenses

☞ Breakdown of the capitalisation of the business

☞ Sales and purchases forecasts

☞ Projected Income Statement and expected income/expenses

☞ Monthly cash flow

☞ Break even analysis

Capitalisation: the costs of purchasing long-term assets, such as vehicles, property, equipment.

Start up expenses: The initial costs that must be paid before the business can open, such as registration fees, accountant's charges, promotion, and training.

ACTIVITIES

A. CHECK YOUR UNDERSTANDING

Planning business activities

1. Define a business plan.

2. Explain the purpose of setting goals.

3. Clearly explain how planning is linked to organisational goal setting.

4. Define the following terms:
    A. Mission statement
    B. Goals
    C. Objectives

Features of business plans

1. Explain the purpose of a Mission Statement.

2. What is a 'start up business'?

3. Compare goal setting and goal ownership.

4. Summarise the main steps in goal setting.

5. What is the function of a business plan?

6. Outline the main sections of the business profile part of a business plan.

7. What is the purpose of the marketing plan?

8. How is the operational plan for a trading business different to that for a manufacturing business? Why does a retail business not include this section in their business plan?

9. Define each of the following sections of the financial plan:
    A. Start up expenses
    B. Breakdown of the capitalisation of the business
    C. Sales and purchases forecasts
    D. Projected Income Statement and expected returns
    E. Monthly cash flow
    F. Break even analysis

10. Is any part of a business plan more important than the others? Why or why not?

B. BUSINESS RESEARCH

1. Download the Business Plan Template from the Small Business Development Corporation website at **www.smallbusiness.wa.gov.au/business-planning**. Create a summary diagram that shows the main sections of a business plan. Compare and contrast this summary diagram with the business plan suggested in this chapter.

2. Choose three large Australian companies, and look up their Mission Statement on their websites. Summarise the main areas that their mission is focused on. As a consumer, have you noticed any aspects of each mission statement when you purchase products from these companies?

3. Access the MyBizPlan app on the Australian Government's small business information website at **www.business.gov.au** (Follow the links through: Howtoguides – Thinkingofstartingabusiness – Whatplanningtoolscanhelpme – Businessplanguidesandtemplates). Use these ideas to create a Business Plan for a local small business of your choice.

C. RESPONSE

1. Write a simple plan for a local or school event that is to occur this year. Set three goals, and then complete a one-page report outlining the following information:

   A. What needs to be achieved?

   B. How will this happen?

   C. Who and where will this occur?

2. Consider Figure 5.1: Business goals. Write four goals each for the following business organisations (remember to use the SMART. Goals):

   A. A research and development firm

   B. A computer servicing and sales business

   C. A cake and biscuit manufacturer

   D. A health food retailer

3. Use Figure 5.2: Steps in goal setting to set goals for Tex, the owner of a small start-up business, which will sell individually designed t-shirts. You may make any assumptions required.

4. Jak and Jil have decided to start a business selling flavoured milk from their specialist dairy in the South West. They own 100 cows, a milking shed and have access to a renovated wooden shed which customers could use as a cafe. Their relatives have offered to provide $5000 seed funding, and they have a friend who will give them two refrigerators. The local bank has set up an interview for them next week. Jak owns a $15,000 car and Jil has $3000 savings.

   A. What forecasts would they want to make in their financial plan?

   B. List all possible start-up costs.

   C. Provide a breakdown of the capitalisation of the business.

5. Business plan case study.

Andy has just finished Year 12 and wants to start his own business. He completed Hospitality studies at school, and has decided to take over an already existing cafe in the shopping strip of his suburb. He has a friend, Stephanie, who has some restaurant management experience. His most direct competition is a nationally franchised coffee shop, and an ice-cream parlour that sells a well known brand of ice-cream, gelati and drinks. Andy's specialities include healthy snacks and unhealthy cakes. The location of the business is shown in the diagram below.

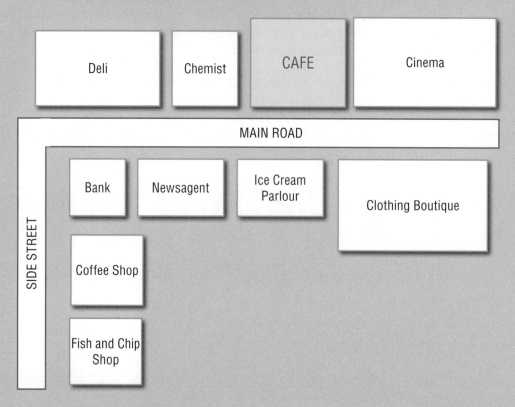

Using additional information from what you know of businesses in your local area, complete a simple Business Plan for Andy.

D. GROUP PROJECTS

I. Analyse a series of business Mission Statements particular to your choice of industry.

A. In groups, collect media articles and samples of Mission Statements from business journals and the business section of newspapers.

B. Summarise the key themes for businesses in a particular industry.

C. Choose one business and rewrite the Mission Statement in simple language.

D. Create three strategic planning goals (follow the steps in goals setting outlined in this chapter) for the business.

E. In pairs, create a poster to be displayed to employees. The poster is to display the Mission Statement and goals in an attractive, eye-catching manner suited to the particular industry.

CHAPTER 6
Operating a Successful Business

'How many people are completely successful in every department of life? Not one. The most successful people are the ones who learn from their mistakes and turn their failures into opportunities.'

– Zig Ziglar –

The operations of small business rely on the business owner having clear aims that enable them to measure their success. Many small businesses fail because of a lack of proper planning or expertise. Knowing the market, and knowing the product, is if vital importance. An additional significant element of small business is sourcing and maintaining funding.

This chapter will examine:

- Business success and failure
- Finance and the business

BUSINESS SUCCESS AND FAILURE

Success: accomplishing a set goal or goals.

Failure: not achieving planned goals.

The difference between **success** and **failure** for a small to medium business can vary depending on the original goals set by the owner. Often, small issues accumulate over a period of time and it is important that the owner can monitor progress in an ongoing way. The definition of "success" will vary between businesses and having a clear business plan with the goals the business wants to achieve, will enable a clear measurement of success.

Success and failure for small business have been compared in the following table, focusing on the areas of finance, planning, skills and marketing.

Table 6.1: Business success and failure

Area	Success	Failure
Finance	Having enough cash to ensure positive cash flow, and being able to make a profit. The business owner must budget carefully.	Not enough reserves of cash, or a misunderstanding of the business' likely cash flow. A business requires enough cash backup to be able to get through issues such as poor creditor repayments and seasonal changes in sales.
Planning	Time for business planning and reflecting on the achievement of goals. This may be difficult for the owner of a small to medium business, as they can often feel overwhelmed by the day to day running of their business.	Poor business planning. The business needs a clear plan for the future, and systematic ways of reviewing if this has been achieved. This will allow the owner to make changes when needed.
Skills	Using outside expertise and mentors. The owner should be able to employ other people for advice in areas that are not their strength.	Knowing strengths and being able to trust other people to assist in areas of weakness. The business should not be over reliant on any one individual.
Marketing	Collecting useful, timely and relevant market research information that can be used by the business to meet customer needs is important. This research should be regularly reviewed.	Poor market research. Before commencing a business, the owner needs to know their customer and to be able to describe their needs. They need to establish that the product or service is likely to be profitable.

BUSINESS CONCEPTS

Isabelle is concerned that her business does not have enough reserves of cash after one year of operation. As she sells bathers, her business enterprise is very seasonally based and she has not predicted the business' likely cash flow correctly. She needs to be wary, as the indications are that she will fail financially in the near future if she does not plan carefully for success.

Avoiding over extension

As a small business starts to grow, the owner may not realise all the challenges that come along with the conversion from a **Small-Medium Enterprise (SME)** to a larger business. Often business expansion can occur quickly and the owner may not have planned for this to happen. This could result in the owner being overwhelmed by the technical, legal and management aspects of expansion and not having the time to focus on important cash flow issues.

> **Small-Medium Enterprise (SME):** an independent business, generally managed by its owners and employing up to 200 people.

The owner might have the exciting possibility of their business becoming very popular early on, however they must ensure that any business growth is sustainable. If the business becomes very popular, the owner needs to be cautious that they do not exhaust all their cash and reduce **profitability**. It would be costly to finance large stock inventories to meet new customer demand, or to purchase new infrastructure or assets to manufacture new stock. If the owner over extends financially, then they are gambling with the future. If customer demand decreases they could find they do not have the cash inflow required to pay back loans.

> **Profitability:** the financial return made from an investment in a business.

Increased customer demand

**Finance stock,
by purchasing a large amount on credit**

Economy or popularity of product declines

Downturn in customer demand

Business loses sales

Business cannot repay loans

Figure 6.1: How a small business can over-extend financially

BUSINESS OPERATIONS

Bec Lennox opened her scrapbooking supplies business Scrappindipity as a home based business. As the business expanded when more product lines were added, she moved to a stall at the markets in Fremantle. The limited opening hours then led to a decision to open a shop in Fremantle. This involved more expansion – as well as new product lines the business started running workshops. The need for growth had to be carefully balanced with the increased costs of renting commercial space. Bec is being very careful, keeping an eye on cash flow and ensuring customers are being listened to when new inventory is purchased. She has been very careful to avoid overextending herself even though the growth of the business is an exciting prospect.

SUCCESSFUL PERSONAL HABITS OF BUSINESS OWNERS

An alert business owner will be aware of their internal motivations and personal goals. People with strong self awareness can identify what they do well and where they need help. They are more able to develop successful personal habits and self management skills, thus having the potential to be more successful as a business owner.

Identifying successful habits

Success can be defined in a number of ways. For many business owners it is the achievement of a goal, and for some it is both the process of working toward a personal goal as well as the final achievement. Allowing the process to be considered as part of the final achievement of success means that the individual can learn from mistakes and setbacks and develop an ability to be flexible in response to change. Being able to not give up is an important part of success.

There are a range of habits, which if practised on a regular basis, can lead to the successful achievement of goals for each staff member.

Table 6.2: Personal habits of success

Visualise	The successful achievement of the goal that has been set.
Challenge	Be on the lookout for positive experiences, helpful people and opportunities that will be of support in achieving business goals.
Responsible	Have ownership of life and of decisions made, do not blame events on other people in an overly focused manner as this is sidetracking.
Believe	Have self belief and use positive self talk. Be realistic but not overly negative about potential.
Listen	Communicate with others carefully and listen carefully.
Plan	Approach each business goal in an active manner, recording in some way the steps required to achieve it.
Enable	Work with others not against them.
Flexible	Be able to adapt and change business path in response to new challenges.

By setting business goals that are in line with their personal goals and then putting priorities next to these, a reflective and self aware business owner can start to enable their success. A habit can be developed and acquired by focusing on successful habits and not negative ones. As a result the workplace will overall become a more positive place.

Self management

Personal time management in the workplace can assist the business owner to manage their stress levels and to gain a greater feeling of being organised and in control of their work day. Figure 6.2 contains some time management tips that an individual would need to consider in order to make their day at work more manageable.

TIME MANAGEMENT TIPS

1. **Prioritise**
   - ✓ Keep 'to do' lists
   - ✓ Complete each item in order of priority
   - ✓ Break tasks into small units of time

2. **Have breaks**
   - ✓ Estimate accurately the time required to finish tasks
   - ✓ Ensure that regular breaks are scheduled
   - ✓ Go for a walk or do something active in a break

3. **Clear work space**
   - ✓ Organise the place where work occurs
   - ✓ Have frequently used items within reach
   - ✓ Keep paperwork filed – preferably electronically

4. **Do not procrastinate**
   - ✓ Recognise when trying to delay something or put it off
   - ✓ Distinguish between 'urgent' and 'important' tasks and prioritise tasks that are both
   - ✓ Handle each piece of paper once

5. **Limit emails**
   - ✓ Do not constantly check email
   - ✓ Have a few times in the day when email is checked
   - ✓ Do not have an 'email conversation' – if replies are going back and forward constantly – speak to the other person instead

6. **Consider time of day**
   - ✓ Work on important or creative tasks in the morning
   - ✓ Leave routine reviewing or checking to low concentration periods such as after lunch and late in the afternoon
   - ✓ Schedule regular meeting and appointment requirements

Figure 6.2: Personal time management tips

FINANCE AND THE BUSINESS

Accounting and finance encompass two important areas of business management. **Accounting** involves recording financial information and presenting this in the form of financial statements so that the business can evaluate and plan. Finance involves how the business sources its funding. There are a number of steps to follow when seeking a source of finance and when deciding between financing alternatives.

Accounting: the process of planning and keeping financial records.

Sources of finance

A business requires funding either to be able to commence as a new entity, or for the expansion of existing business. A source of finance is a supplier of money to the business. Possible sources can include **financial institutions**, hire companies, new investors, the business owner and family members.

A business owner will need to consider several issues when deciding to borrow funds.

Financial institution: a source of funding, such as a bank, credit union or finance company.

Questions to consider when borrowing funds

- ☞ What is the money required for?

- ☞ How long is the money to be borrowed for? The short, medium or long term?

- ☞ How much will interest repayments, or **dividend** payments, cost?

- ☞ How much will be repaid each time a payment is due?

- ☞ What conditions have been placed on the **loan**?

Dividend: an amount of money paid by a company to its shareholders, as a share of the profits of the business.

Loan: money that has been borrowed by the business to be repaid at a future date.

Financing options are usually considered in relation to the amount of time the business has to repay them. They can be short, medium or long term.

BUSINESS CONCEPTS

Amir has owned his painting business for a year now. He has decided that he needs to invest in more equipment, such as drop sheets and spray-painting equipment. In order to do this, he has created a specific list of the items that he requires money for. Then he looks at lasts year's finances and calculates how much money he should be able to repay each month. He looks up banking websites to find out the approximate cost of loans. This enables him to budget the amount of money that he will apply to a financial institution to borrow.

Short term sources of finance

Short term finance must be repaid within the next **one month to two years**. A high rate of interest is usually charged.

Table 6.3: Types of short term finance

TYPE	GENERALLY USED FOR	SOURCED FROM
Overdraft	Seasonal fluctuations, working capital requirements Available for 1-30 days.	Bank, financial institution
Converting assets into cash	Selling stock/inventory, collecting accounts receivable, selling non-current assets	Debtors, customers
Bridging finance	One asset is sold to buy another Available for 1-30 days	Financial institution
Trade credit	Stock purchases, materials Available for 7-60 days	Trade creditors
Loan from family or friends	Small assets	Personal relationships, lawyer
Hire purchase	Vehicle, computing equipment, machinery Business keeps asset	Hire company, bank
Debt financing/Loan	Large non-current assets	Financial institution
Retained profits	Retaining profits in the business, and using these to fund the purchase of assets or repayment of loans	Business

Overdraft: an arrangement with a financial institution where the business can withdraw more cash than it actually has.

Trade credit: occurs when a business allows customers to pay for goods after they have been ordered and delivered to them.

Hire purchase: a business purchases an asset and pays for it over a period of time, with ownership of the asset transferring at the end of the payments.

Medium term sources of finance

Medium term finance must be repaid within the next **two to five years**. A lower rate of interest is usually charged.

Table 6.4: Types of medium term finance

TYPE	GENERALLY USED FOR	SOURCED FROM
Mortgage	Building purchase	Financial institutions
Government loan		Australian government
Venture capital	New and innovative ideas	Business angels, crowdfunding
Loan from family or friends	Small assets	Personal relationships, lawyer
Lease	Vehicle, furniture and fittings, office equipment, machinery Lessor keeps asset	Finance company, bank
Debt financing/Loan	Large non-current assets	Financial institution

Long term sources of finance

Long term finance must be repaid within a term that will be longer than **five years**. A low rate of interest is usually charged.

Table 6.5: Types of long term finance

TYPE	GENERALLY USED FOR	SOURCED FROM
Debentures	Business expansion	A loan from investors, which must be paid interest
Shares/Owner's investment	Business establishment or expansion	Shares are held by shareholders in a company, and are usually paid dividends Owner's investment is additional capital for a sole trader or partnership
Mortgage	Building or land purchase	Financial institutions
Government grant	Government interests such as research and development, exporting, technology	Australian government
Venture capital	New and innovative ideas	Business angels, Crowdfunding

Venture capital: capital which is invested in return for a share in the business, usually in a high risk or very entrepreneurial business.

BUSINESS CONCEPTS

Mai has written her first feature film script. She has approached a number of movie studios with her script, however has not been able to fund the film project. So she has set up a crowdfunding webpage, where investors are invited to invest a minimum of $400 each in the project, with the incentive being a share of the potential returns from future film sales and related publicity. As a result, she has raised the $10,000 initial capital required.

INTERNAL AND EXTERNAL SOURCES OF FINANCE

All financing options are provided either internally by the business and its owners, or externally by creditors and lenders. The investment of money or other assets by owners is their **capital** or share in the business. A loan is an amount of money provided to the business by a financial institution, which must be repaid with interest by a specific date.

Capital: the owner's investment in the business.

INTERNAL FINANCING

Money supplied to the business by the owner, earned from trading, or from selling assets for cash. All within the business.

Capital is not required to be repaid to the owner. It is a type of **EQUITY**.

EXTERNAL FINANCING

Money supplied to the business by a loan provider who is paid interest, or a trade creditor who supplies products before being paid. All outside the business.

A **loan** must be repaid with interest by a due date. It is a type of **DEBT**.

Figure 6.3: Internal and external financing

The equity contribution by a sole trader or a partnership owner of a business is called the capital investment by the owner/s. For a company, this financing contribution is referred to as shares. A proprietary limited company will usually have only a few owners, whereas a public company might have hundreds.

INNOVATION AND OPERATIONS

Wekesa is commencing a high risk marron farm in the south-west corner of WA. In order to be able to fund this new business, he requires external financing from a venture capitalist, and his own internal financing which will be his motor vehicle and a cash deposit he has saved.

Balancing internal and external sources of finance

Comparison of the levels of external sources of finance (or debt) and internal sources (or equity) is very important because the business will not want to have too great a portion of funding coming from external sources unless interest rates are very low. **Gearing** is the relationship between the debt and the equity of a business. If a business has high gearing, there is a high level of borrowed external funds compared to internal equity. A low gearing means that there is a low portion of external debt compared to internally generated equity. This is measured using the **debt to equity ratio.**

$$\text{Gearing} \quad = \quad \frac{\text{Total debt (Liabilities)}}{\text{Total equity}}$$

Debt to equity ratio: a method of measuring the gearing of a business so that it can be compared with other organisations.

A business will usually prefer to have low gearing, because that means that it is providing funds through daily trading and from the owners, who are less likely to require the repayment of capital. When more funds are provided from external debt, there is a requirement to repay this debt at a specific point in time, as well as to pay interest, and this places pressure on the business. The pressure can affect the **cash flow** of the business.

Cash flow: the total amount of cash entering and leaving the business.

A business with high gearing may be able to meet interest payments which is especially useful if interest rates are low. If this business also sells its product very quickly, it will have a more positive cash flow situation.

Monthly cash budget

A business would produce a Cash Budget as part of planning for future operations, and a business owner might be asked to complete a monthly cash budget for the first year of operations by a lender such as a bank. The Cash Budget shows inflows and outflows of the cash of a business, excluding all non-cash items for the period. It provides information that enables the business owner to:

- predict any changes in the total assets of a business,
- consider the financial structure (including liquidity and solvency)
- plan for the business to adapt to changing circumstances and opportunities.

Cash flow information is useful to assess the ability of the business to produce cash and cash equivalents. Historical cash flow information is used as an indicator of the amount and certainty of future cash flows. It is also useful in checking the accuracy of past assessments of cash flows and in examining the relationship between profitability and liquidity.

The cash flow budget is also useful for an individual looking to set up a small business, even for something as simple as a market day stall. It will allow them to plan and set budget targets.

CASH INFLOWS
- Can include asset sales, liabilities such as the receipt of a loan, equity as the investment of capital by the owner.
- Inflows from income are generally in the form of sales or fees, interest earned and other cash coming into the business.

CASH OUTFLOWS
- Can include asset payments such as the purchase of new equipment, liability payments such as the repayment of loans, and equity could include drawings from the owner.
- Most outflows are the payment of cash expenses such as salaries, advertising, transport, telephone, electricity, rent, cost of goods, etc.

Figure 6.4: Examples of cash inflows and cash outflows

Table 6.4: Sample monthly cash budget

MONTH	JAN	FEB	MAR	APR	MAY	JUN	JUL	AUG	SEP	OCT	NOV	DEC
Opening bank balance												
CASH INFLOW												
Cash sales												
Receivables												
Capital investment												
Loan income												
Other												
Total Inflows												
CASH OUTFLOW												
Cost of sales												
Payables												
Selling costs												
Distribution costs												
Administrative costs												
Financial costs												
Acquisition of asset/s												
Repayment of liabilities												
Owner's cash drawings												
Miscellaneous												
Other												
Total outflows												
CASH FLOW												
Closing bank balance												

FEASIBILITY OF FUNDING

When a small business owner applies for finance from a financial institution, that institution will complete a risk assessment before deciding if they will lend the funds. The lender will require some form of **collateral**, or security for the loan. This might include an asset such as property or equipment. If no collateral exists, then the business could find someone who is willing to act as the guarantor for the loan.

The lender will also consider the **credit rating** of the business owner, which is their record of previous debt repayments. They will then look at the capacity the business has to repay the loan, such as any other debts and the ability to make regular cash repayments.

Collateral: an asset that a lender can take if the borrower defaults on the loan.

Credit rating: an evaluation that is used to determine if the borrower is likely to be able to repay their debt.

BUSINESS CONCEPTS

Jeremy owns an orchard and his business tends to be very seasonal. Most income comes in over three months of the year when fruit sales are in full swing. His financial institution has asked him to show how his business will be able to make regular monthly repayments for the full term of his five-year loan.

Figure 6.5: Perceived risk factors

ACTIVITIES

A. CHECK YOUR UNDERSTANDING

Business success and failure

1. Compare the meaning of the terms 'success' and 'failure' for a small business.

2. Summarise the main reasons why a business should avoid over-extending their financing.

3. What is a small-medium enterprise (SME)?

4. List and describe key personal habits which lead to success.

5. Why is it beneficial to the business owner if employees develop good workplace habits?

6. Explain the usefulness of each of the following personal time management tips:
    A. Competing tasks in order of priority
    B. Having active breaks
    C. Ensuring workspace is clear and filing up to date
    D. Handling each piece of paper once
    E. Only checking email a couple of times in the day
    F. Working on creative tasks early in the day

Finance and the business

1. Complete a table showing the following for each different source of finance:
    A. Definition
    B. Advantages
    C. Disadvantages

2. Classify each source of finance from this chapter into internal or external types of financing.

3. Explain the following terms for a business owner who is considering different sources of finance: interest, repayments, loan conditions.

4. Compare short, medium and long term finance. Give two examples of each type.

5. Define 'gearing.'

6. Compare and contrast internal and external sources of finance.

7. What is the purpose of a monthly cash budget?

8. Outline how collateral and a business' credit rating are relevant when applying for funds.

9. Summarise the elements of a risky business investment.

B. BUSINESS RESEARCH

1. Collect five media articles about small local businesses. Consider the four areas of business success and failure in Table 6.1: Business success and failure.

   A. Which of your five businesses is most likely to succeed in one year's time?

   B. Why?

   C. Rank the businesses in order of their likely success or failure within the next twelve months.

2. Access the websites of four major financial institutions and look up their interest rates for business loans. What conditions do each place on the loans? Which loan do you recommend and why?

C. RESPONSE

1. For each of the following examples, outline the critical issue affecting the business' success or failure, then decide if the owner is likely to succeed or fail in this business:

   A. A business has just completed its monthly Cash Flow Statement, and does not have enough cash to meet this month's creditor repayments.

   B. An owner has no time to plan for the future of the business, as they are so busy responding to daily issues.

   C. A business employs outside experts with skills to manufacture a specific technical component of their product.

   D. An owner has just completed intensive market research on the needs of consumers.

2. Alex owns a small home based business, selling bike parts over the internet. Demand for these bike parts has grown so much that he is going to expand to provide bike repair services and finance this by applying for a loan. The business will need to move to new premises. Using Figure 6.1: How a small business can over-extend financially, explain any problems that Alex needs to anticipate.

3. Using the information provided on borrowing funds, look up the website of a financial institution and write a summary of how long it would take to repay a business loan of $1,000,000 over a period of ten years.

4. Define each of the following business acquisitions. Then suggest the best possible source of finance, explaining why.

   A. Machinery

   B. Photocopier

   C. Materials required to manufacture product to fill a new order from a customer

   D. Office building

   E. Marron farm in a tourist area

   F. Shop shelving

   G. Inventory

H. New medical breakthrough that is at the forefront of research and development

I. Purchase of computing equipment while waiting for the sale of stock to be processed

J. Purchase of a fleet of five motor vehicles that will be obsolete in ten years' time.

5. Your friend Helen owns a computer service business, and relies on her vehicle to transport her and her equipment, as well as repaired computers, to customers. Her vehicle requires replacing, and she has the following options:

- hire purchase of a new vehicle
- leasing
- an unsecured loan
- a secured loan (at a lower per annum rate and with her mother acting as guarantor).

Consider the 'questions to consider when borrowing funds' from this chapter. Recommend to Helen her best course of action.

6. Eric is the owner of a business which sells BBQs and outdoor settings. The business has a high gearing ratio. Write a report for Eric, and include answers to the following questions.

A. What does 'high gearing' mean?

B. How could the ratio be made lower?

C. What is an acceptable range for the gearing ratio in times of high interest rates?

D. GROUP PROJECTS

1. Irene is an artist who creates unique, one-off pieces of jewellery. She currently advertises her jewellery in the local lifestyle magazine, and through personal contact and parties. She has sales outlets in five small wineries and gift boutiques dotted throughout WA. She is going to expand her business, including employing some assistants, and would like your advice.

A. How can Irene ensure she is successful in the areas of finance, planning, skills and marketing?

B. Access the websites of three financial institutions and research the main forms of finance available to Irene, and explain to her how she should avoid over extending her financing.

C. How will Irene need to develop her management roles to plan, organise, control and lead as she expands her business?

2. Sources of funding case study.

You are going to open a new business in the local shopping centre in your town/suburb. You have estimated that you require $10 000 for fittings and fixtures, $7000 for office equipment such as an integrated computer/cash register/fax/photocopier, and you can potentially purchase a second hand vehicle for $12 000. Before approaching any financial institutions or friends for extra funding you need to consider all your possible sources of finance.

Complete the following in pairs:

A. Research the current cost for the assets you require, or use the dollar amounts listed above (discuss this with your teacher).

B. List and define all possible sources of finance for your new business.

C. Rank these possibilities in order from the most to least optimal.

D. Explain why you ranked the best and worst sources in that order.

E. If you decided to form a company instead of operating as a sole trader, how would your ranking change? Explain.

MANAGEMENT CROSSWORD

Across

5. The method of product distribution
6. A business which sells goods directly to the customer
11. Information collected directly from another organisation or within the business, usually for market research purposes
12. Name, symbol or design used to identify a product
13. A long term loan used to purchase land or buildings
14. Borrowed money
16. The section of the market to which the product aims to appeal
17. Information collected directly from the consumer, usually for market research purposes
18. Accomplishing goals results in this
19. The good or service that will be marketed
20. Type of promotion where the media runs stories about the business
21. Share of the profits paid to shareholders

Down

1. A business proposal that aims to give direction for the achievement of the business owner's goals and objectives
2. A statement about the main overarching purpose of the business
3. Visual characteristics of a good or service
4. An arrangement when more money is taken out of a bank account than in actually in the account
5. The financial return made from investing in a business or other opportunity
7. The physical and human capital needs of the business
8. The amount a customer is willing to pay for a product
9. Gathering information about the marketplace, consumers and competition in order to identify the target market and their needs and wants
10. The majority group of potential customers who might wish to purchase a good or service
15. Dividing up the market

SECTION C: PEOPLE

CHAPTER 7
The Role of Human Resource Management

'Organisations which are committed to excellence understand that employees can be their single greatest asset and foundation for long-term success.'

– www.merchandiseinfo.com –

> **Human resources:** the people of an organisation including their knowledge, skills and abilities.

There are many resources within a business. However, people are the vital living resource that 'makes or breaks' a business. Every business, big or small, has a complex organisational structure which requires a combination of skills, aptitude, creativity, initiative and enterprise to operate effectively.

This chapter explores human resource management (HRM) in a small business context. It aims to reveal the importance of people to a business. Within the chapter we identify what is HRM, the role of HRM, HR guidelines and the HRM process within a business. In this process we identify how to effectively manage the employees of a business to reap the full benefit from their skills and knowledge as well as how to guide and motivate them to aid business success.

BUSINESS CONCEPTS

Michael who lives in Albany, a regional country town, worked with the help of his brother Mark to purchase a van and modify it as a mobile coffee shop. Every weekend the brothers take turns to drive the van to local venues. Coffee to Go[1] is now a famous name among the coffee lovers in Albany. The success of this small business is due to the commitment and skill of the two brothers, the human resources of this business.

THE VALUE OF PEOPLE IN BUSINESS

Businesses are a product of human thought, creativity and skill. People are required to operate within a business by completing tasks to make the product or provide the service. Without people a business cannot exist therefore the **human resources** element of the business needs to be carefully managed.

---

1   Coffee to Go – Coffee Van, Albany, Western Australia.

HUMAN RESOURCE MANAGEMENT (HRM)

Human resources are the people of a business, that is the employees. This includes the employees' knowledge, skills and attitudes. Human Resources are the living breathing aspect of the business; consequently the beliefs, values and life style factors of the people influence the workforce as a whole. This is referred to as 'Human Capital' due to its value and importance to the business. Human capital is often considered the most important asset in small businesses. Small business employees have a direct impact on the working environment that is created, the way the business runs and ultimately whether it produces successful outcomes or not.

Figure 7.1: Overview of human resource management

Human Resource Management (HRM): the process of acquiring, developing and maintaining an organisation's human resources for the purpose of achieving organisational goals and objectives.

Human capital = Human resources of a business.

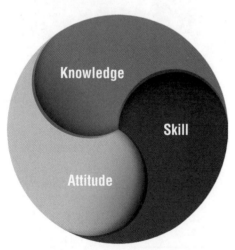

Employee (the human resource)

Figure 7.2: Elements of human resource management

BUSINESS CONCEPTS AND BUSINESS IN SOCIETY

Cosis Café[2] is a small business operated in Albany that is more successful than most of its counterparts. It serves breakfast, lunch and cakes with tea and coffee as most cafes do. The key to Cosis Café's continued success is the great food it serves and the personalised service it provides. The business is owned and operated by a husband and wife team.

Clearly two people cannot be everything. To excel in all aspects of the café business they have a team of cooks, kitchens hands, waiters, baristas, cake makers and so on. Each of their contributions is vital as the customers experience their output first hand. Even though there is no formal HR department for the café business, the owner is conscious about the value his staff adds to the business. Therefore he is fully engaged with selecting a team of employees that suit the Cosis Café's culture and are excellent in their areas of work. He encourages and supports them on a daily basis, making them feel valued and part of the café. As a result every member of staff, regardless how minute their role may be, takes pride in their job, resulting in an excellent final output. Therefore the business operates smoothly on a daily basis.

---

2   Cosies Café, www.facebook.com/cosiscafe, accessed 07 May 2014.

ROLE OF HRM IN SMALL BUSINESS

In a small business environment where there is no capacity to host large departmentalised operations, the role of a HR department is absorbed by the business owner itself.

BUSINESS CONCEPTS AND INNOVATION AND OPERATIONS

Organisations such as Gloria Jeans[3] coffee group have a team of employees as the Human Resource Management Department. These groups assess and provide required instructions to the management of the organisation on how to control and manage staff. In small business ventures such as Venice Restaurant[4] the owner and manager Guy Lembo has to undertake all the human resource management aspects of his small but highly successful restaurant. He claims that careful selection of his staff and training are the basis for success. He communicates to his employees about their performance and rewards them where appropriate, encouraging positive workplace behaviour and outstanding performance. Guy's mantra is successful business begins with good people and good products.

Figure 7.3: HR roles of a small business owner

TABLE 7.1: HRM Responsibilities of the small business owner

Responsibility	Includes...
Overall management and control of staff	• Manage the welfare of employees. • Guide employees towards achievement of organisational goals.
Job designing and job planning	• Identify the duties of a job. • Identify skills and knowledge needed to complete those duties. • Match skills and knowledge requirements to the job.
Recruitment and selection	• Identify suitable applicants.
Training and development	• Provide required training and development for the employee to complete his or her job effectively.
Performance appraisal	• Review employee performance to monitor performance level. • Review the job to identify changes and highlight training needs.
Management of reward systems	• Identify effective rewards and compensation methods to suit the particular job.
Occupational Health and Safety (OHS)	• Identification, implementation and evaluation of OHS practices.
Industrial relations (IR)	• Provide consultation on IR issues.

Recruitment: a process undertaken by businesses to attain staff.

Compensation: reimbursement or a reward provided by the business to employees for their services.

---

3   Gloria Jeans Coffee, www.gloriajeanscoffees.com.au, aAccessed 11 May 2014.
4   Venice Restaurant, www.facebook.com/The-Venice, accessed 11 May 2014.

Human resource guidelines

Employees of a small business hold all the keys to its operations, production, marketing and sale. Therefore they are a key ingredient. It is essential that they feel valued by their employer. Employees must also understand what is expected of them and how their contribution is expected to influence the future of the business. The **Human Resource Guidelines** assist in helping employees understand their obligations and provide a clear avenue for the small business owner to communicate their expectations. There are many benefits from setting clear guidelines and communicating them to employees. These benefits are highlighted in the diagram below.

Human Resource Guidelines: A set of rules and expectations that assist in helping employees understand their obligations and provide a clear avenue for the small business owner to communicate their expectations.

Human resource guidelines assist small businesses keep track of their employee management and ensure they are operating within the legal expectations of employee management requirements. **Equal Employment Opportunity** and **Employee Relations** aspects of the HRM guidelines do this. Further details on the components of the Equal Employment Opportunity and Employee Relations matters were discussed in previous chapters of this text.

Figure 7.4: Benefits of HR guidelines

Equal Employment Opportunity: Policies and practices adopted by organisations due to legislation and the value the community has placed on anti-discriminatory work practices.

Under Australian law all businesses, including small businesses and sole traders, are liable for the rightful management and treatment of their employees. Therefore having a clear set of procedures, that is guidelines, on how human resources are managed help operate a transparent business. Effective HR guidelines are developed with employee input and regularly updated to ensure they are up to date with the changes in the law and people's expectations, as well the changes the business is experiencing.

Employee Relations: Skills and practices related to the maintenance of employer-to-employee relationships that contribute to satisfactory productivity, motivation and morale.

Employee workplace rules and procedures

Employee workplace procedures are a set of quick reference guides the workplace uses to provide information to employees. These contain information regarding the daily duties, process of work practices and standards, expectations of behaviour and dress, and leave and disciplinary procedures.

Figure 7.5: Common employee workplace guideline topics

BUSINESS CONCEPTS AND BUSINESS IN SOCIETY

Alex joined a fancy local restaurant as a barista with the aim to earn some extra money during his university study break as he has had professional café barista training. He was hoping to present his customers with some high quality coffees as discussed during his interview with the restaurant owner. However, Alex never received a formal statement explaining his duties nor did the manager ever clarify to him what other duties were expected of Alex other than making coffees. On a daily basis, Alex was asked to do various other jobs that ranged from waiting at tables, cleaning the restaurant, helping out in the kitchen, doing delivery and sometimes making purchases. At the beginning Alex didn't mind this, however as time went on he felt as if he didn't know what his actual role at the restaurant was, especially when the manager would complain about how the coffee station was not managed well, regardless of the fact Alex was assigned to do other duties and abandon his role as barista. Frustrated, Alex left his job at the restaurant.

If Alex was given a clear outline of his duties and the expectations of the restaurant had of him, he would have had the opportunity to better organise his day and negotiate his duties with the manager, rather than being hired for a particular role but being assigned varying roles on a daily basis, which resulted in confusion and frustration.

Figure 7.5 depicts some commonly found workplace procedures. These are legally binding. Therefore it is vital that the information is accurate and expectations are realistic and fair. In small business environments this information tends to be presented in the form of random posters or single page documents that are filed. This makes it difficult to access them or to ensure which of the posters hold important information that is legally binding. It is advisable that businesses carefully assess what information their employees should be given and make it available in a clear and concise form that is accessible and understood. It is the responsibility of the employer to ensure that this information is up-to-date and distributed to employees during their recruitment process. Due to the legally binding nature of these procedures, it is also the responsibility of the employee to ensure they operate within the procedures. If for any reason, whether it may be health or cultural reasons, an employee cannot obey a particular aspect stated within the guidelines, they may negotiate a suitable outcome for both parties.

In summary, the purpose of **human resource management** is to assist both employers and employees in understanding the following:

- the importance of working within the requirements of the business
- the role of position descriptions and significance of performance appraisals
- the importance of developing effective strategies for working effectively in the work place.

HUMAN RESOURCE MANAGEMENT PROCESS

Human resource management has previously been considered a business component that applies only to large corporations. However, contrary to popular belief, efficient and correct management of the human element is vital to small business success. A small business is made up of three key aspects; its employees, the good/service it offers and its customers.

Human Resource Management (HRM) is the process of **attaining, managing, developing** and **evaluating** a business's human resources for the purpose of achieving business goals and objectives.

In small business, the small business owner takes responsibility for executing the components of the **HR process**, as stated previously in this chapter. The following sections of the chapter explores what is involved in each of these stages and the benefits that embracing this process bring to small business.

Figure 7.6: HRM Process

1. Attaining human resources

Attracting, selecting and attaining employees are components of the **recruitment** process in business. This component is discussed in detail in **Chapter 8: Recruitment** in this text.

2. Managing human resources

Managing employees effectively is vital for small businesses to attain the most out of their employees. It is a three-step process, which is the responsibility of the business owner.

MANAGING EMPLOYEES

☞ **Communicate** business goals and expectations clearly.

☞ **Understand** employees' own needs and expectations.

☞ **Provide** work conditions suited for the job.

Business goals and expectations

A clear articulation of the business's goals and its plan to achieve those helps employees identify their job expectations easily. When managing employees, employers need to be using language and documentation that is concise, clear and written in a tone of language that is suitable for the audience; that is, the target employee group.

WORKPLACE RULES

1. Treat each other with respect.

2. Work independently or ask help from supervisor.

3. Attend work only in full uniform.

4. Do not leave the cash register unattended.

BUSINESS CONCEPTS

Staff at the coffee kiosk at the Princess Royal Harbour in Albany[5] are constantly changing as the business provides employment to tourists who visit the town. The business owner finds it easier to have a set of simple rules and expectations posted on the wall as a regular reminder to his ever-changing staff, and it's easier on him too.

Understanding employee needs

Small businesses can take steps to ensure that the needs of their employees are met by the business. Understanding people for who they are and maintaining equity are essential factors. There are elements that business owners can concentrate on to ensure employee satisfaction, and these are identified here.

Figure 7.7: Key elements to understanding employees

---

5   Coffee Kiosk, Princess Royal Harbour, Albany, WA.

BUSINESS CONCEPTS

Tammy works at a florist. Her job involves picking up flowers from farms and delivering flower arrangements. She also assists with day to day operation of the shop and flower arrangements in between pickups and deliveries. Tammy, who is also a prominent sports woman, hurt her ankle during a competition and was unable to drive or put weight on her feet. Her employer recognised that Tammy's need to stay employed and earn an income. Therefore her duties for the next three months were altered, so she would be in charge of placing flower orders and taking booking requests as well as attending to the cash register. These were all duties she is able to do seated and using a phone and laptop. This is an example of understanding employees' needs and having a response strategy to suit the employee.

Job oriented values: values or beliefs that are directly connected to a job position.

Response strategy: a technique adopted as a solution to the needs of the employee's situation.

3. Developing human resources

Developing the employees of a small business involves three key elements of training and development.

- Orientation
- On the job training
- External training

Figure 7.8: Training and developing employees

Orientation

When a new employee is hired by a business, the small business owner provides them with an overview of the business operations, the new employee's job role and an introduction to other employees and their roles. This process is commonly known as **orientation**.

This is an opportunity where the new employee will be given their uniforms and safety apparatus, where this applies. Employees are generally given a tour of the factory or farm environment if the small business is in the manufacturing, production or agricultural industries.

Orientation is where a small business owner explains to the employee the **workplace procedures** and **human resource guidelines** the business operates under, such as hours of work, wages and work conditions.

Orientations are also an opportunity for the new employee to clarify information and raise any concerns. Figure 7.9 on the following page provides some examples of this.

BENEFITS OF ORIENTATION TO EMPLOYEES

- ☞ Learn in detail about the job role and duties
- ☞ Awareness of the workplace procedures
- ☞ Become informed of the HR guidelines that dictate the job and work conditions
- ☞ Other benefits and rewards of the job, such as staff discounts
- ☞ Opportunity to raise concerns regarding the duties
- ☞ Opportunity to request any needed training and guidance
- ☞ A forum to make the employer aware of any personal needs and circumstances that may influence the job

Figure 7.9: Benefits of orientation to employees

On the job training

On the job training is where a new employee is given training in their duties while they are employed and performing some duties. This is the most common form of training in small business. It is both cost and time efficient. Most of this training is provided by the small business owner themself or one of the experienced staff.

External training

Small businesses embrace external job training opportunities for their employees in areas where the business does not have adequate resources to provide such training. This is common in trade industries such as building and construction.

BUSINESS CONCEPTS AND INNOVATION AND OPERATIONS

Victoria is hired as a waitress at a restaurant and her job involves working with the 'Group bookings and functions staff', while making fresh juices for the daily customers at the restaurant. Victoria has never worked in a formal dining environment. Her training in formal dinner table setting was done while she was employed. Another waitress taught Victoria everything she needed to know while on the job, by teaching her what to do and how to do it. This is on the job learning.

BUSINESS CONCEPTS

Thomas has always envisioned becoming a builder, just like his uncle Paul. When Paul acceptedk Thomas as apprentice at the age of 17, he instructed Thomas to enrol in a Certificate IV in Building and Construction course at the local trade school. This is because Paul is able to teach Thomas the practical skills, however he does not have a legal authority or the other required skills to educate and certify Thomas as a builder in the long run.

4. Evaluating human resources

Evaluating an employee's performance involves reviewing their performance and managing it, as well as providing feedback. Terms such as **Performance Management**, **Performance Review** or **Performance Appraisal** are used. This allows the employees to identify their actual contribution to business, which promotes motivation. These appraisals, or reviews, can be done formally or informally. In either form it is most beneficial if these are conducted in set cycles such as six monthly or annually.

Performance management

Performance management is a process of reviewing an employee's performance over a period of time and giving feedback, which includes praising them for a job well done and providing positive criticism on areas which need improvement or disciplinary action where necessary. Performance management also includes providing the employee means as to how to improve their weaknesses. These could entail assigning mentors, further training opportunities and so on.

PERFORMANCE REVIEW AIMS

- Monitor employee performance
- Identify key strengths and weaknesses of the employee
- Identify changes in the job role and changes in working conditions and knowledge requirements
- Identify training and development required
- Match appropriate rewards and compensation for performance

Figure 7.10: Aims of a performance review

PERFORMANCE REVIEW BENEFITS

- They are a source of information for both the employer and employee.
- They provide a set time line to assess the performance of the employee.
- They identify employee performance in relation to the business performance and needs.
- They provide an opportunity to raise concerns regarding performance with legitimate evidence.

Figure 7.11: Benefits of a performance review

BUSINESS CONCEPTS AND BUSINESS IN SOCIETY

Max has been an employee of the local accounting firm in Bussleton for the last twelve months. In that time due to his diligent work the firm has had an increase in clients and the management has received messages of commendation from existing clients regarding Max as well. Marcus, who has been an employee since the start of the accounting firm, is continuously lagging behind in his work and needs regular reminders to attend the firm's weekly briefing and so on.

The firm's management saw potential in Max and hoped to one day promote him as a partner. They however never mentioned this to Max nor did they pass on the messages of commendation to Max. Max felt he was unrecognised for his efforts and commitments and being financially rewarded equal to Marcus who performed below average made this situation worse. At the end of 24 months Max left the firm.

Due to the management's oversight in providing feedback, and lack of proper performance management, they have lost a valued staff member.

Employee Evaluation

Work quality	5
Knowledge of job	5
Work skills	5
Enthusiasm	5
Initiative	
Judgment	

PERFORMANCE REVIEW TIPS

✓ Don't wait till a review to provide praise or feedback – do it on the spot – because this is much more effective

✓ Prepare for the reviewing of employees

✓ Enable preparation for the review from the employee as well

✓ Be specific

✓ Be constructive (honest and sincere, because this develops trust)

✓ Ensure the employee is clear about their duties and expectations

✓ Provide procedures on how to improve: mentors, training, education and so on

✓ Take action: reward improvements

Figure 7.12: Performance review tips

BUSINESS CONCEPTS AND BUSINESS IN SOCIETY

Tenniella was employed as an accountant responsible for accounts receivable two years ago by a small business. As the business grew Tenniella had to prepare some accounting reports and forecasts for the business. After six months completing new responsibilities she was feeling anxious as she was not certain how effectively she was performing. She was also stressed due to the increased work load but lack of increased time or pay.

The business conducted a performance review of Tenniella's position and identified the changes in her job role and provided her with necessary training, revised her job role and responsibilities and her pay structure. Now Tenniella is a happy committed staff member who is contributing to the success of the business.

Barriers

From the business owner's point of view, the biggest barriers for effective performance management are time and communication skills. Firstly, some small businesses consider that taking time away from the daily duties to review an employee's performance is not worth its return; a big mistake.

Secondly, most individuals find it challenging to communicate the weaknesses of another person or realise the value of praise when it is due. A simple set of questions could be used at the performance review interview to assist with this. Examples are given in Figure 7.13 below.

Figure 7.13: Sample performance review questions

PERFORMANCE REVIEW INTERVIEW QUESTIONS	
INSTRUCTIONS: ☐ Please ensure you allocate adequate time for this interview. ☐ Refer to the responses of the employee on their Performance Review Questionnaire. ☐ Make written remarks of the verbal responses of the employee.	
QUESTIONS	COMPLETED
1. What did you feel was your biggest achievement for the year?	
2. How do you feel about your overall performance?	
3. In what areas do you feel you didn't perform well?	
4. What can you do to make your performance better?	
5. What can I do to assist you in improving your performance?	
6. What areas would you like to focus on for development next year?	
7. What will you need to achieve this?	

In conclusion, it is essential to recognise the importance of effectively managing the *people* in a business. This process includes recognising the business focus, identifying job roles within the business, analysing these roles and developing job descriptions. Following this, the HR manager, or the business owner in a small business, engages in the demanding task of seeking out and sourcing the work force of the business. This is done through interviewing and selecting people with the right skills, knowledge and attitudes to suit the business's requirements. The HR manager continues pastoral care of employees by conducting performance reviews, identifying the needs of both the business and employees, and facilitating training and development opportunities to attain the goals of the small business as well as the employee.

ACTIVITIES

A. CHECK YOUR UNDERSTANDING

Value of people in business and HRM

1. Define the term 'human resources'.

2. What are the four areas of HRM that are explored in this chapter?

3. What are the three key elements of human capital that affect the business?

Role of HRM in small business

1. What human resource roles does the small business manager assume?

2. List six HRM duties of the small business owner and explain each of those.

HRM guidelines

1. What are human resources guidelines?

2. What are the three key features of a human resource guidelines?

3. Give five benefits of having HR guidelines in place.

4. What does employee workplace rules and procedures mean?

5. List seven workplace rules and procedures a commonly found in workplaces.

Human resource management process

1. What is meant by the 'human resource management process'?

2. What is entailed in the four sub-processes of the HR process?

3. What are the three steps in managing employees?

4. List seven important aspects to understanding employees.

5. List three elements of developing HR.

6. Explain what the following terms mean.

   A. Orientation
   B. On the job training
   C. External training

7.   What are three benefits of orientation?

8.   What is 'performance management'?

9.   List and explain the 'performance review' process.

10.   What are the reasons for performance review?

B. BUSINESS RESEARCH

1.   Read one of the articles on **Performance Review** on **http://careerplanning. about.com**. What would you do to ensure your performance review would be a success if you are the employee being reviewed?

2.   Select a **Performance Review Template** on **www.businessballs.com** and review it.

3.   What are the advantages and disadvantages of this template?

4.   View the video on **How to Prepare for a Performance Review** on **http://careerplanning.about.com**. List 10 steps to assist with performance reviews.

5.   Download your very own Employee Handbook from **www.biztree.com** and fill in the blanks and print it. During this process identify the **Employee Workplace Procedures** that are embedded within the handbook.

6.   Prepare an **Employee Needs Survey** using the sample survey questions provided within the **www.custominsight.com** website. Your teacher may wish to guide you as to the type of business the employee is working at.

7.   Select an existing sample **Employee Needs** survey on **www.custominsight.com** and complete this survey. If you have a casual or part time job, pretend you are completing this survey for this job; if you are unemployed you can complete the survey from an imaginary perspective.

C. RESPONSE

1. HRM case study

   Human Resources, or Human Capital, is the most important ingredient in the business. In a small business, employees are its life line. Their abilities, commitment and attitude affect its success level. In small business the roles and responsibilities of managing the human resources are undertaken by the small business owner. Managing the employees well is the biggest challenge for small business owners.

   A. Why are correct human resource management practices vital to a business's success? Discuss this with reference to evidence from the chapter.

   B. Lucia has just commenced managing an electrical goods store, and wants to know how she can understand her employees' talents, capabilities and aspirations. Construct your answer with reference to Figure 7.7 Key elements to understanding employees.

   C. Explain how employing the services of an HR manager, rather than the Small business manager performing these roles, can be beneficial to a small to medium business in relation to the human resource process, drawing examples from Figure 7.3 in relation to the benefits mentioned in Table 7.1.

   D. Discuss the role of small business owner assuming the duties of a human resource manager in the following businesses:

      i.   An accounting firm

      ii. A gold mine

      iii. A machinery manufacturer

      iv. A hotel

2. You are the newly promoted supervisor of the local fast food restaurant; you must now conduct a **performance review** on two cashiers.

   A. Discuss the benefits of conducting performance reviews for a small business.

   B. Referring to 'Figure 7.12: Performance review tips', explain how you would conduct this performance review session and give reasons.

   C. What advice or guidance can you provide your employer about the employee you have reviewed, and their job, after the appraisal?

   D. Discuss the following quote in relation to the types of questions that should be asked in an interview, and in a performance review:

      'I believe everybody is creative, and everybody is talented. I just don't think that everybody is disciplined. I think that's a rare commodity.'

      Al Hirschfield

D. GROUP ACTIVITY

Case study

James Cornwell and Emily Panizza are two high-performing staff members at Legal Eagles Inc. James has been with the company for 10 years and Emma for seven years. Emma's area of speciality is industrial relations and James specialises in business practices. The company is conducting interviews within the organisation to fill a vacant position. This is a senior position and any applicant will have to demonstrate commitment and capability in their current position. The senior position will involve dealing with clients of the business and working closely with the directors of the company. A representative from an independent organisation is conducting performance reviews to evaluate the skills and interest levels within Legal Eagles.

Complete a performance evaluation for these two employees who will be interviewed for the promotion.

A.   Identify the process involved in conducting a performance review.

B.   What information will be sought from James and Emily during the performance review?

C.   How will a job evaluation be advantageous in determining the job requirements of the promotional position?

- What level of human relations skill is needed? Will ordinary courtesy do? Does the job require a good communicator, or does it require an ability to motivate and lead people?

- What is the structure of the job? Where are the boundaries? What instructions, procedures or goals define the work?

- What are the boundaries of the job holder's authority to make decisions?

- What are the most difficult parts of the job? What kinds of challenges arise? How demanding is the thinking needed to solve these problems?

D.   Once you have each answered the questions and identified all the criteria for the position, work together to prepare a portfolio including the job description, interview criteria, and induction manual.

CHAPTER 8
Recruitment

'Choose a job you love and you will never have to work a day in your life.'
– Confucius –

Human resource ranagement (HRM) involves attaining, managing, developing and evaluating **people**. To ensure the business success the first step of HRM, **Attaining,** needs to be done correctly. Businesses engage in the **recruitment process** to ensure that the business attracts, interviews and employs the right individuals for the right job. This is tedious but a vital role any HR manager or, in this case, small business owner.

This chapter focuses on the process of employee recruitment in small businesses. In an effort to provide an in-depth understanding of all other key factors that influence the success of recruiting the right employee, the chapter also explores the process of job design, job evaluations and job descriptions as crucial elements of employee attainment, development and retention. Recruitment and selection reveal the benefits and the necessity of matching individuals to their capabilities and explores the sub-processes which precede recruitment, such as advertising, various job markets and interviews.

This chapter will address the recruitment process, as summarised in Figure 8.1

Figure 8.1: Recruitment process

JOB IDENTIFICATION

The success or failure of a business depends upon having the right work done by the right people in the right way. A lot of resources, especially financial ones, are allocated to compensate people performing duties and the business needs to receive a return for this outlay. It is also important that employees enjoy their jobs and are satisfied.

In an effort to match the employee with the right set of skills and other attributes with the right job, the business owner or a manager who has the role of recruiting engages in a process known as **job identification (JI)**. This process allows the business to identify the tasks within that job, the set of jobs, and the **job roles** that could overarch these required skills.

Once this is done they are able to write a job description and engage in various other processes required in recruiting future employees. This is a somewhat back to front approach, in the sense that it is easier to identify the job roles, identify the job sets within the job role and finally examine the individual tasks within each of those job sets. These are defined with examples in Table 8.1.

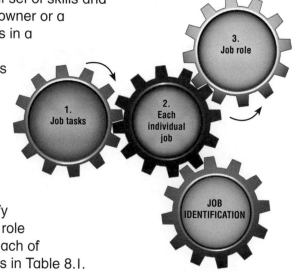

Figure 8.2: Job identification process

TABLE 8.1: Job identification process components and examples

JI process component	Example	
Job tasks: a single specific tasks	Making transactions: • Greeting the customer • Scanning the products being sold • Stating the total cost • Clarifying the mode of payment (cash, EFTPOS, credit, etc.) • Taking the payment and giving change if necessary • Issuing a receipt • Thanking and farewelling the customer	**Job identification:** recognising a particular job role, its duties and responsibilities, how the job is conducted, the working environment and conditions, and the skill and knowledge requirements.
Job sets: each individual set of jobs that comprise a range of Job Tasks	• Receiving the daily cash • Making transactions • Making deposits • Closing the till	**Job role:** a set of tasks which together make one job.
Job role: a set of tasks which together make one job	Teller machine operator	

BUSINESS CONCEPTS

A job description for a pizza delivery driver would outline the type of drivers' licence required, length and the intensity of driving experience required, customer service skills required and so on. Furthermore, it would define duties such as picking up orders, being able to read maps, ensuring accurate delivery and basic cash management.

Job description: a brief summary of a particular job. It defines and describes the job role as it is actually performed.

Job identification process

Table 8.1 outlined the most basic form of job identification. If a small business is employing staff for 10 or more roles, it is wise to pay a little more attention to this process, given that the costs of making a mistake is immense. Where possible, engaging in a job identification and job structuring process would benefit the business largely in the long run.

Figure 8.3: Job identification and structuring process

1. Job analysis

Job analysis involves identifying and describing what is happening on the job. A job description is the product of job analysis. This section outlines the job analysis process, what is entailed and the reasons for performing a job analysis. It also discusses who conducts a job analysis and how they obtain their information.

Job analysis identifies the:

- required tasks within a job
- knowledge and skills required
- working conditions needed to complete the job.

An orchard worker's job involves tasks such as pruning trees, picking fruit to specifications and fertilising. They require knowledge of the particular type of fruit they are dealing with, picking styles and requirements. They require the pruning skills and picking skills to complete the job effectively. Their working conditions include outdoor weather such as cold rainy days and hot summer days and carrying heavy produce, fruit. To complete the job effectively these conditions are improved by providing the workers with suitable equipment and clothing such as hats, rain courts, pickers' bags, ladders for pruning and picking, etc.

Reasons for job analysis

The work roles and related jobs that an organisation requires employees to perform are identified for many reasons.

- **Internal equity:** analysis determines the position and the ranking of a job within the overall structure. Work can be described and employees assisted to perform their job effectively as they are well aware of their tasks, who they report to, and what they are responsible for.

- **Compensation:** to ensure employees are paid fairly they must be compensated appropriately. Identification of the tasks that form a job will provide information on the level of commitment and effort, knowledge and skills required.

> **Compensation:** salary structure and reward systems of a business.

- **Change:** jobs change and evolve over time as the business changes. Analysis uncovers the change in tasks within the job, the change in the level of skill and knowledge required, and the change in working conditions for the particular job. The employee will then be able to perform their job effectively.

BUSINESS CONCEPTS AND INNOVATION OPERATIONS

At Munch Lunch, a local lunch bar there are four staff members, the cook, two waitresses and the manager, who is also the business owner. In this small business the job roles of the two waitresses are placed after the manager and the cook. This is because those positions are viewed to be more permanent and vital to the business, whereas the waitresses' positions are casual positions.

BUSINESS CONCEPTS AND INNOVATION OPERATIONS

Twenty years ago a secretary's job role involved taking notes, editing on a note pad then typing on a typewriter, and filing a record in the archives room. The same job position has dramatically changed in the twenty-first century. Today a secretary would transfer speech notes from a voice recorder into the computer and electronically edit and transfer the file to his/her manager. Record keeping would involve electronic database management and file management.

The change in the task sets in the same job has resulted in change to the skills and knowledge required to complete the same job position.

Performing a job analysis

A range of information related to the job and the employee who is to perform the work is collected. Information is gathered from employees or the job holders, through an interview process, a survey or via an informal conversation. If there are discrepancies these are resolved through discussion with managers or other businesses in the same industry. See Figure 8.4 presented on the following page.

In Step 4, information can be gathered through a range of different methods.

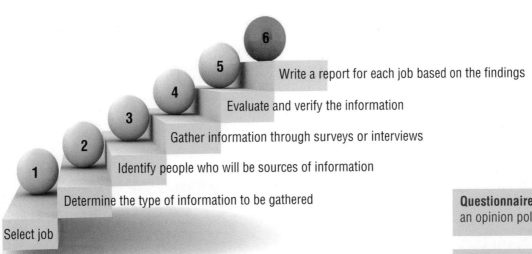

Figure 8.4: Job analysis

6	Write a report for each job based on the findings
5	Evaluate and verify the information
4	Gather information through surveys or interviews
3	Identify people who will be sources of information
2	Determine the type of information to be gathered
1	Select job

Questionnaire: a survey or an opinion poll.

Checklist: a list of elements to be checked

Diary: a record or a log.

Observation: watching, reflection or study

These include:

- questionnaires
- checklists
- diaries
- observations.

Job analysis, which involves identifying and describing the job in relation to the tasks involved, knowledge required and working conditions, has been outlined. Following job analysis, the next step is preparing role or job descriptions. Job descriptions are vital to employees, employers and interviewers as they provide insight into key skills, knowledge and attitudes to look for during an interview.

2. Job description

Job descriptions are also known as role descriptions or position descriptions. All have the same purpose, just different formats. A job description is a detailed outline of work involved in a particular position within the business. Every business should have a role or job description for each position to ensure that each employee is fully aware of their role and responsibilities. When recruiting new staff, the **recruiter** is able to refer to the job description to match the skills of the applicant to the requirements of the job role. During employment **trainers** are able to use this document.

Recruiter: involved in hiring or employing new staff.

Trainer: provides knowledge and skills through their expertise to assist an employee to improve their performance.

INNOVATION AND ENTERPRISE

When an application is received by the manager for a vacant position, he or she would match the skills and knowledge of the applicant to those outlined within the JOB DESCRIPTION. If there is a match of skills and knowledge between the applicant and the job requirements then he or she will be called in for an interview.

Level of authority: the amount of power or rights one has over another to control and manage the other person; the extent to which a manager can control the behaviour and performance of an employee.

Scope: the capacity, extent or range of duties within a job.

Essential functions: key duties or responsibilities.

Organisational chart: a visual representation of a business' management structure.

Job environment: workplace, its surroundings and atmosphere.

Writing a job description

A job description includes information such as duties, responsibilities, **level of authority** and position within the business hierarchy. It consists of statements which identify and describe the **scope** and content of a job. It does not describe all the details but is an outline of the **essential functions** and major duties of a particular job.

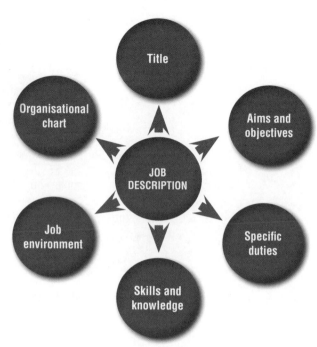

Figure 8.5: Information found in a job description

Questions answered by a well-designed job description

☞ Why does this job exist?

☞ Where does it fit into the business? How does it relate to other jobs?

☞ What is expected? What is affected, and what is the nature of that effect?

☞ What specialist skills are needed?

☞ What has to be managed, and what managerial/supervisory skills are needed?

☞ What level of human relations skills is needed?

☞ What is the structure of the job? What instructions, procedures or goals define what the employee has to think about?

☞ What are the boundaries of the employee's authority to make decisions?

☞ What are the most difficult parts? What kinds of challenges arise? How demanding is the problem solving required?

Figure 8.6: Elements of a well-designed job description

The sample job description in Figure 8.7 outlines an example of job information for a fast food restaurant employee.

JOB DESCRIPTION

JOB TITLE: **FAST FOOD CREW MEMBER**

JOB PURPOSE: **PREPARE FAST FOOD ORDERS**

- Stocktaking, ordering, preparing and stocking items at beginning, during and end of shift
- Selecting, assembling, measuring, heating and cooking food
- Maintaining control
- Maintaining a safe and clean working environment by removing spills on a regular basis.

ESSENTIAL FUNCTIONS:

Significant percentage of the shift is attributed to the following tasks:

1. MAINTAINING CUSTOMER SATISFACTION AND CONFIDENCE
    - Meeting food quality and service standards, finding ways to satisfy customer expectations

2. STOCKING FOOD PREPARATION LINE
    - Stocktaking, ordering, preparing and stocking inventory prior to, during and after shift

3. FILLING FAST FOOD ORDERS
    - Checking orders then selecting, assembling, measuring, heating and cooking food as per orders
    - Placing orders on ready racks

4. MAINTAINING FOOD PREPARATION LINE
    - Maintaining the process during shift to ensure effective work flow
    - Removing spills

5. KEEPING FOOD PREPARATION EQUIPMENT OPERATING
    - Following equipment operating instructions
    - Carrying out proper steps during breakdowns or malfunction of equipment
    - Maintaining supplies
    - Using preventative practices in work place safety and maintenance
    - Advising superiors on repair requirements

6. MAINTAINING SAFE AND HEALTHY FOOD PREPARATION ENVIRONMENT
    - Occupational health and safety standards and procedures as outlined
    - Complying with food handling and sanitation regulations

7. IMPROVING FOOD JOB KNOWLEDGE
    - Attending training sessions

8. CONTRIBUTING TO ORGANISATIONAL SUCCESS
    - Accepting related, different and new requests in food orders
    - Assisting others in the team

JOB QUALIFICATIONS:

- As stated in the essential functions above. An employee must be able to accomplish the essential functions in order to be competent in the job.

Figure 8.7: Sample job description

It is the responsibility of the employer to provide the employee with a job description outlining essential information. The employee has the right to request a job description if he or she has not been provided with one. The employer and employee must keep track of changes in the work role as jobs change for various reasons. Changes may be in the form of skill requirements, the job process or the time line for completing a task. Over time job descriptions need to be reviewed and amended to reflect the changing nature of the particular position.

3. Job evaluation

Job evaluation is a methodology used to evaluate and rank jobs within a business to assign hierarchy and value. It is performed by comparing jobs in relation to the varying levels of importance and then **ranking** them on this basis.

Ranking: rating or positioning.

The purpose of job evaluation is to maintain **equity** and fairness in the reward system of the business. Job evaluation ensures that jobs are valued correctly by the business owner.

Equity: fairness or equality.

4. Job structure

Job structure: the formation of a set of duties to form a particular job.

Award: a reward for services provided by an employer, in the form of a rate of pay set by the government for a particular job.

Job structure is the way in which a set of tasks form one particular position. This is the end product of the job identification process. Prior to creating a job, the position is analysed, then it is described through a job description to enhance the understanding of the job. Then the job is evaluated to determine its place within the business and assigned an **award** rate, its position within the business is confirmed and the title of the position is assigned.

BUSINESS CONCEPTS and INNOVATION AND OPERATIONS

Fort Café is small business owned by Elly. The café is staffed by the Manager, Brianna and waitress, Karly. Joan joined the business as a second waitress to ease the work load. The new job role needs to be fitted in to the business. This has created the need for Elly to review and identify the duties and responsibilities so as to position each job effectively.

Elly will compare each job role, and its duties and responsibilities with other jobs within the business. She will also compare the knowledge and skill requirements of each job role. Based on revealed information Elly will position the new job in the business hierarchy.

BUSINESS CONCEPTS

Adam is a chef who manages the commercial kitchen of a popular boutique restaurant in Perth. As a chef his job involves preparing menus, identifying meal requirements, preparing orders for inventory needed for meal orders, cooking food, deciding on appropriate accompaniments, presenting meals in a way that appeals to consumers, and maintaining a safe and hygienic working environment.

As the person in charge of the kitchen Adam has to manage and control all operations of the kitchen and staff. Being in charge means Adam has to maintain a budget, control food processing, minimise wastage, ensure a safe and cooperative working environment, prepare rosters for shifts, communicate with management to ensure goal achievement and plan for events.

All these are key duties that make up Adam's JOB POSITION as the head chef of the restaurant. Without these requirements his job position would not exist. Therefore, it is essential to understand how these small duties together form a major job position.

Jobs are identified, analysed and structured using the job identification process. This is time consuming and demanding, and involves matching the requirements of the job to an individual who has the capabilities to fulfil requirements. This is the beginning of the recruitment, or the staff selection process, where the individuals are matched for jobs based upon their capabilities.

JOB MARKETS

Securing the right employee for the right job is vital to the success of small business. This requires a significant investment of time and resources in the **job market**, to ensure that the small business is able to secure the employee with the right skills, knowledge and attitude. In reality small businesses have to compete with big companies for the best employees and they are limited in both time and resources.

A job market is not a physical location, but a concept. It is a marketplace where employers search for employees and employees search for jobs. The following tips outline some key strategies to attract the right employee.

> **Job market:** a marketplace where employers search for employees and employees search for jobs.

BUSINESS CONCEPTS and INNOVATION AND OPERATIONS

Some small business owners assume that advertising job vacancies are an expense. Therefore they tend to opt for the easy and cheap options such as advertising in the shop window or the local community paper, which charges a minimal fee. This restricts the audience to the job advert. Wine Yard owner James, however, advertises the vacancies of his business on online job seeker websites, wine industry publications and websites, and on travel websites. The cost of these adverts are higher, however they help him reach a target audience with specialist skills and also those overseas travellers seeking employment for minimal wages with other benefits. This allows James to attract well-suited employees from a vast pool of applicants.

TIPS TO ATTRACT AND HIRE THE TOP APPLICANTS

✓ Be on the lookout for high performers.

✓ Be ready and able to hire quickly when the suitable individual is found.

✓ Pre-identify what needs to happen to assure that the business can extend good offers to talented applicants.

✓ Get the business name in front of the target applicants:
  – Make presentations at professional organisations.
  – Write articles for trade publications.
  – Attend meetings to meet potential employees.
  – When you meet a potential applicant, don't get bogged down in formalities.
  – Take advantage of the interview process to show the business's strengths and to introduce the applicant to other top performers.

TIPS

Online markets: Recruitment sites

Job markets are present in various forms such as print media, digital media and the local community. Accessibility and usability of technology has levelled the playing field for small businesses with large corporations, in attracting and selecting suitable employees from a larger pool of applicants both local and international due to the emergence of **online job markets**.

A list of the popular job seeker websites are presented below.

www.jobsearch.gov.au

www.careerone.com.au

www.downundr.com

http://jobs.com.au

www.monster.com

www.seek.com.au

BUSINESS CONCEPTS and INNOVATION AND OPERATIONS

A small boutique winery in the Great Southern has seasonal work. Labour hire of Australian employees is extremely costly to small enterprise owners. Advertising the vacancies online allows the winery owner to attract overseas labourers. People who are intending to either migrate or travel Australia seek such opportunities and apply. This allows the winery owner to attract and employ labour at a much more affordable rate.

Please note that all overseas employees must be employed under proper migration visas and are to be compensated according the standards of Australian law.

Social media as a recruitment tool

Technology and online recruitment sites such as these provide an opportunity to research potential employees in more detail. This is due to the popularity of social network sites such as Facebook, LinkedIn and Twitter. These social networking sites provide both a personal and professional insight to the potential employees' values, interests, life style. They also reveal past and present aspects of their life, allowing the employer to grasp a much deeper understanding of the employee than what a traditional reference check would provide.

Some of the top social media sites include:

- FB
- Twitter
- LinkedIn
- Pinterest
- Google+
- Tumblr
- Instagram

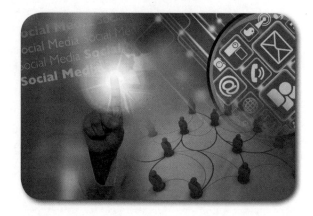

BUSINESS CONCEPTS and BUSINESS IN SOCIETY

Adam Rifkin , co-founder, director and CEO of PandaWhale had more LinkedIn connections in 2011 than the 640 most powerful people on Fortune Magazine's lists than any other human being. He built a network of contacts that included the founders of Facebook, Netscape, Napster and Twitter.

Adam's experience is proof that online networking sites are the new place to link employer and employee and successful business contacts. Adam was a small scale operator and due to his networking using such sites has given him the opportunity become one of the super successful business owners in the world.

JOB INTERVIEWS

The job interview is the second last step in attaining employees for a business. Small businesses operate with minimum budget and resources on a daily basis, therefore the time and effort placed on interviews is important. For long term success, ensuring the interview is conducted efficiently and gathers as much information as possible about the applicant or future employee is vital for a small business.

The **interview** is usually a personal meeting between the applicant, or **interviewee**, and the small business owner or **interviewer**. During this interview session the interviewer finds out information about the interviewee by asking relevant questions. Questions need to be relevant to the job, and might ask the interviewee how they have previously handled specific work situations.

Recruiting new employees is usually a good sign that the business is flourishing and additional resources are required to maintain its success. Once a business has identified the jobs within it that requires people to complete them and identified the skills required to complete these jobs, the business owners could begin the interview process utilising the applicants list they have gained through the job advertisements they have run.

However, making the right decision and recruiting the right employee can always be a lot more difficult than originally conceived. Some applicants may seem like great options during the interview, however it's quite impossible to truly evaluate their performance until they are working in the role they were recruited. A careful selection of interview questions would make this process a little bit easier.

> **Interviewee:** the person being interviewed. An applicant who has expressed their interest in fulfilling the job requirements.

> **Interviewer:** the recruiter conducting the interview.

BUSINESS CONCEPTS and INNOVATION AND OPERATIONS

Jo Black is preparing to conduct an interview to appoint a new accountant to JB Accountants, a popular accounting firm in the Great Southern. It is important that the new recruit be competent, self-driven, devoted and, most importantly, a team player. To seek out information about each applicant, Jo Black would use a particular set of questions such as:

- Why would you like to join JB Accountants?
- What will you be offering to JB Accountants?
- Describe a situation showing your experience in commercial accounting.
- What are your strengths?
- What do you see as a weakness you have and how do you overcome this?
- Tell me about a situation where you have worked in a job sharing arrangement.
- Describe a complex problem that you have solved using accounting software.
- What do you aim to achieve by being a part of JB Accountants? What are your career goals?

The purpose of these questions is to probe the interviewee about their personality and skills. The responses to these should reveal their values and motives. Using that information the interviewer could make decisions on who is more suited to the position and the organisation as whole.

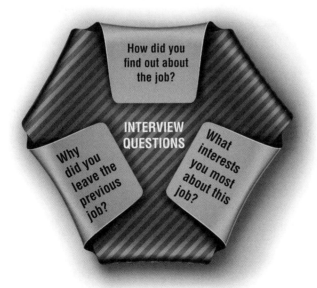

Figure 8.8: Essential interview questions

A person's responses to questions that probe their values, motives and intentions provide the interviewer with an opportunity to identify whether this applicant's personality would suit the role/position they are aiming to fill. Table 8.2 contains a descriptive outline as to how these questions reveal vital information about the applicant.

TABLE 8.2: Interview questions

Question	Why this question	What is revealed
How did you (applicant) find out about the job?	It's important to consider the recruitment process from the applicant's point of view. The applicant may have found out about the job though an unexpected source.	The applicants' preferred style of job search could reveal the emphasis they have placed in seeking this particular job. It could also reveal their commitment in the long run.
What interests you (applicant) most about this job?	Provides insight to the applicant's ambitions. Some may try to be neutral in their response, however a focused individual would be able to make clear links to their attraction towards the job.	Promotes honesty and transparency in the eyes of the applicant. Provides the employer the opportunity to identify applicants who are aware of their future job role and expectations.
Why did you (applicant) leave your last position?	May reveal the true motive for seeking the job.	May reveal whether there were personality conflicts or performance issues, based on the manner of the response.

These questions would assist a small business owner to identify some important personality and workplace traits of the applicant. In some cases the applicant will leave their role for a better position or more money. However, a lot of individuals leave their jobs due to the role being too demanding, or because they have internal issues with the business owner or other employees. With that in mind, the interviewer should not make their mind up too early, but should try to identify any trends in the employment history that can be traced.

In small business it is important to get the right mix of employees, rather than the most skilled employees. Recruitment is a costly process. It is better to have committed and reliable employees that can be trained to perform a particular role, rather than hiring the wrong individual who could cause internal conflict.

BUSINESS CONCEPTS and BUSINESS IN SOCIETY

Small business owners Robin and Allen who runs a successful hairdressing and beauty company Renew Salon Spa decided to hire the best personality applicant rather than the best skilled applicant for the senior hairdresser position. Robin approached ex-barista Jason and made a proposition for him to undertake a training course for hair dressing under her mentorship, with the commitment to working with her company for a certain agreed duration after his completion of the training. The reasons behind approaching him were that he had an outstanding commitment to service, excelled at customer care and took pride in his job.

After five years on the job, Jason has become the senior hairdresser and the most committed and reliable employee of the business. Robin views him as her protégé. The costs of training and development have been overshadowed by having an outstanding member of staff.

Types of job interviews

With the aid of technology, interviews can be done in various modes. Technology tools such as Skype and teleconferencing enable businesses to meet and assess future employees from across the world, without the hassles of costly time consuming travel.

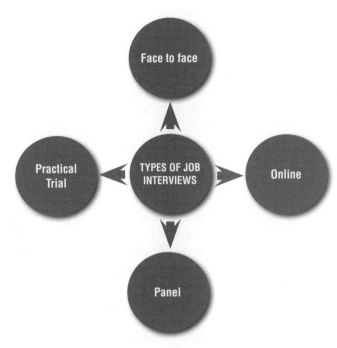

Figure 8.9: Types of job interviews

Face to face interviews

Face to face interviews are the oldest form of interviews. The **interviewer**, that is the business owner and **interviewee**, that is the future employee, meet with each other in person in a professional location. This is generally the business itself. However, on some occasions the small business owner may choose a neutral location such as a café, depending on the nature of the workplace environment.

Panel interviews

A group of individuals assume the role of interviewer. Most of them take the role of posing questions to the interviewee. There could be some panel members who are there to observe the applicant. Small businesses generally entertain this type of interview structure when seeking employees for administrative or management roles.

Online interviews

These interviews take place via an Internet-connected facility such as teleconferencing or video conferencing. A common example is Skype. These sorts of interviews are conducted mostly when the interviewer and the potential employee are in locations far from each other, such as inter-state or overseas. This method has become prominent over the years as Australia has allowed small businesses to hire labour from overseas labour markets.

Practical interviews

These are interviews that contain a component where the applicant is required to perform a part of his or her job duty as part of the interview. These interviews take place in the work place itself and these are performance based interviews. These are common in high-order restaurants and in industries that require specialist skills or personalities.

APPLICANT BACKGROUND CHECKS

Employees can come from far and wide. With new immigration laws even small businesses haves the opportunity to employ people from a distance. Some of these individuals could be backpackers, holiday or work visa users, or individuals who the small business owner may import primarily to work in the small business establishment.

No matter the background of the future employee, it is good practice to do a background check. Background checks need to be conducted with full disclosure and applicant permission, and they are an important part of the recruitment process.

Figure 8.10: Employee background checks

It is important the employees are properly qualified or have immigration visas, and detailed information is available on federal government websites. Police checks are particularly relevant to businesses that deal with finances or security where the business could be at risk of financial fraud or similar.

RECRUITMENT

The **staff selection** process is where a business matches people to its operational requirements. Recruitment involves advertising positions, attracting applicants and conducting interviews to select the most suitable employee out of the interested applicants.

> **Staff selection:** a way in which employees are chosen for a particular position or job.

BUSINESS CONCEPTS and INNOVATION AND OPERATIONS

A commercial cleaning business would have not lost its major client if they had performed background checks when hiring new cleaning staff. A major client of the business made a complaint stating that their petty cash had been skimmed on a regular basis and ended the business relationship with the cleaning company. If they had background checked, they may have realised they had employed a petty criminal who was fired from his previous job for similar offences and who has various contacts with many anti-social groups.

Matching capabilities to roles

The recruitment process firstly involves the small business owner evaluating applicant resumés. They then select a set of people who have potential to fulfil the requirements of the job. Following this, applicants are contacted and invited to attend an interview session.

TOP 10 TIPS FOR HIRING NEW STAFF

1. Recruit based on attitude and passion, not qualifications
2. Broaden the search
3. Look for referrals
4. Clearly define the requirements of the job
5. Don't hire a clone of the business owner
6. Be thorough
7. Utilise the existing employees for assistance: ask them about the job and type of person right for the job as they know the job more than the business owner
8. When possible, give potential employees a realistic preview of the job
9. Be open about remuneration
10. Don't be intimidated. Hire people more capable than the business owner

INNOVATION AND OPERATIONS

Ann and Sue are business partners who operate H Recruitment Services. They are currently involved in appointing a new secretary to the local accounting firm. They are in the early stages of the process, reviewing applications in an attempt to choose a set of appealing applicants who can be called in for an interview.

During this stage they both read each resumé to identify applicants with the skill and knowledge requirements highlighted in the job description. Following this matching process the applicants with the most common skills and knowledge that satisfy the needs of the job are contacted for an interview.

Resumés

Resumés are a source of information for recruiters. A resumé contains vital information about the applicant. This might include personal details such as age, gender and marital status (though these are not legally required), and other information such as academic qualifications, work experience, and achievements. A resumé is the primary information source about the personality capabilities and strengths of the applicant. A sample resumé is provided in Figure 8.11 on the following page.

Employment contracts

Small businesses can sometimes be very informal in employment agreements. In today's workplace the importance of having every aspect of business management from daily work plans to **Employee Contracts** drafted and presented in a formal manner is immense due to legal and legislative requirements.

RESUMÉ

1. PERSONAL DATA:

- Name
- Address
- Phone numbers (home, mobile).

2. CAREER OBJECTIVE OR SUMMARY

A statement that informs the recruiter about the job the applicant wants.

Example: a customer service position using my skills in researching customer information and resolving problems to the customer's satisfaction.

3. WORK EXPERIENCE

Past jobs and accomplishments arranged in order. Focuses on the accomplishments most related to the job being sought, to enhance applicant's suitability.

Addresses each of the criteria contained in the job advertisement.

Example: for the position of a sales person in an electronic shop, particular notes on keyboarding skills and understanding and ability to use computers and other technology tools.

4. SKILLS

Specific skills relevant to the job. Key words, such as the names of equipment, software, or special knowledge, are important.

5. EDUCATION

Include the names of schools and tertiary institutions attended, degrees and major areas studied as well as any courses taken and the results. A recent graduate will place education before work history.

6. EXTRA CURRICULAR

A brief list of other activities, memberships and volunteer activities. These would inform the recruiter that the applicant is a well-rounded person with a variety of interests and skills.

7. REFEREES OR REFERENCES

People who can be contacted to discuss the applicant.

Figure 8.11: Sample resumé

Small businesses usually create formal, written employment contracts that state the specific terms of their **employment agreement** for senior job positions. It is important to note that the hiring, managing, promoting or redundancy of an employee can be expensive, whether it is a senior management role or a regular part time employee, if the process is not managed correctly. In Australia employment contracts provide a legal and formal record of expectations and agreements between the employer and employee at the time of recruitment.

A clear and simple statement outlining the expectations, work conditions and remuneration are generally sufficient.

> **Employment contract/Agreement:** a legally binding contract between the employer and employee at the time of recruitment that states the exact nature of their business relationship and each other's responsibility towards each other. It includes the remuneration the employee will receive in exchange for specific work performed.

Further to recruitment the employee can be provided with a copy of Employee Workplace Procedures as a further reference on the workplace **code of practice** and expectations.

Code of practice: a certain set of workplace behaviours and mannerisms as well as presentation that is expected of employees.

INNOVATION AND OPERATIONS

Jim Brickson is a builder in need of three labourers to assist with a new building project. Ryan Jackaroo appeared to be a suitable applicant and was hired for the job. After attending work for a fortnight and receiving an advance payment of his next pay, Ryan failed to present himself at work. Ryan claimed he no longer intended to work for Jim, even though he owed Jim money and a formal notice of resignation.

However, as Jim never made a formal offer of employment or got Ryan to sign a contract, Jim does not have a leg to stand on when fighting for his rights as he is not an employer in the eyes of the law.

TABLE 8.3: Key information to be found within an employee contract

Employee contract essentials

Information	Examples
Specific job position offered and accepted, including job title	Nursery worker
Primary job duties and responsibilities of this position	Pruning, soil preparation, planting, repotting, composting and other general garden maintenance
Amount and type of compensation agreed to by both parties	Hourly pay rate
Duration of employment	Not stated/flexible
Types of benefits offered and accepted	Paid time off; holidays, sick leave. Superannuation. Bonuses or other rewards. Employee family discount. Other insurance plan
Restrictive covenants: Statements that stipulate what the employee can and cannot do during employment and within a particular time after terminating employment.	The employee cannot go to work for a competitor or start a competing business within a certain time period (such as one year) after leaving the business

A standard contract can be created for all employees and customised for specific jobs. This contract might include the information in Table 8.3. Some employment contracts define a specific time or duration of employment, or the contract can be written to be more open ended where either party has the right to terminate employment at their will, without violating the terms of contract. Employer and employee rights are further discussed in **Chapter 9** of this text.

ACTIVITIES

A. CHECK YOUR UNDERSTANDING

Job identification, job roles, job descriptions and job evaluations

1. List the four steps of recruitment?

2. What are the three stages of job identification?

3. What is a job analysis?

4. What information is identified through a job analysis?

5. What is compensation?

6. What is a job description?

7. What information is mainly found in a job description?

8. What is the purpose of a job description?

9. What is job evaluation?

10. What is job structure?

Job mMarkets

1. What is an online job market?

2. Give three handy hints for recruiting top applicants through these online job markets?

3. Give three examples of online job markets?

4. What is the role of social media in selecting employees?

Job interviews

1. What is a job interview?

2. Why conduct a job interview?

3. Differentiate between the interviewer and interviewee.

4. What are three vital interview questions?

5. Define the following three types of job interviews
    A. Face to face interview
    B. Panel interview
    C. Online interview

6. Give three reasons for performing a background check on an applicant.

Recruitment

1. Define recruitment.

2. What is a resumé?

3. What are the key features of a resumé?

4. What is the purpose of a resumé for the recruiter and the applicant?

5. What is an employment contract?

B. BUSINESS RESEARCH

1. Access the following online job description websites and complete the questions which follow.
    * **www.seek.com.au**
    * **www.careerone.com.au**
    * **www.jrmi.com**
    * **www.businessballs.com/jobdescription.htm**
    A. What information features in all job descriptions?
    B. Create a template that could be used for any job description.

2. Guidelines on various job evaluation methods can be accessed on the HR Guide website at **www.hr-guide.com/jobevaluation.htm**

    Choose a particular job position you are familiar with, then conduct a job evaluation of that position. Report your findings to the class using a slide presentation.

3. Visit one of the listed online job markets/recruitment sites from the text.

    A. Select three jobs and identify two common aspects within the job adverts.
    B. Prepare a suitable application for one of the jobs. Select the job advert under your teacher's guidance. You may use the skills you have learned in other subjects to assist with your application.

4. Based on a job you have found that interests you from one of the online job sites that was referred within the text, complete the following:

    A. Write 10 interview questions you might pose to the applicant if you were the interviewer or business owner.

B.   Write three questions you would pose to the interviewer if you were the applicant.

5.   Build your online resume on Australia Online. Templates and instructions on resumé construction are found on their website.

C. RESPONSE

Job identification, roles and descriptions

1.   Choose three simple job roles within a small business and in a table such as the one below, present it in the form of the job identification process, for example job tasks, job sets, job role

EXAMPLE Job Role #:	Teller Machine Operator
Job tasks	**Making transactions:** • Greeting the customer • Scanning the products being sold • Stating the total cost • Clarifying the mode of payment (cash, EFTPOS, credit, etc.) • Taking the payment and giving change if necessary. • Issuing a receipt. • Thanking and farewelling the customer
Job sets	• Receiving the daily cash • Making transactions • Making deposits • Closing the till

Job role 1:	
Job sets	
Job tasks	

Job role 2:	
Job sets	
Job tasks	

Job role 3:	
Job sets	
Job tasks	

2. Use the flow chart in Figure 8.4: Job analysis to analyse the part time job of a family member or friend.

3. Collect job descriptions for a range of different positions. Using these and the example found in Figure 8.7: Sample job description, summarise the requirements of these jobs in a table, using the following headings:

   • Title
   • Objectives
   • Duties
   • Skills required
   • Knowledge required
   • Job environment
   • Structure
   • Organisational chart

4. Your teacher will provide three sample job descriptions per pair of students.

   • Identify the similarities and differences within these job descriptions and list five of each.
   • Evaluate two of the jobs using the processes of job evaluation.

5. Focus on the structure of the local pizzeria.

   • Refer to 'Diagram 8.2: Job identification' and 'Table 8.1: Job identification process components and examples' to assist with this task.
   • Identify five key job roles within this business and list them.
   • Identify the job tasks and job sets for each of those roles.
   • Present your response in a table format.

Job markets

1. Complete the self review form using the Career Planning template at **http://careerplanning.about.com/od/performancereview/Performance_Reviews.htm**.

   A. What are the advantages and disadvantages of this template?
   B. Consider your
      i. Accomplishments and strengths
      ii. Areas for future improvement and explain how this information could be useful for the human resource management of your workplace.

Job interviews and recruitment

1. You are applying for a casual position at the local fast food restaurant. The vacant cashier's role requires you to have excellent interpersonal skills, basic mathematical skills and the ability to work in a team and provides flexible working hours.

    A. Make a list of the skills this position would require you to have.
    B. Match your skills to suit the skills required for the job.
    C. Prepare your resumé for this job.

    The following website may be of assistance – Review Resumé formats on:
    http://jobstar.org/tools/resume/res-what.php

2. Prepare a set of possible questions that the interviewer may pose to you when you attend an interview for the above job role. Construct your answers. Interview another member of the class for the job, then swap roles and become the interviewee.

3. Why are references or referees an important aspect of your resumé? Discuss.

4. Discuss this statement in a small group:

    'I believe in the adage: Hire people smarter than you and get out of their way.'

    Howard Shultz
    CEO of Star Bucks Coffee Chain

D. GROUP PROJECTS

1. Participate in an interview panel.

    Two groups of students are assigned as Team X and Team Y. Each team chooses a job position and studies that position and the organisation well. Draw a one-page flow chart, showing how external recruitment for this position would have to proceed.

    *   **Interviewers:** list 10 questions that could be asked of an applicant in the interview. Allocate questions to different members of the interview panel.

    *   **Interviewee:** create a short resumé for the application.

    *   **Observer:** identify likely verbal and non-verbal cues to be looking for in the interview.

Each group member takes it in turn to be on the interview panel, interviewing one member of the opposite team. They can also be the interviewee when the situation is reversed. For example, the students of Team X are required to prepare a set of interview questions to ask a member of Team Y during the interview. Team X is also required to prepare to face an interview by Team Y. Remaining team members from the group being interviewed are observers, and they take notes on the interview process, and verbal and non-verbal cues given off by participants, and give feedback at the end.

2. Select a local small business and research the role of its employees. In order to do this research you might be able to interview the business owner, otherwise complete research over the telephone or Internet. Create a job portfolio for this business.

In pairs, select two job descriptions. Each person is to answer the questions below based on the information provided within the job description. Do not make assumptions. Compare answers and clarify you are both in agreement. Resolve any issues. Identify the depth of information provided by each job description and identify the differences.

- Why does this job exist? Where does it fit into this local small business? How does it relate to other jobs?

- What are the expectations of the job? What does it affect, and what is the nature of that effect?

- What specialist skills are needed to do the job? How deep must they be? How broad?

- What elements of planning, organising, evaluating and innovating are present?

- What has to be managed, and what supervisory skills does this imply?

CHAPTER 9
Employer and Legal Obligations

'No employer today is independent of those about him. He cannot succeed alone, no matter how great his ability or capital. Business today is more than ever a question of cooperation'

– Dr Orison Swett Marden –

People are the most vital resource of a small business; therefore, ensuring their wellbeing is vital to business success. Both employer and employees have obligations towards each other as a result of their bond due to employment. These obligations are legally bound and are a social expectation as well. This chapter explores employers' responsibilities and obligations towards their employees from a legal and social perspective.

Furthermore, the chapter examines areas that are important to small businesses such as payroll tax, superannuation, leave entitlements and working conditions set out by both state and federal Australian law.

EMPLOYMENT AND LEGAL OBLIGATIONS

A successful and cooperative workplace is achieved through developing a mutually respectful working environment for both small business owners and employees. Where an employer and employee fulfil their rights and responsibilities, a positive and productive work environment is created.

The government, as a main stakeholder of the business environment, **legislates** and provides a framework outlining the rights and responsibilities of both employees and employers. This section of the text focuses on such duties for the business owner and managers.

Legislate: to impose a rule or right by law.

Figure 9.1: Components of this chapter

The rights of employees

Employees have many rights in the work place, as result of industrial and other laws. In Australia small businesses and sole trader operations must observe these laws which require these businesses to operate in a transparent manner.

Figure 9.2 explores some of the common workplace rights of employees that are regulated under various laws. Providing a safe workplace ensures that employees are able to focus on the task at hand without concern for their personal health and wellbeing. This also reduces the risk of workplace injuries and future illnesses that the employer may be held responsible for.

Abiding by wage standards set by law and rewarding employees appropriately results in employee satisfaction and retention. Providing them access to training ensures that the employees are skilled for the job they are expected to perform and their performance will be of a higher standard.

Operating a workplace with positive morals and respect for everyone without bias for gender, sexuality or race creates a harmonious workplace. Happy employees are committed employees.

There are a range of laws and legislation in place to protect the rights of employees in both state and federal levels. These laws and details as to where to locate further information on these rights are mentioned in a later chapter.

> **Employee right:** an employee's moral or legal entitlement to be treated in a fair and just manner in the workplace.

Figure 9.2: Rights of employees

Safe workplace

Respect and dignity

Suitable remuneration

RIGHTS OF EMPLOYEES

Access to training and development

The obligations of employees

> **Employee obligation:** an act or course of action to which an employee is morally or legally bound, during their employment.

In a workplace arrangement the responsibilities are not just of the employer. Employees also have to be responsible employees if they are to continue to be employed by any business. Laws protect both employees and employers.

BUSINESS IN SOCIETY

The recent newspaper article 'Carabooda raids: Numerous charges after WA operation targets organised crime' [1] reveals that the main operation targeted a market garden compound at Carabooda, where more than 130 foreign nationals were taken into custody. It turns out that most of these workers were employed under very poor conditions and were treated abusively.

This case is evidence that along with government bodies private sector groups such as Walk Free Foundation [2] are exposing the exploitation of labour in the modern workplace. Such measures are aimed at protecting the rights of both national and international employees working in Australia.

---

1   www.abc.net.au/news/2014-05-05/ten-charged-after-carabooda-raids-uncover-foreign-workers/5429852, accessed 15 May 2014.
2   Walk Free Foundation, www.walkfreefoundation.org, accessed 15 May 2014.

Employees who abide by workplace expectations and laws have the benefit of becoming trusted and reliable employees in the view of the small business owner. These employees would be recommended for promotions and rewards. These employees help facilitate a work place that is transparent, supporting, nurturing and welcoming. This results in overall improvement in employee attitude, morale and performance.

Therefore it is beneficial for business owners to encourage and demand their employees abide by their obligations to the business and the laws that govern its operations.

The following could result in termination of employment:

- committing a criminal offence

- negligent and careless behaviour to the extent of causing an accident (lack of **duty of care**)

- acting disloyally such as by disclosuring confidential information and stealing.

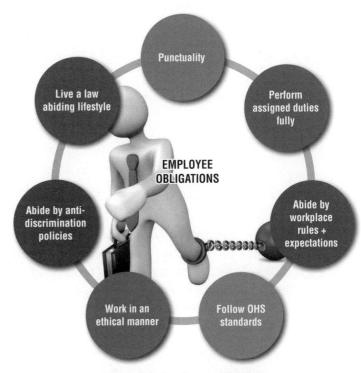

Figure 9.3: Employee obligations

> **Duty of care:** the responsibility or the legal obligation of an employee or a business to ensure the safety or well-being of others.

The rights of employers

Employers have the right to expect their employees to attend work and perform their duties to the expected standard for the agreed number of hours. They also have the right to expect all employees to follow business guidelines and instructions in completing tasks and to engage in safe work practices. Failure to abide by business practices results in an employer having to discipline the employee and potentially even suspend benefits.

Employers have the right to expect that employees...

Figure 9.4: Employers' expectations of their employees

Workplace employee procedures outline the rights and responsibilities of employees that belong to a particular business. Small business could provide this information to their new and existing employees at the recruitment stage or ensure this information is readily available.

Rights of employer: an employer's moral or legal entitlement to expect their employees to perform and behave in a certain manner that is appropriate for the workplace.

The obligations of employers

Employers also have obligations towards their employees These are enforced by Common Law[3] and are also beneficial for the employer in promoting a positive work environment. These obligations and duties are designed to protect employees and maximise productivity in the workplace.

These obligations are explored in detail in the next section, with particular attention to payroll tax, superannuation and leave entitlements.

Employer obligation: an act or course of action that is expected of the employer towards their employees according to moral and legal codes of practice.

EMPLOYMENT OBLIGATIONS

The topic of employment obligations builds on requirements for good workplace conditions in Australian businesses, including elements such as working conditions, and legal requirements of employers and for employees. Business obligations including **payroll tax**, **superannuation**, **leave entitlements** and **conditions of employment** are legislated in Australia. Therefore this segment of the chapter explores the effects of these **legal employment obligations** in relation to full time, part-time and casual employment arrangements.

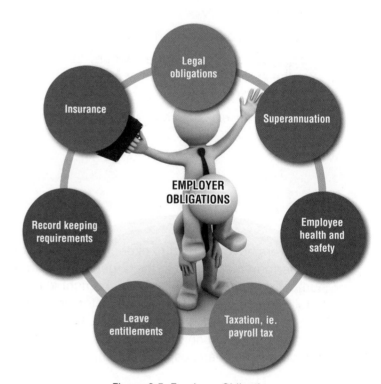

Figure 9.5: Employer Obligations

---

3   Australian Government's Principal Business Resource, www.business.gov.au & Small Business Development Corporation, www.smallbusiness.wa.gov.au, accessed 25 May 2014.

Legal obligations

The level of employee commitment and work ethic is influenced heavily by the business owner's approach to managing his or her staff. Legal obligations of small businesses are stated in the State labour relations system. Obligations are dictated by a range of sources, as outlined in Figure 9.6.

Laws and events that dictate legal obligations

- National laws
- State and territory laws
- Industrial awards and agreements
- Industrial tribunal decisions
- Contracts of employment

Figure 9.6: Laws and events that dictate legal obligations

The Department of Commerce in Western Australia has a range of information for small business owners on labour relations to assist with complying with these obligations.

The legal obligations of a small business owner include:

- paying correct wages
- reimbursing employees for work-related expenses
- ensuring a safe working environment
- not acting in a way that may seriously damage an employee's reputation or cause mental distress or humiliation
- not acting in a way that damages the trust and confidence necessary for an employment relationship
- not providing a false or misleading reference
- forwarding PAYE tax instalments to the Taxation Office
- making appropriate payment under the Superannuation Guarantee legislation.

Record keeping obligations

Small business owners are required to maintain a range of records relating to the employment conditions of their employees under Australian law. The most common types of employee records that are expected to be maintained are presented in the following diagram.

Figure 9.7: Employment condition records

Time and wages records must be kept for at least seven years following the termination of employment with the business. Records should be in clear legible form so that anyone could easily read and interpret them.

The main reason for such strict enforcement of record keeping is to ensure that all employees have been paid correctly, have received all relevant entitlements and that taxation and superannuation have been correctly accounted for. This also ensures that employees are hired and managed in a legitimate manner and that they are treated equally and fairly.

Further information on **employee record keeping** can be obtained from the Taxation Department website.

Employee health and safety obligations

Employee health and safety is primarily the responsibility of the small business owner. There are strict guidelines and laws that dictate the requirements. This vital aspect of OHS is discussed in other chapters of this text.

Insurance obligations

Small business owners are expected to maintain up-to-date insurance policies for their employees. The business owner is responsible for employee's **workers compensation insurance,** to protect the employees and the level of liability for the business in the result of workplace injury, illness or death. This insurance is compulsory under Common Law.

> **Workers compensation insurance:** form of insurance providing wage replacement and medical benefits to employees injured in the course of employment.

Taxation obligations

Small businesses have various taxation obligations to employees. Depending on the recruitment status of the employees, for example employee or contract worker, the taxation obligation differs.

Payroll tax

Payroll tax is a state government tax paid by employers when their annual payroll bill exceeds relevant thresholds. In Western Australia this applies to any business that has an annual payroll exceeding $750,000[4].

Payroll tax is self-assessed. The employer calculates how much is owed and pays the appropriate amount to the government. This is the **tax liability** which can be paid in a monthly, quarterly or annual return. If the wages paid by the business exceed $750,000 the business must pay payroll tax.

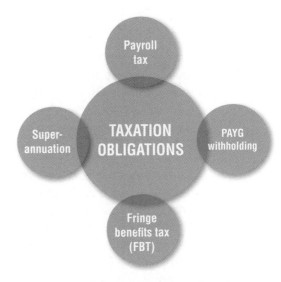

Figure 9.8: Taxation obligations of employers

Tax liability: amount of tax owed.

Pay As You Go (PAYG) withholding

Pay As You Go (PAYG) is a tax withholding system where the small business owner withholds a certain amount of the taxation contribution they make on behalf of the employee. The aim of this withholding is to assist the employee and the small businesses meet the end of the year taxation liabilities. The business owner must make an application to the Australian Taxation Office if they are intending to register for PAYG status for their taxation payments for their employees.

Fringe benefits tax (FBT)

A fringe benefit is a **payment** to an employe, that the small business owner makes other than their salary or wages. These payments can be viewed as extra benefits or rewards for saving as an employee of the business. However not every work related expense or minor benefits is considered for FBT. The Australian Taxation Office provides specialised systems to calculate FBT taxes.

Examples of FBT include:

- using a work car for personal use
- facilitating a personal loan for employee
- providing employee with health or travel insurance
- providing recreation, food and drink and so on.

---

4   The Office of State Revenue, www.osr.wa.gov.au, accessed 15 April 2014.

Superannuation

The superannuation guarantee levy is a major taxation obligation of the small business owner. There are various sub components of superannuation, shown in Figure 9.9.

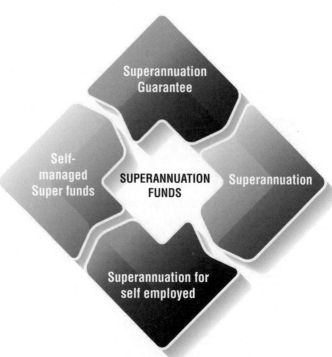

Figure 9.9: Sub components of superannuation funds

Superannuation is a system where money is placed in a fund to provide for a person's retirement. Contributions to this fund can be made by both employer and employee. It is mandatory for an employer for every employee earning more than $450 per month[5]. The business is liable to pay 9.5% superannuation. This contribution has to be paid directly into a complying **superfund**. These are known as managed superfunds. It is essential that employers keep good records of all superannuation payments as they can be fined significant amounts[5] for not meeting their superannuation obligations. Superannuation fund managers are regulated by the Australian Prudential Regulation Authority (APRA)[6].

Super fund: retirement fund.

Superannuation is savings put away for the employee during their working life for when they retire. At present in Australia there is approximately $700 billion in accumulated super funds. Since the federal government of Australia introduced 'Super Choice', employees are able to choose which super fund their money is paid into by their employer. For those who don't want to choose, the employer will put the money into a fund on their behalf.

Superannuation for self-employed individuals

If a person is self-employed there is no legal requirement for them to contribute money to a super fund. However, there are a number of good reasons to do so. Businesses treat superannuation as an operating cost which means if a person has their own business and pay superannuation they can claim it back as a business expense.

BUSINESS CONCEPTS and BUSINESS IN SOCIETY

The Association of Superannuation Funds of Australia (ASFA) is the peak industry body for the superannuation sector, representing all types of superannuation funds. ASFA[7] predicts that by the year 2020 there will be $1699 billion in super funds. According to ASFA a 25-year-old today earning $30,000 will have around $142,000 in super when they retire at the age of 60.

Australia is the fourth largest nation of savers thanks to compulsory superannuation and small business owners have a smaller super balance per person than employees. Small business owners only have $39,800 stashed away whereas employees have $49,900.

---

5   Australian Tax Office: www.ato.gov.au, accessed 15 April 2014.
6   Australian Prudential Regulation Authority (APRA), www.apra.gov.au, accessed 26 May 2014.
7   Association of Superannuation Funds of Australia (ASFA), www.superannuation.asn.au, accessed 20 May 2014.

It can also be a great way to save assets. Superfunds are taxed at a lower tax rate, resulting in potential tax savings for the individual.

Superannuation is important for asset protection, as creditors usually cannot access it in the event of bankruptcy. If the business is profitable, by moving some profits into super, the business owner can realise that asset. This assures that profits earned will benefit the business owner in the future.

Self-managed superfunds

Small business owners or an employee who chooses to manage their own superfunds, rather than nominating an existing superfund service provider, have a **self-managed superfund**. The Australian Taxation office regulates self-managed superfunds, not the **Australian Prudential Regulation Authority,** which normally regulates superfunds.

> **Self-managed superfund:** superannuation monies that are managed by the individual who controls the funds.

Leave entitlements

Small business employees can take leave or time away from work for many reasons. All planned leave should be mutually agreed between the small business owner and the employee. Leave must be previously approved by the business, unless it is a result of unforeseen absence, such as absence due to illness.

All leave, planned and unplanned is to be recorded in the employee records of the business and maintained correctly. The state and national system requires that all attendance time and wages records must be kept for at least seven years and records relating to calculation of long service leave should be kept for at least 10 years.

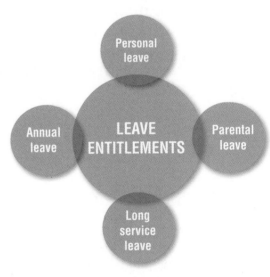

Figure 9.10: Types of leave entitlements of employees

There are various types of workplace leave. Leave is part of the National Employment Standards (NES), overseen by the Fair Work Laws. Therefore, NES applies to all employees covered by the national workplace relations system, so understanding employees' personal leave entitlements is important for employers.

Personal leave

Personal leave is a type of leave entitlement where the employee is eligible to be absent from work while being paid, when he/she or an immediate family member or household member is sick, injured or has an emergency.

Personal leave can be obtained in the forms of:

- sick leave
- carer's leave
- compassionate leave.

On most occasions personal leave is assigned for an unexpected circumstance. However, where possible, it is required that the employee gives as much notice as possible to the business owner. If the leave has begun due to an unexpected situation, but the employee is aware of the extent of the leave required, it is recommended they inform their employer. This allows the employer to plan for the absence and facilitate better support and assistance to the employee. This promotes workplace harmony as fellow employees do not get burdened by the absent employees' duties without notice or reason.

The small business owner has the right to request a medical certificate as evidence of illness or injury, if the leave duration exceeds a significant number of days of work. These terms can be stated in the employment contract; if not, the Fair Work Laws take precedence.

Minimum pay requirements and time entitlements for personal leave

When paid personal/carer's leave is assigned the minimum requirement is that an employee must be paid at their base rate of pay for the ordinary hours they would have worked during that period. This does **not** include wage loadings, fringe benefits, overtime payments and such.

All employees except casual employees are entitled to a minimum of 10 days paid personal leave annually. This includes sick leave and carer's leave as for the National Employment Standards (NES).

Sick leave

Sick leave applies when an employee is absent from work due to illness. Commonly, sick leave is unplanned, however there are circumstances when the employee's sick leave is preapproved as the illness is known to the employer.

Sick leave is separate to worker's compensation, which is paid to compensate for an injury or illness that occurred while at work.

BUSINESS CONCEPTS

Harry, a baker, got a severe fever one evening and was due at the bakery for the 4 am shift the next morning. Without delay Harry contacted his employer and told her about his illness. He was told to take a day or two off work to recover. When Harry got his pay he was paid for the two days he missed work, as he was assigned sick leave.

Carer's leave

Carer's leave is available to an employee for the care or support of an ill family or household member, or if an unexpected emergency affects a family or household member. It is typically part of personal (sick) leave and is dealt with similarly to above.

BUSINESS CONCEPTS

Jared a child care worker had to leave his work one morning to collect his daughter from school, as she had taken ill. Jared's absence was considered carer's leave as he was absent to care for his child.

All employees, including casual employees, are entitled to two days' unpaid leave for each occasion to care for a member of their family or household who is sick or affected by an unexpected emergency.

Compassionate leave

Compassionate leave is paid leave taken by an employee to spend time with a family member/member of the employee's household, who has a personal illness or injury, or after the death of a family member/member of the employee's household.

Each employee is entitled to a period of two days paid compassionate leave for each occasion where a family member has died, or the employee needs to spend time with a seriously ill family member. Additional unpaid leave maybe granted at management discretion. Casual employees are entitled to two days' unpaid compassionate leave for each occasion.

BUSINESS CONCEPTS

Isabella, a sales assistant, requested two days of compassionate leave to accompany her housemate Jane to her mother's funeral. This leave was approved as Jane had a long journey to get to her home and was quite distraught, Isabella was her only close friend able to care for her in this instance.

Annual leave

All employees are entitled to a set amount of days as annual leave per year, except employees hired on a casual basis. This is based on their normal hours of work and it is pro-rata for part-time employees. Leave entitlements are calculated from the date they started work and accrue over time of their employment with the small business.

ANNUAL LEAVE ENTITLEMENTS

A full time employee of a small business is entitled to[8]:

- 4 weeks annual leave for each 12 months of service; or
- 5 weeks annual leave for some shift workers for each 12 months of service.
- Annual leave is usually paid at the same rate as ordinary hours.

Part-time employees are entitled to:

- 4 weeks annual leave but paid on a pro rata basis.

Casual employees are entitled to:

- These workers are not eligible for annual leave but are paid a loading on top of their normal rate of pay to compensate.

... in accordance with the National Employment Services. An annual leave entitlement that comes from an award or agreement between the employee and the employer may be different, but cannot be less than the NES entitlement.

Applications for annual leave need to be lodged in advance; the timeline for such notifications is agreed between the employee and the business owner at the time of recruitment.

In some circumstances, leave in advance of what leave has accrued may be approved. This is conditional on the employee agreeing to the business deducting any advance in the event of termination, or on the employee accepting leave without pay.

---

8   National Employment Services, www.nesa.com.au; FairWork Ombudsman, www.fairwork.gov.au, accessed 10 May 2014.

Long service leave

Long service leave is an entitlement of full-time, part-time and casual employees[9] due to their continued service to the same business. Annual leave is counted towards continuous service, when calculating **long service leave**.

Long service leave is eight and two-thirds weeks of paid leave for an employee after 10 years' continuous service working in the same business. For every five years of continuous employment after this initial 10 years, an employee is entitled to four and one-third weeks of paid long service leave. To calculate the long service leave entitlement for a casual employee the hours the employee has worked per week for the entire duration of employment is averaged.

Parental leave scheme

All employees are eligible for unpaid parental leave when a new child is either born or adopted, including small business employees.

The **Australian Government Paid Parental Leave Scheme** is a system where employees are paid during their leave, as an extra entitlement. This scheme has been active since 2011, providing for eligible employees who are parents and the primary carer of the child. The scheme provides government funded wages to the employee at the National Minimum Wage standard. An employee is eligible for paid parental leave under certain criteria.

AN ELIGIBLE EMPLOYEE FOR THE PPL SCHEME

✓ Is the primary carer of a new born child or adopted child

✓ Has worked for the business for at least 12 months before the expected date of birth or adoption

✓ Will be the business' employee for their paid parental leave period

✓ Works in Australia

✓ Is expected to receive at least eight weeks of parental leave pay

Figure 9.11: Eligible Employee for PPL Scheme

Dad and partner pay

This is another scheme where the government funds leave for either the father or the partner of the child's primary carer if they are an eligible employee. This leave scheme facilitates two weeks of government funded wages at a national minimal wage standard. This program has been operating since 2013.

---

9 Long Service Leave – Employer Obligations, Department of Commerce – WA, www.commerce.wa.gov.au, accessed 15 July 2014.

Small business owners are responsible for identifying the eligible employee and reporting to the Department of Human Service[10] about the upcoming leave requirement of the employee. The government debits the payment to the business and the business owner is responsible for distributing the payment in the same way they normally distribute their wages, that is weekly, fortnightly or monthly basis. An eligible employee can choose to receive parental leave pay before, after, or at the same time as employer-provided paid leave such as recreation or annual leave and employer-provided parental leave.

It does not require the business to make superannuation contributions on Parental Leave pay, nor will it increase payroll tax liability or workers compensation premiums. The business is expected to withhold the usual Pay As You Go (PAYG) tax when distributing these payments. It is not an added cost to the business, instead it has many value-added components.

BUSINESS IN SOCIETY

Bubba Do is a small child care service. It employs a group of 11 employees, both male and female. When Jemima and Ja`c was nearing the birth of her first child the business owner made two claims with the Department of Human Services. These included a claim for 18 week paid parental leave for Jemima and two weeks of partner leave for Ja`c, upon the arrival of their child.

BENEFITS TO SMALL BUSINESS OWNER IN FACILITATING PPL

- ✓ Helps the business retain valuable and skilled staff by encouraging them to stay connected to the business when they become parents
- ✓ Receiving the Federal Government payments
- ✓ No extra cost to business
- ✓ No changes to payroll operations
- ✓ Benefit in the long-term through the increased workforce participation of parents
- ✓ Increased employee morale
- ✓ Positive perception of the business from a public perspective

Figure 9.12: Benefits to small business owner in facilitating PPL

AUSTRALIA'S NATIONAL WORKPLACE RELATIONS SYSTEM (ANWRS)

Australia's National Workplace Relations System (ANWRS)[11] is an Australian government service for both business owners and employees about workplace relations laws. Australia's workplace relations laws provide a framework which encourages cooperative, flexible and productive practices in workplaces.

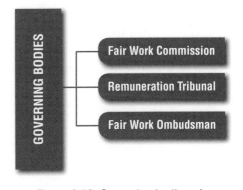

Figure 9.13: Governing bodies of Australian workplace laws

10 Department of Human Service, www.humanservices.gov.au, accessed 13 May 2014.
11 Department of Employment, https://employment.gov.au, accessed 10 April 2014.

Services and information provided by ANWRS include:

- agreements, awards and contracts
- conditions of work for employees
- pay and conditions for Australian work places and where to get assistance and information
- employee entitlement schemes.

Fair Work Commission[12]

The Fair Work Commission is an independent national workplace relations tribunal. It has the power to carry out a range of functions in relation to workplace matters such as the safety net of minimum conditions, enterprise bargaining, industrial action, dispute resolution and termination of employment.

This commission is responsible for setting and adjusting the Australian federal minimum wages, including:

- the federal minimum wage for juniors, trainees, school-based apprentices and employees with disabilities
- minimum wages for piece workers
- casual loadings.

Remuneration Tribunal [13]

This tribunal controls the pay of federal officers such as judges, senators, members of Parliament, government chief executive officers, heads of departments and other full-time and part-time public officers.

Fair Work Ombudsman [14]

The ombudsman helps employees, business owners, contractors and the wider community to understand their workplace rights and responsibilities and enforces compliance with Australia's workplace laws.

---

12 Fair Work Commission, www.fwc.gov.au, accessed 07 April 2014.
13 Remuneration tribunal, www.remtribunal.gov.au, accessed 27 May 2014.
14 Fair Work Ombudsman, www.fwc.gov.au, accessed 27 May 2014.

ACTIVITIES

A. CHECK YOUR UNDERSTANDING

Employee rights and obligations

1. What is an employee right?

2. List four employee rights in the workplace.

3. How are these rights enforced?

4. What is an employee obligation?

5. List six employee obligations.

6. Define duty of care.

Employer rights and obligations

1. What is meant by the term 'rights of an employer'/

2. List four rights of an employer.

3. What is an employer obligation?

4. List six employer obligations.

5. List five influencing factors that have shaped employer obligations in small business operations.

6. What are the legal obligations of a small business owner, list at least five obligations.

7. What five areas are essential for the Record Keeping Obligations of a small business?

8. List the four taxation obligations of a small business.

Payroll obligations

1. What is payroll tax?

2. Who pays payroll tax?

3. What is the payroll threshold in Western Australia?

4. What does the acronym PAYG stand for?

5. What is PAYG?

6. How can a small business attain PAYG status?

7. What is the benefit to small business in attaining PAYG status?

8. What does the acronym FBT spell out?

9. What is FBT?

10. Give four examples where FBT applies.

Superannuation obligations

1. Define superannuation.

2. How much superannuation must the business pay, according to the Superannuation Guarantee obligation?

3. Who is eligible for superannuation?

4. Who can choose to pay superannuation and who must pay superannuation?

5. Where does the employer pay superannuation contributions to?

6. Who regulates the superfund managers?

7. What is the impact of the Australian government's introduction of 'SuperChoice'?

8. Does a person who is self-employed have to make superannuation contributions to themselves?

9. List the benefits of making a super contribution by the self-employed?

10. What is self-managed superfund?

Leave entitlements

1. What is personal leave?

2. Who is entitled to personal leave?

3. What other types of leave come under the personal leave criteria?

4. How much personal leave is an employee entitled to annually?

5. Define sick leave.

6. Explain carer's leave.

7. What circumstances entitle an employee for compassionate leave?

8. Define annual leave and state the entitlement.

9. Define the long service leave entitlement.

10. What is the paid parental leave scheme?

B. BUSINESS RESEARCH

Employee and employer rights and obligations

1. Visit the following web resources to research and respond to the following questions.

   - Western Australian Small Business Development Corporation website: **www.smallbusiness.wa.gov.au**
   - Department of Commerce website: **www.commerce.wa.gov.au**
   - Work Cover WA website: **www.workcover.wa.gov.au**

   A. What are the responsibilities of the small business owner when hiring a new employee?

   B. What are the legal obligations of a small business, in relation to their employee? List and give examples.

   C. What are the insurance obligations of a small business owner?

   D. What obligations does the employee have towards the employer?

2. Following a thorough study of the information within the following websites, respond to the questions in relation to taxation obligations of small businesses in Western Australia, with references.

   - Australian Tax Office: **www.ato.gov.au**
   - The Office of State Revenue: **www.osr.wa.gov.au**
   - Department of Commerce WA: **www.commerce.wa.gov.au**
   - and one more website you choose under your teachers guidance.

   A. What taxation obligations does a small business have towards its employees?

   B. What is payroll tax and what are the employee entitlements.

   C. How does a small business calculate payroll tax?

   D. What is PAYG and what are the employee entitlements?

   E. What is fringe benefits tax and how does it affect the employee?

   F. What aspects of employment are regulated under the WA Department of Commerce?

   G. What is the basis upon which various wage or pay rates are set and why?

   H. What is the role of 'Wage Line'?

3. Visit the following websites and research the responses for the following questions.

   - Australian Tax Office: **www.ato.gov.au**
   - Australian Prudential Regulation Authority (APRA): **www.apra.gov.au**
   - Association of Superannuation Funds of Australia (ASFA): **www.superannuation.asn.au**

   A. What is the purpose of superannuation? Should it be compulsory? Why or why not?

   B.   How do superannuation regulations in Australia affect a self-employed
        person?

   C.   What is the role of the remuneration tribunal?

4. Visit the website of the Department of Treasury at:
    www.treasury.wa.gov.au. Answer the following questions.

   A.   How does a small business pay payroll tax?

   B.   What are the rates of payroll tax in WA?

   C.   What does the government do with the revenue raised by payroll tax?

5. Visit the National Employment Services website: **www.nesa.com.au** and FairWork
    Ombudsman website: **www.fairwork.gov.au** when responding to the following
    questions.

   A.   What is the role of National Employment Services in influencing the
        workplace leave entitlements for small business employees?

   B.   How does the FairWork Ombudsman enforce that employees are assigned
        their legal leave entitlements?

C. RESPONSE

1. Merle Berry is a blueberry farm owner who has recently set up a café in her farm to
    attract locals and tourists. Since setting up the BlueBird Café at Bird & Berry Farm,
    she had to employ more staff. Merle is hiring both local people and backpackers on
    a part-time and casual basis. These employment structures are new to Merle and
    she is mindful of the need to find out about her obligations to her employees.

    Following is a statement on Bird & Berry Farm's (including BlueBird Café) employee
    structure, outlining their employment basis. Staff are employed under one contract
    and business title, 'Bird & Berry Farm', even though some now work in the café as
    well or only at the café.

Employee	Job	Employed to work at	Employment basis	Pay rate
James (32 yrs)	Grower	Farm	Full time	$50,000 p/a
Michael (27 yrs)	Farm hand	Farm	Full time	$32, 000 p/a
Helena (17 yrs)	Berry picker	Farm	Casual (7 hrs per day, four days a week for a total of 8 months a year)	$14.50 p/h
Jose (22 yrs)	Berry picker	Farm	Part time (9 hrs per day, four days a week for a total of 8 months a year)	$ 19.45 p/h

Employee	Job	Employed to work at	Employment basis	Pay rate
Maggie (43 yrs)	Cook	Café	Part time (4 hrs per day, 3 days a week plus 5 hours on Saturdays & Sundays)	$21.40 p/h – Weekdays $32.60 p/h – Weekends
Novak (21 yrs)	Waiter/ Barista	Café	Casual (5 hrs per day, 2 days a week plus 5 hours on Sundays)	$23.50 p/h – Weekdays $27.67 p/h – Weekends
Pinto (23 yrs)	Waiter/ Barista	Cafe	Casual (5 hrs per day, 3 days a week plus 5 hours on Saturdays)	$26.51 p/h – Weekdays $31.82 p/h – Weekends
Mie`le (14 yrs)	Waitress	Cafe	Casual (5 hrs per day, 1 day a week plus 5 hours on Saturdays & Sundays)	$11.00 p/h – Weekdays $13.15 p/h – Weekends

Considering the number of employees Merle has under her and the various structures, their age groups and commitments, make recommendations on the following.

Present your findings in the form of a report with properly assigned subheadings, rather than question numbers. Your teacher may assist you with selecting your headings.

A. Explain to Merle her employer obligations for staff under various contracts.

B. What are the leave entitlements that are relevant to Bird & Berry Farm and how do they apply to these employees?

C. Check that Merle is paying her employees the right wages, taking into consideration that they are paid at different levels for similar work. Refer to the Wage Line on the Department of Commerce website to support your claims.

- Explain how and why Pinto and Novak, who perform the same job, may be entitled to different pay scales.

- Why might Mie`le be paid a different rate for her work in the café? Support your response with evidence from the wage laws.

2. What is the paid parent leave scheme? Write a statement explaining the impact of the paid parental leave scheme on small businesses and on employees. In your response, explain how the scheme operates.

3. Alex is preparing an employee workplace procedures document for his new business, Pie Café. Outline all relevant leave requirements, taxation obligations and any other related entitlements that he should be mentioning in this document.

D. GROUP PROJECT

Staff at 'Steaks n Spud' met for beer at the local pub to discuss some concerns they have regarding their welfare and entitlements at work. They have decided that it is better to raise their concerns with the manager as a group rather than individually. They have asked the three of you to attend this informal meeting to guide them on their entitlements and rights. Following is a list of facts about employment structures and conditions you have picked up during this meeting.

- Jack, assistant chef, 34 years of age, full time employee, 12 hours a day 5 days a week – including weekends, very much in need of a holiday, married with one child and second child is due in 5 months, been with the business for over 10 years. When the head chef is away performs all those duties, without extra pay or recognition.

- Marla, head waitress, 26 years of age, 6 years of experience on the job, part time employee, works 8 hours a day – 6 days a week – includes alternate weekends, newly married, intends to take a vacation overseas in the near future but does not want to quit her job.

- Kim, 17 years of age, kitchen hand, casual employee, works 5 hours a day 4 days a week – including weekends, lives at home with parents, earning extra cash before university studies, sometimes helps out waiting in the restaurant.

- Julie, waitress, 19 years of age, has five years of experience, Part time employee, able to perfrm all the responsibilities of the restaurant waitressing roles, lives in a share home with other young people. Works 6 hours a day five days a week – alternate weekends. Sometimes works more hours if she is filling in for the head waitress and manages the till.

- Kate and Amanda, 18 year old waitresses, new to the job, works 5-6 hours a day 5 days a week – including every weekend.

- None of the staff are provided uniforms but are required to wear appropriate clothing such as chefs' uniforms, aprons, black pants with white shirts, safety boots for kitchen staff, etc.

- Restaurant is open all year long and closes for 10 days in winter. This the time employees normally take their holidays, however out of this 10 days they are expected/required to attend to work the first day it's closed for a clean-up of the restaurant. This is not considered as hours of work where they are paid.

1. Please advise the employees on their legal entitlements from their employer at 'Steaks n Spud'. Make sub reports to each employee outlining their personal entitlements and obligations under the following categories:
   - Entitled rate of pay
   - Entitled conditions of work
   - Superannuation entitlements
   - Types of leave entitlements and how much
   - Other benefits and entitlements

2. Make a general statement on the employees' legal obligations towards the employer. Within this statement explain clearly why the employees must abide by these obligations. Also outline how failure to do so would affect their employment status.

3. In your opinion is the business 'Steaks n Spud' breaching any laws in its obligations to its employees? Justify your response with evidence to support your claim. Draw evidence from Western Australian and federal laws, and rules set out by these laws, as to employees' rights in the workplace.

PEOPLE CROSSWORD

Across

2. Monies put aside for retirement
7. Employees as an investment
10. A type of benefit employer offers employee
11. Appointing someone to a job
13. A rule or right imposed by law
14. Employees of a business
16. A source of information for recruiters
18. A person's approach to a project is a reflection of this
19. When you know something you have ...
20. The entitlement of an individual

Down

1. A person's or a business' duty
3. Identifying and exploring a job
4. When one can do something they have...
5. A meeting to explore the suitability of a person to a job
6. A list of things to be done
8. To abide by
9. Formation of a set of duties
12. A state government tax associated with employers' wage costs
15. Someone who performs tasks for another for a wage
17. Someone who has others working for them

UNIT 2
SECTION A: ENVIRONMENTS
CHAPTER 10
Business in the Community

'It has become dramatically clear that the foundation of corporate integrity is personal integrity.'

— Sam DiPiazza,(CEO of PriceswaterhouseCoopers) —

Businesses have a public image or a reputation that is created by how its employees treat people. The interactions between people also create business opportunities. Consistency is also important. Business owners and operators need to have plans and policies in place to set standards for how employees, customers and suppliers are treated and for how communications are to be conducted.

The topics in this chapter are:

- Business networks
- Business ethics
- Employer/Employee behavior
- Business/Client relationship
- Business protocols

BUSINESS NETWORKS

Business networking is where a group of people meet either in person or through social media to exchange ideas and information. Networking is about interacting with people for mutual benefit. Networking can help establish a new business or grow an existing one.

The aim of networking in business is to build working relationships with others, promoting products and services and making contacts that could lead to sales. It is also an opportunity to improve industry and business knowledge and to learn from others.

BUSINESS IN SOCIETY

A group of teenagers who assemble at a skate park every weekend to practice and show their skills will share their opinions on one another's performances. Their sharing of similar ideas, interests and thoughts is an example of networking.

Networking can be either formal or informal, as illustrated in Figures 10.1 and 10.2.

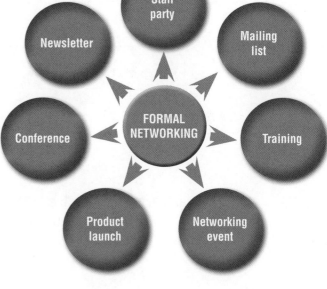

Figure 10.2: Informal networking

Figure 10.1: Formal networking

BUSINESS IN SOCIETY

There are groups in WA that organise regular business networking events. Local councils, the state government and Chambers of Commerce organise events to encourage business owners to work together to grow the local economy. These include networking events, seminars, breakfasts with guest speakers, dinners and award nights. The events create opportunities for formal and informal networking.

Some tips about networking:

- **Build profile:** as a business and as an individual. Attend industry networking events, workshops and conferences and contribute to online discussions and groups. Start a blog about current and emerging problems and interesting topics and become a source of information to others in the industry.

- **Plan a networking strategy:** identify people to network with and what outcomes to achieve. Think about networking opportunities and set dates. Prepare for networking by identifying topics to talk about and questions to ask.

- **Business cards:** have them ready to give to people when networking. Business cards are reminders about who to follow up and also provide contact details.

- **Follow up:** use social media or email to follow up an informal contact. Deliver on the promises or agreements made, whether it's a phone call or a special offer. Keep in regular contact to maintain business networks.

- **Etiquette:** shake hands confidently, smile and look people in the eye when talking to them.

BUSINESS ETHICS

Business ethics is about doing the right thing, to look beyond personal gain and profit and consider the impact of individual decisions on society and the local community. Ethical business practices are part of building a workplace culture. A business owner demonstrates expected ethics and conduct to staff and reinforces a commitment to ethical practice.

Areas of ethical business practice include:

- **Environmental:** thinking about the environmental impact of a business, for example its carbon footprint.

- **Local community:** considering the contribution a business can make to employment, health and the quality of life of the local and broader community.

Figure 9.3: An example of a business network:

- **Workplace:** treating employees with respect, valuing diversity and providing equal opportunity to work/life balance, rewards and career development.

- **Clients and customers:** maintaining safety of products and services, not hiding terms and conditions, providing value for money and keeping promises.

- **Compliance:** committing to complying with laws, regulations and industry codes and standards.

A business owner can also show commitment to ethics by establishing policies and procedures in the workplace such as a code of ethics.

A code of ethics details the rules and expectations for the business. It states the ethical principles staff are expected to have and the values of the workplace culture. A code of ethics provides clear standards for staff on how to do their jobs and make business decisions.

The code of ethics applies to all working relationships; employees working together, dealing with customers and working with suppliers. A code of ethics may cover:

- workplace conduct
- receiving gifts from customers and suppliers
- bullying
- language
- dress standards
- use of phones and the internet at work
- work-related social events.

BUSINESS IN SOCIETY

ANZ[1] has a Code of Ethics. When an employee is not sure if they are doing the right thing they need to ask these questions:

- Does it feel like the right thing to do?

- What would an ANZ customer or shareholder expect or want me to do in this situation?

- What would the reaction be if this was reported in the newspapers?

- Would my colleagues or manager consider my behaviour appropriate?

- What impact might this have on ANZ and its commitment to shareholder value?

---

1 www.anz.com/documents/au/policies/ANZ-Employee-Code-of-Conduct.pdf

A code of ethics must be enforced and there must be consequences if an employee breaks the rules. By doing this the ethical values are reinforced and an ethical workplace culture is made stronger.

EMPLOYER/EMPLOYEE BEHAVIOUR

Employees generally expect that they should be provided with safe working conditions, job security, good pay and fair treatment from management. The employer will usually expect that employees will work to the best of their ability, communicate effectively and complete work as required.

An ethical business is built when employers treat their employees ethically and do not ask them to compromise their ethics in their job. If employees and employers act ethically then they will treat clients and customers ethically.

Privacy is an important ethical issue in the workplace. Employers should discourage employees from gossiping about co-workers and sensitive personal and health issues that have an impact on work performance should be kept confidential.

BUSINESS/CLIENT RELATIONSHIP

Having a code of ethics is one way a business can show clients their commitment to ethical practice. Consistent ethical conduct and dealings with clients will build a reputation and a good public image for the business. This will lead to customers referring their family and friends to the business and the business being their preferred option. A customer can compare how they are treated against the code of ethics of the business.

A client must not be promised products, services or prices that the business cannot deliver. Clients should not be deceived into a sale. This is illegal under consumer law as well as being unethical.

BUSINESS PROTOCOLS

Protocols: rules or guidelines in a workplace that all staff must follow.

What the business owner does and how they deal with people creates a perception about the business and a public image. How a person dresses, how they greet and speak to people and the language used when communicating, all make up business **protocols**. They are often detailed in documents such as a code of conduct or a dress policy. Their aim is to ensure there is consistent behavior in the workplace and that all employees create a good impression when dealing with each other, with customers and with suppliers.

BUSINESS IN SOCIETY

A survey by Servcorp International[2] of 700 business people in 13 countries found that the top 5 most hated business behaviours are:

- using swear words (79%)
- people arriving at work and not acknowledging fellow workmates (77%)
- speaking loudly across the room (66%)
- not offering office guests a beverage (51%)
- taking calls on speakerphone (47%).

2   main.servcorp.net/newsletter/2009/1/eu/index.html

Businesses may even have scripts to guide how to greet customers, answer phone calls or how to deal with customer enquiries and complaints. Businesses may have sample letters that can be modified for different customers and situations.

EXAMPLES OF GOOD BUSINESS ETIQUETTE

✓ Use people's names when greeting them.

✓ Treat people with respect and courtesy.

✓ Be punctual and notify the other person if being late is unavoidable.

✓ Apologise if a mistake is made.

✓ Return phone calls and emails as soon as possible after receiving them, don't leave people waiting.

✓ Never use slang or text abbreviations in business communications, even in emails.

✓ Avoid taking or making texts and calls when in a meeting or in a conversation.

✓ If a call is important, apologise and ask permission before taking it.

Netiquette

Netiquette: rules or guidelines for communicating online.

Netiquette is an important part of building a public image and reputation for a business. It is important to plan how and what will be communicated. Once it is published online it cannot be taken back, it can be shared easily and quickly and stored for a long time.

It is a good idea for a business to have a policy regarding communicating online that sets protocols for email and social media content, signatures and to make what not to do clear to employees.

TIPS FOR USING EMAIL AND SOCIAL MEDIA IN BUSINESS

TIPS

✓ Check spelling and grammar.

✓ Double, triple check before sending.

✓ Include a signature in emails to clearly identify the person and the business.

✓ Don't post confidential or personal information.

✓ Don't use email or texts for things that would be better discussed face to face.

INNOVATION AND OPERATIONS

A local Council has the following four rules regarding netiquette:

1. Respect
2. Keep it clean
3. No spam
4. Stay on topic

Social media policies

Social media is a very useful tool in marketing. It can be used to build a community around products and brands, to create awareness and desire for products and services, and to understand customers so marketing strategies can be better targeted.

But social media must be managed to ensure these benefits are gained. Employees must use social media carefully and consistently to support marketing plans and to help build a positive public image and word of mouth.

A business should have a clear social media policy that sets rules and standards for content and the ways social media is used in the business. There may be rules limiting personal social media use in work time but social media business use should be a part of the marketing plan. This is to avoid having the business reputation damaged by negative comments posted by employees on social media sites.

Employers can be held responsible for workplace bullying if they haven't done enough to control how employees use social media.

Research carried out in 2013 found:

- 10% of people had experienced a manager using information from a social media site against them or a colleague.

- 20% of respondents were not protected from cyber-bullying because workplaces did not have a policy to cover it.

- 50% of those surveyed believed their company was responsible for the online behaviour of employees during work hours if they were using their personal social media accounts.

Businesses are including clauses about social media in employment contracts such as 'comments made via social media that refer to their employment or personal life, on sites such as Facebook or Twitter, could result in disciplinary action up to and including termination'.

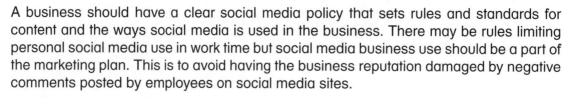

BUSINESS IN SOCIETY

Some recent examples of poor netiquette include:

- An employee at an electrical appliance shop is dismissed after using a Facebook status to complain about an error in his pay.

- Two employees are sacked after posting pictures of themselves planking at work in the warehouse.

- A bartender is sacked after his employer sees Facebook pictures of him celebrating New Year's Eve after calling in sick.

ACTIVITIES

A. CHECK YOUR UNDERSTANDING

Business in the community

1. How can a business owner benefit from their business network?

2. What is formal networking?

3. What are some examples of informal networking?

4. Why is having a networking strategy important?

5. Explain two areas of ethical business practice.

6. What is a Code of Ethics?

7. Describe one example of an ethical dilemma in business.

8. Discuss the relationship between an employer and an employee.

9. What are business protocols?

10. List examples of protocols in schools.

B. BUSINESS RESEARCH

1. Make a list of local and community groups in your area that could provide networking opportunities.

2. Choose one country and make a brochure for business people which covers business customs and etiquette for that country.

3. Research online for two examples of a Code of Ethics of Australian businesses. What are the main topics they cover? What consequences or enforcement strategies do they use?

4. What does 'conflict of interest' mean? Describe an example of conflict of interest in a small business.

5. Find two examples of social media policies for workplaces in Australia. Is there a policy in your school? Describe a recent case of an employer taking action over an employee's use of social media. What is your opinion of the situation? Was action warranted? What could the employer have done to prevent the problem?

C. RESPONSE

1.   Use the following diagram to show your personal network:

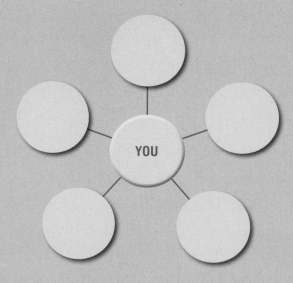

2.   Why is it important for a business to have a clear code of conduct for staff? What are some of the benefits?

3.   Think about a goal you could achieve. It could be focused on achievement in school, sport or other interests. Plan a networking strategy to help you achieve the goal. Prepare a plan using the following headings:

Person/Organisation	Event/Opportunity	Benefits – how will it help?	Follow up

D. GROUP WORK

1.   In small groups develop a code of conduct for students and one for teachers. Produce a poster or brochure for each. Include an introduction to explain the purpose and benefits of the code. Include a section on how it will be enforced.

2.   Working in pairs, create a slide presentation that is aimed at the employees of a specific small business. The presentation is to communicate:

   • business protocols
   • appropriate language
   • business etiquette.

CHAPTER 11
The Legal Framework of Business

> 'I have found no greater satisfaction than achieving success through honest dealing and strict adherence to the view that, for you to gain, those you deal with should gain as well.'
>
> – Alan Greenspan –

Governments have laws that aim to protect workers and to set standards for business operations. Employers and business owners have legal obligations that must be managed as part of running a business. In this chapter we look at areas of business law such as taxation, occupational health and safety and equal opportunity.

The topics in this chapter are:

* Taxation
* Workplace laws

TAXATION

Governments collect tax to fund what they do. It is a complex system and small businesses pay tax and the business owners also pay tax. Small businesses must be registered with the Australian Tax Office (ATO) to make the tax system work.

Small businesses must register for:

* Tax file number (TFN)
* Goods and services tax (GST)
* Pay-as-you-go tax (PAYG)
* Fringe benefits tax (FBT).

Tax File Number (TFN)

A TFN identifies individuals and businesses to the ATO. Sole traders operate using their personal TFN. Partnerships have their own TFN and the partners lodge tax returns using their personal TFNs. Private companies and incorporated not for profit organisations have their own TFN.

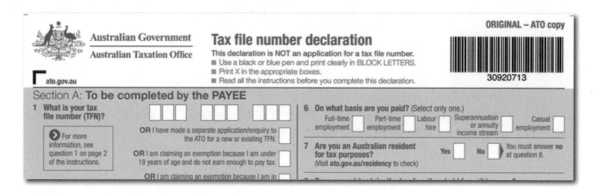

Goods and Services Tax (GST)

The GST is a 10% tax on most goods and services sold in Australia. Businesses must register for the GST if sales will be $75,000 or more. A business needs an Australian Business Number (ABN) to register. Small businesses may register for the GST even if they won't earn $75,000. Businesses that are registered can get refunds from the ATO for GST paid on business expenses. Invoices given to customers must clearly show the amount of GST included in the price.

Pay As You Go (PAYG) Tax

PAYG tax is the amount of tax a business takes out of employee pays to send to the ATO. Businesses that employ people must register for PAYG tax with the ATO.

> **Fringe Benefits Tax:** tax paid when an employee receives their salary in another way, eg. gym membership, school fees, health insurance or a work car. Even though it isn't cash the ATO still sees it as salary.

Business Activity Statement (BAS)

The BAS is the way small businesses report their taxes to the ATO. The BAS includes the GST, PAYG tax and other taxes including the **Fringe Benefits Tax (FBT)**. The BAS can be lodged monthly, quarterly or annually. Most sole traders and partnerships are required to complete a BAS quarterly; it depends on the size of the business. Completing a BAS will help the ATO work out whether the business needs to pay tax or if it will receive a tax refund. An example of a BAS form is provided on the following page.

C

Office use only

[barcode] 41950901

Business Activity Statement

Document ID

ABN

Form due on

Payment due on

GST accounting method

Contact phone number

Contact person who completed the form

When completing this form, please
- use a BLACK pen only (to help with processing)
- leave boxes blank if not applicable (do not use N/A, NIL)
- show whole dollars only (do not show cents)
- do not use symbols such as +, –, /, $

Please read *BAS Basics* before completing this form

Goods and services tax (GST)

Complete Option 1 OR 2 OR 3 (indicate one choice with an X)

Option 1: Calculate GST and report quarterly

Total sales	G1	$	.00
Does the amount shown at G1 include GST? (indicate with an X)		Yes ☐ No ☐	
Export sales	G2	$	.00
Other GST-*free* sales	G3	$	.00
Capital purchases	G10	$	.00
Non-capital purchases	G11	$	.00

Go to *summary* over the page to report GST on sales at 1A and GST on purchases at 1B and then complete the other sections

OR

Option 2: Calculate GST quarterly and report annually

| Total sales | G1 | $ | .00 |
| Does the amount shown at G1 include GST? (indicate with an X) | | Yes ☐ No ☐ | |

Go to *summary* over the page to report GST on sales at 1A and GST on purchases at 1B and then complete the other sections

OR

Option 3: Pay GST instalment amount quarterly

| | G21 | $ | |

Write this amount at 1A in *summary* over the page (leave 1B blank) OR if varying this amount, complete G22, G23, G24

| Estimated net GST for the year | G22 | $ | .00 |
| Varied amount for the quarter | G23 | $ | .00 |

Write the G23 amount at 1A in *summary* over the page and then complete the other sections

| Reason code for variation | G24 | | |

PAYG tax withheld

Total salary, wages and other payments	W1	$	.00
Amount withheld from payments shown at W1	W2	$	.00
Amount withheld where no ABN is quoted	W4	$	.00
Other amounts withheld (excluding any amount shown at W2 or W4)	W3	$	.00
Total amounts withheld (W2 + W4 + W3)	W5	$	.00

Write the W5 amount at 4 in *summary* over the page and then complete the other sections

NAT 4195-9.2001

Small businesses that do not submit a BAS will face a penalty. Every 28 days late results in a $110 fine up to a maximum of $550.

Employer obligations for taxation are discussed further in a later chapter.

WORKPLACE LAWS

The government's role in regulating workplaces is to protect employees and consumers and to provide guidelines for business practices. Two important areas are equal opportunity and occupational safety and health.

Equal Opportunity Act 1984 (WA)

The Equal Opportunity Act (EOA) 1984 came into operation in July 1985. Its aims are:

- to eliminate discrimination in the areas of work, accommodation, education, the provision of goods, facilities and services, access to places and vehicles, land and the membership of clubs

- to eliminate sexual and racial harassment in the workplace, educational institutions and accommodation

- to promote community recognition and acceptance of the equality of men and women, and the equality of people of all races, regardless of their religious or political convictions, their impairments or their age.

The aim of the Equal Opportunity Act 1984 is to prevent and punish discrimination, sexual harassment and racial harassment. Discrimination occurs when one person or group is treated unfairly because of a characteristic that is protected under the law. For example:

- gender and gender history
- marital status
- pregnancy or breast feeding
- family responsibility or family status
- race
- religious or political conviction
- impairment
- age.

The EOA also created the position of the Commissioner for Equal Opportunity. The Commissioner investigates complaints lodged by people who believe they have been discriminated against. Complaints must be made in writing to the Commissioner. Complaints are assessed and investigated. The Commissioner will try and resolve the complaint by bringing the parties together to discuss it. If unsuccessful, the matter is referred to the Equal Opportunity Tribunal to make a decision.

Employers have legal responsibilities under the EOA.

Discrimination can be direct and indirect:

BUSINESS IN SOCIETY

The NBN Co[1] has an Equal Employment Opportunity Policy that covers all employees and potential employees. Its purpose is to 'give everyone a fair chance to obtain employment and gain promotion according to their abilities and qualifications'.

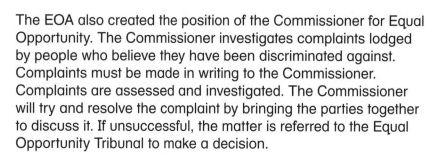

Direct	**Indirect**
When a person treats another person less favourably than someone else in the same circumstances.	When a business practice or policy that appears to be fair discriminates against people who share a characteristic.

---

1   www.nbnco.com.au

Table 10.1: Examples of direct and indirect discrimination

Direct discrimination	Indirect discrimination
• An employee tells her manager she is pregnant and applies for parental leave. Her employer fires her because she is pregnant.	• To pass probation all new employees must pass an eye test, even though there isn't a clear link to the job. An employee has a vision impairment and fails the test and remains on probation.
• A man asks a business about applying for an advertised receptionist job. They tell him not to bother because they are looking for a female receptionist.	• A shop advertises for a bookkeeper. It is on the second floor with only stairs to get to it. An applicant who is the best candidate and in a wheelchair does not get the job.
• An employee has young children. Her manager says she will not get a promotion because her family responsibilities will make it difficult for her to do the job.	• An employer advertises that applicants must have a valid drivers' licence even though driving is not a core task of the job. People with disabilities cannot apply for the job because they may not be able to drive.

Responsibilities for business

Business owners must review their policies and procedures to remove all direct and indirect discrimination. The areas where discrimination may exist include the following.

Advertisements

It is unlawful to publish or display an advertisement that shows an intention to discriminate. This includes television, newspaper, online, email and radio advertisements and circulars, newsletters, catalogues and price lists.

Unlawful acts

Under the Equal Opportunity Act 1984, a business owner who instructs or permits an employee to do something illegal shall be considered to have done the act themselves. For example, if an employee discriminates against someone in a job interview the business is regarded as being discriminatory. The business owner will be held liable due to **vicarious liability**.

> **Vicarious liability:** an employer may be legally responsible for the discrimination and harassment of employees unless it can be shown that they made all reasonable steps to prevent it.

Victimisation

Victimisation includes threatening, harassing or punishing a person because they have objected to or complained about the discrimination they have received. Victimisation also applies to anyone giving evidence about a complaint.

Recruitment and selection

The selection process must be free from discrimination. Selection decisions must be made only on merit and based on job and workplace requirements. Application forms and interview questions must not be discriminatory. Discrimination is present if applicants are asked about such things as their marital status, intention to have children, sexual preference or union membership.

Exemptions

The Equal Opportunity Act 1984 recognises that in some very limited situations discrimination is necessar such as:

- when a characteristic such as race or sex is a genuine qualification for the job
- when an employer is wishing to provide employment opportunities or put in place measures intended to achieve equality for a particular group.

Businesses and organisations can apply to the Equal Opportunity Commission for an exemption.

A charity organisation may want to focus on working with refugees which will mean that their services will be focused on a certain ethnic group. A school may want to employ an Aboriginal Education Officer which means they can specify an ethnic background for applicants. A social club for seniors will discriminate based on age.

BUSINESS IN SOCIETY

Section 11 of the Equal Opportunity Act 1984 (WA) makes it unlawful for an employer to discriminate against a job applicant because of their gender. An exemption was requested to increase the number of female Senior Prison Officers at Bandyup Women's Prison. By allowing 8 of the 13 positions to be filled by women, the employee ratio of men and women would be improved and female prisoners would be looked after better by women Officers. The Commissioner for Equal Opportunity supported the application and an exemption was granted.

Bullying

Bullying involves the tormenting of others through verbal harassment, physical assault or other more subtle methods such as manipulation. In colloquial speech, bullying often describes a form of harassment where an abuser has more physical and/or social power than the victim. The victim of bullying is also referred to as a 'target.' The harassment can be verbal, physical or emotional.

Bullying occurs when the employee is exposed, repeatedly and over time, to **negative actions**. Bullying can occur in any setting where human beings interact with each other.

This includes the workplace and home. Bullying generally exists where there is a perceived power imbalance. The effects of bullying can be serious and even fatal. There is a growing body of research which indicates that individuals who are persistently subjected to abusive behaviour are at risk of stress related illness which can sometimes lead to suicide.

Negative actions: when a person intentionally inflicts injury or discomfort upon another person, through physical contact, words or other methods.

Types of bullying

There are two different types of bulling:

1. **Direct bullying:** direct bullying involves a great deal of physical aggression such as shoving and poking, throwing, slapping, choking, punching and kicking, beating, pulling hair, scratching, biting and scraping.

2. **Indirect bullying (social aggression):** social aggression or indirect bullying is characterised by the victim being forced into social isolation. This isolation is achieved through a wide variety of techniques including spreading gossip, refusing to socialise with the victim, bullying other people who wish to socialise with the victim, and criticising the victim's manner of dress, race, religion or disability. Other forms of indirect bullying which are more likely to be verbal include name calling, the 'silent treatment', manipulation, false gossip, lies, rumours, staring, laughing, saying certain words that trigger a reaction from a past event and mocking.

Characteristics of bullies

Adults who bully are authoritarian with a strong need to control or dominate. A deficit in social skills and a prejudicial view of subordinate employees can be particular risk factors. Envy and resentment may be motives for bullying, however bullies do not usually suffer from a deficit in self-esteem. There are instances where bullying takes place for humour, or if the individual is quick to become angry, uses force, shows aggressive behaviour, mistakes actions as hostile and is concerned with their self image.

Workplace bullying

In the workplace bullying is a serious issue that can have serious penalties. Bullying is the repeated mistreatment of one employee by one or more other employees with intimidation and sabotage of performance. Statistics show that bullying is three times as common as discrimination and many times more prevalent than workplace violence. While few employees become a victim of workplace violence one in six experience bullying at work. Bullying is also far more common than sexual harassment and verbal abuse. Unlike the more physical form of schoolyard bullying, workplace bullying often takes place within the established rules of the organisation. Bullying actions are not necessarily illegal and may not even be against the firm's regulations; however, the damage to the targeted employee and to workplace morale is huge.

Cyber-bullying occurs in electronic space. It involves the use of information and communication technologies such as email, mobile phones and social media to belittle and humiliate another person.

BUSINESS IN SOCIETY

A $9 million damages claim was made by a senior manager in the underwear division of a clothing manufacturer in Australia due to workplace bullying and intimidation. The nationwide problem of workplace bullying has led to new laws to protect workers in Australian workplaces.

Cyber-bullying: use of information and communication technologies to bully someone.

Hazing and ragging

Hazing has been reported in a variety of social contexts including sports, universities, associations, school bands and workplaces. Hazing may constitute harassment, abuse or humiliation with requirements to perform meaningless tasks, sometimes as a way of initiation into a social group.

The term can refer to either physical or mental practices. Problems range from hazing which is somewhat abusive to rites of passage which are essentially bonding activities. It can be degrading and harmful abuse that should not be tolerated even if accepted voluntarily. Serious but avoidable accidents happen.

Occupational Safety and Health Act 1984 (WA)

The *Occupational Safety and Health (OSH) Act 1984* regulates occupational safety and health in most workplaces Western Australia. There is also the *Mines Safety and Inspection Act 1994* that covers safety and health in all mining workplaces. The purpose of the OSH laws is to protect the health and safety of employees across WA. It sets standards for safe and healthy workplaces and enforces them through penalties and workplace inspections. It ensures that **hazards** and **risks** to health and safety are identified, eliminated or minimised.

> **Hazards:** anything in the workplace that could cause harm or injury, eg. toxic fumes, a slippery floor, damaged power cord, cables across a walkway.

The OSH Act 1984 also gives the regulator, WorkSafe, powers to enter workplaces, investigate complaints and give employers improvement notices. The Act established the Commission for Occupational Safety and Health which researches and improves safety and health laws and regulations.

> **Risks:** how likely it is that the hazard will cause harm or injury and how severe the harm or injury would be, eg. a car accident may be rare but with serious consequences.

The Act includes duties of care for employers and employees. Both have legal duties to maintain a safe and healthy workplace. Section 19 details the duties of employers and Section 20 the duties of employees. For example:

Table 10.2: Duties of care

Employers – Section 19	Employees – Section 20
• Maintain safe systems of work. • Provide information, instruction, training and supervision. • Consult employees and encourage cooperation. • Provide personal protection equipment.	• Follow safety and health instructions of the employer. • Use personal protective equipment. • Report hazards. • Cooperate with employers in safety and health processes.

Under Section 19 employers have a legal duty to provide safe systems of work. This includes having policies and procedures for identifying hazards and acting on hazards that have been reported. They must have ways to report hazards and regular workplace inspections. It is part of their duty to maintain a safe and healthy workplace.

Safety and health responsibilities

Under Section 20 employees have a legal duty to follow safety and health rules and procedures and safe systems of work. This includes the duty to report hazards that they find in the workplace. If a hazard is spotted employees are required to report it so it can be managed. This would involve following the procedure and using the correct form.

Employers also have a legal duty to provide safety and health instruction and training to staff. This includes inductions for new staff, training for new work sites and equipment, instruction on how to use tools and equipment safely, including personal protective equipment (PPE), and ongoing safety awareness. Employees have a legal duty to participate in training and instruction and to follow the training and information given.

In terms of identifying and managing hazards in the workplace, WorkSafe WA have identified a three step process, The SAM Strategy:

1. Spot the hazard
- Look around the workplace to identify anything that may cause harm or injury
- Report it

2. Assess the risk
- How badly could it hurt someone?
- What are the chances that someone will get hurt?

3. Make the changes
- Make changes to remove the hazard or lower the risk
- Use safety equipment or change the way the job is done

Overall, employees must work ethically. In terms of safety and health this means that they must consider their safety and the safety of others while performing their job. It also means that they must follow the instructions, training and procedures of their employer. If there is a conflict between getting a job done and getting it done safely, the ethical approach is to choose the safe way. An ethical approach will result in employees consistently working safely and leads to a workplace culture committed to safety.

Most states and territories have adopted national work health and safety laws. WA workplaces are still operating under the state OSH Act. If and when WA will move to the national *Work Health and Safety Act 2011* is uncertain.

ACTIVITIES

A. CHECK YOUR UNDERSTANDING

Taxation

1. Discuss two requirements under the taxation system for small businesses.

2. What is a tax file number and why is it important?

3. What is a BAS?

Workplace laws

1. What is the purpose of the EOA Act 1984?

2. List three characteristics that are protected from discrimination.

3. Explain the difference between direct and indirect discrimination.

4. Give an example for direct and indirect discrimination.

5. What is vicarious liability?

6. What are two examples of the duties of care for employers and employees?

7. What is the purpose of the OSH Act 1984?

B. BUSINESS RESEARCH

1. Research local and Australian businesses to find out at least two equal opportunity policies or codes for managing diversity. What is their purpose? What are some of the common elements or key points in them?

2. Using online research find an example of vicarious liability where an employer has been found to be responsible for the discrimination or harassment of employees. Present a report on the example. Describe the scenario and explain why the employer was found to be liable. Discuss what reasonable steps the employer could have taken.

3. Design and produce training materials on one of the following topics. It should be something that can be used to raise awareness and increase understanding. Create a slideshow that could be used to present an overview of the topic and a brochure or a poster that will remind people of key points and responsibilities. Include important facts, key points, useful contacts and examples.

   - Discrimination in the workplace
   - Taxation rules for small business
   - Duty of care

C. RESPONSE

1. Read the following ethical dilemmas. Discuss why it would be difficult to make a decision and the impact the decision would have on the workplace. What would you do?

   - Going to work when you are sick and possibly contagious.
   - Telling an insecure co-worker their work is good when it is not.
   - Voicing support for a decision you don't really support because there is no more time for discussion.
   - Ignoring a co-worker's chronic lateness because the employee is your friend.

2. In the following examples list what the employer should do and what the employee should do to keep the work and workplace safe.

Example 1

Example 2

3. Identify the following as either direct or indirect discrimination by ticking the correct box. For each example, explain how a small business owner could take steps to ensure this does not occur in the future.

Scenario	Direct	Indirect
A manager tells an employee they will not be trained to work on the new machinery because they are too old to learn new skills		
An employer has a 'no part time work' policy		
A real estate agent tells an African man the property is taken. An Australian man looks at the property and is offered a lease		
All information and signs about safety and health in a workshop are printed in English		

4. Create a health and safety poster for a small business of your choice. The poster must include information on:

    - how to report workplace hazards
    - the importance of being correctly trained to perform duties
    - any two other hazards or risks. (Use the Worksafe website for ideas.)

5. Select one of the following topics, and create a diagram showing why it is unlawful to discriminate in this area, and how an employee could submit a complaint about this type of discrimination. (Use the Equal Opportunity Commission website for ideas.)

    - age
    - family responsibilities
    - marital status
    - pregnancy
    - race
    - religion
    - sex.

D. GROUP WORK

1. **Ethical dilemma**

    The cruise ship is sinking and there is one lifeboat left. The lifeboat holds five people. There are eight people who want to get into the lifeboat. The four people who stay on the ship will certainly die. The ten people are:

    - woman who thinks she is six weeks pregnant
    - two young adults who recently married
    - senior citizen who has fifteen grandchildren
    - nurse
    - lifeguard
    - primary school teacher
    - thirteen year old twins
    - the captain of the ship

    In your group discuss who should be saved by getting into the lifeboat. Explain how you made your decisions.

2. **Workplace code of ethics**

    Develop a code of ethics for teachers at your school. It should have an introduction that explains the purpose of the code and clear statements about the ethics, protocols and conduct of teachers. Topics for the code should include:

    - ethical practices
    - communication guidelines
    - discrimination
    - safety and health
    - making complaints.

CHAPTER 12
Rights of Consumers

'Our personal consumer choices have ecological, social, and spiritual consequences.
It is time to re-examine some of our deeply held notions that underlie our lifestyles.'
– David Suzuki –

Consumers have rights that are consistent across Australia. The Australian Consumer Law (ACL):

- gives consumers the same rights and protections wherever they are in Australia
- simplifies the law from 20 national, state and territory laws to a single national consumer law
- grants consistent enforcement powers for consumer protection agencies.

This chapter examines how the ACL works to protect consumers and what businesses must do to comply with the laws. The topics in this chapter cover the customer complaint process, returning faulty goods and lay-by agreements.

MAKING A COMPLAINT

There is a range of options available to consumers if they believe they have been misled by a business. When making a complaint the first step is to talk to the business involved to try and resolve the problem. If the business does not resolve the complaint, formal action may be necessary.

Under ACL all products must be:

- of acceptable quality
- safe
- durable
- free from defects
- **fit for purpose**.

> **Fit for purpose:** the product does the job the consumer was told it would do.

If there is a problem consumers should keep everything in writing: receipts and invoices, emails and records of phone calls and any letters sent and received. This is evidence of the complaint and shows what the consumer has done to try and resolve it.

Consumer Protection WA

If the problem cannot be resolved with the business, Consumer Protection WA can help the consumer making the complaint. They will give the consumer advice about which ombudsman or industry body to go to. If the problem continues, a formal complaint can be made using the Consumer Protection form.

Government of Western Australia
Department of Commerce
Consumer Protection

Complaint Form

Please use a pen and write clearly using BLOCK LETTERS and tick ☐ where required.

If you need help in completing this form please contact our Advice Line on 1300 30 40 54 between 8.30am - 5.00pm Monday to Friday (excluding public holidays) or visit the office nearest to you.

Complaint made by (your details)

Preferred title   Mr ☐   Mrs ☐   Miss ☐   Ms ☐   Other _____

Family Name   _____

Given Names   _____

Consumer Protection Division
Department of Commerce
Ground Floor
"Forrest Centre"
219 St George's Terrace
Perth WA 6000

Postal Address
Locked Bag 14
Cloisters Square WA 6850

Email: consumer@commerce.wa.gov.au
General Advice Line
1300 30 40 54
8.30am to 5pm
Monday to Friday
(excluding public holidays)

Once the form has been submitted the consumer will receive a reference number. The time it takes depends on the complexity of the complaint and the cooperation of the business. If Consumer Protection can't resolve the complaint, legal action must be taken.

Legal action

A person who is a victim of misleading conduct by a business is entitled to take legal action to get the dispute resolved by a court. The law courts can order **damages** or **injunctions** and other orders against a business found guilty of engaging in misconduct or for breaking consumer protection laws. Most disputes will be heard in the Magistrates Court. The Magistrates Court deals with disputes between consumers and businesses regarding claims up to $75,000. If the dispute involves a claim of more than $75,000 but less than $750,000 the customer needs to take the action to the District Court. If the matter involves a claim over $750,000 the legal action must be taken to the Supreme Court.

Damages: compensation for loss or damage or reimbursement of costs.

Injunction: an equitable remedy in the form of a court order that requires a party to do or refrain from doing specific acts.

ACCC assistance

The Australian Competition and Consumer Commission (ACCC) can take legal action against businesses. Generally, legal action is taken against large businesses that have used misleading advertising. Legal action would result in an injunction to stop the advertising. A small local business could also potentially be taken to court if they advertised deliberately in a misleading manner.

Industry ombudsman

Some industries have a complaints process. They have an **ombudsman** to investigate complaints if the problem cannot be resolved with the business. There is the Telecommunications Industry Ombudsman, Postal Industry Ombudsman and the Financial Industry Ombudsman. The Western Australian Small Business Commissioner helps consumers and small business owners with disputes over contracts for the supply of goods and services, franchise disputes, intellectual property disputes and unfair market practices. An ombudsman will only take action if the consumer can show that they have done everything they can to fix the problem with the business.

Ombudsman: impartial mediator to help resolve disputes between businesses and consumers.

FAULTY GOODS

Customers have rights if the product they buy is faulty. The responsibility is with the business that sold the product to handle the complaint.

If a product is faulty the customer has the right to request:

- a refund
- a replacement product
- repairs to the product.

BUSINESS IN SOCIETY

It is illegal for a shop to have a 'no refunds' sign; it is an offence under the ACL. Even if a shop has a no refund sign, consumers still have the right to a refund if the product is faulty.

It is the responsibility of the business to return goods to the manufacturer for repair. If it is a minor fault the customer has the right to have it repaired within a reasonable time. If it is not repaired within a reasonable time the customer can request a refund. Customers are not entitled to a refund if they just change their mind or find the product cheaper in another shop.

A product is faulty if it:

- does not do what it's supposed to do, for example a television doesn't display channels
- has a defect, for example the dial on a washing machine falls off
- is damaged or scratched
- is unsafe, for example sparks come out of a heater
- isn't durable, for example a vacuum cleaner breaks down after using it three times.

MISLEADING AND DECEPTIVE CONDUCT

Consumers are also protected against misleading and deceptive conduct. It is illegal for a business to make statements that are incorrect or create a false impression. A business must not make false or misleading claims about the quality, value, price or benefits of products or services.

This applies to product labels and advertisements in print, radio, television, social media and online. It also applies to what sales staff and managers say to customers.

A focus of the ACCC and Section 18 of the ACL is to prevent misleading and deceptive conduct; to stop businesses lying to customers to get sales. Examples of illegal conduct under the ACL are:

Table 12.1: Misleading and deceptive conduct

BAIT ADVERTISING	**Advertising a discounted product that is not in stock** Bait advertising is when an advertisement shows a very low price for a product that is very attractive to customers. The aim is to lure customers into the shop with the promise of a bargain, to take the bait, and when they can't buy the advertised special they buy something else at full price. Special prices can only be advertised if the business has the item in stock.
COUNTRY OF ORIGIN	**Making false claims about the country of origin of products and their ingredients** Phrases such as 'Australian Made' and 'Product of Australia' and similar logos and labels cannot not be used to mislead the public. Some products include claims on their labels such as 'Proudly Australian owned' or '100% Australian owned'.These are about the ownership of the business and do not mean that the product itself is sourced in Australia. Two criteria must be met to be labelled 'Product of …' or 'Made in …': 1. Each significant component or ingredient must originate from the country or state of the claim 2. All of the production or manufacturing processes must take place in that country or state. If you want food that was grown or sourced in Australia, look for: 'Grown in Australia' or 'Product of Australia' If you want food that has been made in Australia by Australian workers, look for: 'Made in Australia', 'Grown in Australia' or 'Product of Australia' A product with a 'Made in Australia' label may contain ingredients from overseas.
SCIENTIFIC CLAIMS	**Making scientific claims about products with no proof** Businesses must be able to prove their products have the characteristics that are being promoted. For example, claims such as 'not genetically modified', 'recycled', 'sustainable', 'reduces wrinkles by 40%', 'decreases cholesterol by 20%' or 'environmentally friendly' must be backed up by scientific proof. Many products claim that their benefits are 'clinically proven'. Scientific data must be provided to back up the claims.

FINE PRINT	**Using small print and disclaimers to hide information and mislead customers**
	This refers to the fine print included in advertising. Often when promoting phone deals or service arrangements business will include details about the price and additional fees and charges in very small print. There may also be warnings and safety information hidden in this way. The ACCC now requires businesses to make these details clearer and easier for customers to see and understand.
WRONGLY ACCEPTING PAYMENT	**A business must not accept payment for goods or services if it does not intend to supply the goods or services or knows it cannot supply the good or service**
	It is an offence if a business sells a product online or in a shop with the intention of taking the customer's money without supplying the goods, or knowing that they would not be able to supply the item in a reasonable time.
OFFERING GIFTS AND PRIZES	**A person that offers rebates, gifts, prizes or other free items in connection with the sale of goods or services must honour that offer**
	Gifts and prizes are often used to entice customers to enter a shop or to provide their personal information to be used for direct marketing. The ACL prohibits a person from offering rebates, gifts, prizes or other free items in connection with the supply or possible supply or promotion by any means of goods or services: • with the intention of not providing them • not providing them within a reasonable time.

'Puffery' are exaggerated claims about a product or service. For example, a restaurant advertises that they have the 'best desserts on Earth', a drink has the 'freshest taste ever' or a cafe has 'the best coffee in the world'. These types of statements are not considered to be misleading because no one could possibly treat them seriously.

BUSINESS IN SOCIETY

An advertisement for Olay Regenerist Face Cream was banned for using false scientific claims. The ad claimed that 'pentapeptides' could reduce the appearance of visible lines and could be used as a substitute for cosmetic surgery. The company was not able to provide any evidence to support the claim.

LAY-BY AGREEMENTS

A lay-by is a contract between a customer and a business where:

- the customers pays for the goods in two or more instalments
- the customer does not receive the goods until the full price has been paid
- a deposit is an instalment.

Consumers should read and agree with the terms and conditions of a lay-by before they sign the contract. In particular, look at payment dates, instalment amounts and any termination charges. It is a good idea for the consumer to keep copies of the agreement and the receipts for the deposit and instalments paid in case there is a problem later.

Lay-bys help customers to budget and afford to buy goods. Instead of paying the whole price up front a customer is able to spread the cost of an item over weeks or months. An example is the expensive Christmas hampers that can be ordered in January and paid off with direct debits and delivered in time for Christmas. It encourages customers to buy products, but two disadvantages are:

- This delays cash flow to the business.
- A business must store the products until they are paid off.

Under Australian Consumer Law:

- Lay-by contracts must be in writing.
- Contracts must provide clear details of all the terms and conditions.
- The contract must include all details of any termination charges.
- The business must give the customer a copy of the lay-by contract.

If a customer cancels a lay-by contract the business must refund all money paid to date. The business may charge a termination fee. The business can cancel a contract but only if:

- the customer has missed a scheduled payment
- the business closes down
- the goods are no longer available due to unforeseen circumstances, for example a fire or water damage.

BUSINESS IN SOCIETY

A customer used lay-by to purchase a $400 stereo. The customer paid it off and went to the shop to pick up the stereo. The customer was told the stereo had been lost and was offered a different stereo with fewer features. The store had the originally-ordered stereo on the shelf but said it would now cost $500 and could not be discounted. This store was acting illegally and the consumer was entitled to the stereo for $400 or a full refund.

INTERNATIONAL PURCHASES

A customer may purchase something from a business overseas. That business must comply with the consumer protection laws of the country in which they operate. It is also important that the consumer reads the terms and conditions regarding shipping, refunds and returns.

The ACL in Australia does apply to purchases from international businesses because they are delivered to Australia. If there is a problem or dispute it will be difficult to enforce Australian consumer protections because of the time difference, language barriers and distance.

One way to manage this issue as a consumer is to make purchases through an online payment service such as PayPal. They offer a complaints and dispute resolution process that can result in a refund. Banks also offer a dispute resolution process for purchases made on their credit cards.

There is also a website, www.econsumer.gov for international consumer complaints.

Consumer alerts

Consumer Protection WA publishes alerts as a way to warn consumers about businesses that are unethical or that mislead and deceive customers. Alerts also tell consumers what action has been taken against the businesses.

Example 1

An alert from January 2014 warned customers about a furniture maker in Port Kennedy that took over $22,000 in deposits from customers and failed to complete the orders.

Example 2

A backyard dog dealer in Spearwood was convicted of 17 animal cruelty charges and permanently banned from keeping more than one dog, Consumers who have bought dogs have been warned to get them checked and vaccinated as diseased dogs were sold.

ACTIVITIES

A. CHECK YOUR UNDERSTANDING

Rights of consumers

1. Under the ACL what must all products be?

2. What does 'fit for purpose' mean?

3. What is an injunction?

4. What are two reasons for a customer to request a refund?

5. How does a lay-by contract work?

6. What should a consumer do before signing a lay-by agreement?

7. Why would a lay-by agreement be terminated?

B. BUSINESS RESEARCH

1. Design and produce training materials on one of the following topics. They should be something that can be used to raise awareness and increase understanding. Create a slideshow that could be used to present an overview of the topic and a brochure or poster that will remind people of key points and responsibilities. Include important facts, key points, useful contacts and examples.

   - Consumer rights – faulty goods
   - Making a complaint

2. Find an example of a lay-by policy for an Australian business. Does it comply with ACL? How could it be improved?

3. Consumer survey

   Select a particular product or service that you are familiar with.

   A. Research the marketing techniques used to attract consumers.

   B. Develop a set of key questions to ask the consumers of the product or service in order to identify what motivates them to purchase that item.

   C. Set up the questions in a survey format.

   D. Carry out the survey with a target consumer group. Evaluate the findings by categorising the responses.

   E. Analyse the findings and prepare an information brochure for businesses on what strategies are effective and what strategies require changes.

4. Visit SCAMwatch on the ACCC website to find out how to protect consumers from scammers. Complete these questions:

   A. How do scams generally work?

   B. Summarise five psychological tricks that scammers rely on.

   C. How can a scam be reported through the SCAMwatch website?

   D. Which government agencies which can help the consumer, and the business owner?

   E. Summarise three victim stories from people who have been targeted by scammers and 'The little black book of scams'.

C. RESPONSE

1. Describe how PayPal protects consumers against deceptive seller conduct. How does the policy work?

2. Explain the benefits to businesses and consumers of having national consumer protection laws instead of different laws in different states.

3. Search for a recent example of a breach of the ACL. Look for cases reported in the media or in government websites. Describe the situation, the laws that appear to be breached and what penalties the business may face.

4. In terms of faulty goods, describe what a minor fault is and what constitutes a major fault. What remedies are available to customers in each situation?

5. Consumer law case study

   During Christmas Charlene and Mark, a newly married couple, received a range of gifts from family and friends. Charlene decided to return the sandwich maker her grandma gave her and use the refund to purchase another item. As it is a gift she has no proof of purchase, however she is aware of the exact retailer her grandmother made the purchase from. Her husband Mark decides to return the electric drill as it does not seem to operate properly. He took the electric drill to the retailer with the copy of the receipt he received from his father.

   After Christmas is one of the busiest times of year for retailers, and it is a time where consumers return faulty or 'not quite what I wanted' gifts. Returning products to a retailer can cause disagreement between a store and a customer. Although some stores will allow products to be returned if a consumer simply changes their mind, other may not allow this practice. Is it or isn't it a legal requirement for them to do so? Referring to the information presented within the chapter and on the ACCC website on consumer rights and responsibilities on return and refunds on purchased product and services, answer the following questions.

   A. What are Charlene's rights in this situation?

   B. Is Charlene eligible for a refund?

   C. Did Charlene follow the right protocol in returning her gift?

   D. What are Mark's rights in this situation?

   E. Is Mark eligible for a refund or an exchange?

   F. Did Mark follow the right protocol?

6. Kimberley had a pair of shoes on lay-by for three weeks. She decided to cancel the lay-by because she had seen a better pair of shoes online. She approached the sales assistant and asked for a refund of the money paid so far.

    A.   Is Kimberley entitled to a refund?

    B.   What charges or fees may Kimberley need to pay if she cancels her lay-by?

7. Describe a situation where a product is not 'fit for purpose'.

D. GROUP WORK

I. Produce an information kit to educate consumers on their rights and protections and how to make a complaint under the ACL. Your information kit must contain:

    • a slideshow

    • a poster

    • a brochure.

2. In groups collect advertisements, guarantees and warranty information of a selection of products. Allocate each group member a type of product or service to focus upon, for example electrical, food, clothing. It is better to take notes on advertising campaigns for these products and services on electronic forms.

    A.   Once the group has at least 10 or more samples, prepare a Y chart for these products. A starting point is preparing answers to the following questions.

        i.   What aspects of the advertisement send out a *positive* message about the product or service it is advertising?

        ii.   What aspects of the advertisement send out a *negative* message about the product or service it is advertising?

        iii. What elements of the advertisement appeal to me?

    B.   Split into pairs within your group. Each pair is responsible for constructing solutions to one of these questions using your collection of sample advertisements.

    C.   Summarise your comments.

    D.   Meet back together as the whole group and discuss your findings.

    E.   Prepare an informational presentation for the class on your findings. Suitable topics of discussion can be:

        i.   Guarantees and warranties

        ii.   Misleading customers

        iii. Influencing tactics

ENVIRONMENTS CROSSWORD

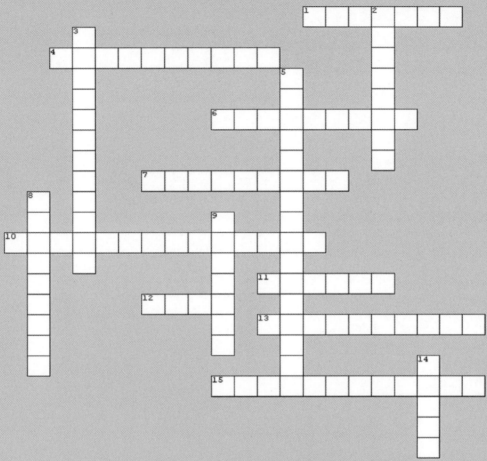

Across

1. Business contacts that work together for mutual benefit
4. An opportunity for formal networking
6. An impartial mediator that resolves disputes
7. Rules for communicating with customers, suppliers and others
10. Treating people unfairly because of a characteristic
11. Considering the impact of business decisions on the community
12. Pay as you go tax from employee wages
13. Court order to stop or restrict business conduct
15. Legal duties for employees and employers to maintain a safe workplace

Down

2. Workplace safety and health regulator in WA
3. Written rules for conduct and decisions in the workplace
5. Laws to prevent discrimination and harassment
8. Standards of behaviour that are generally accepted
9. Compensation for loss, damage or a reimbursement of costs
14. Contract for a customer pay off a purchase over time

UNIT 2
SECTION B: MANAGEMENT

CHAPTER 13
Competition and Consumers

'The most meaningful way to differentiate your company from your competitors, the best way to put distance between you and the crowd is to do an outstanding job with information. How you gather, manage and use information will determine whether you win or lose.'

– Bill Gates –

Any small business owner will want to determine their competitive advantage, which is what makes their businesses product unique in the market. They can use market research and their understanding of the market to establish their special positioning. For a service business, the expanded marketing mix including people, processes and the physical presence of the business are strategically important elements of the process. Knowing the factors that influence consumer purchasing decisions will give valuable insight into the marketing process.

COMPETITIVE ADVANTAGE

A competitive advantage exists when a business has a product that is unique in the market, or when the business earns profits that are above average compared to its competitors. For as long as the business can sustain a competitive advantage, they can often demand a premium, and receive a good return from their good or service. Often, though competitors will perceive the competitive advantage and they may move into the same market, meaning that customers can substitute another product or service for that offered by the business. The business will try to keep its competitive advantage for as long as possible.

There are two main types of competitive advantage: cost and differentiation.

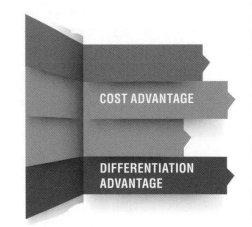

Figure 13.1: Competitive advantage

If the business can provide the same item as its main competitors but it can do this with a lower cost or provide better benefits, then it has a competitive advantage. The business is creating a better product and better profits. The business should aim to sustain this competitive advantage over time.

Good market research will enable a small business owner to identify what their competitive advantage is. The owner should research questions about competitors, costs and points of difference.

INNOVATION AND OPERATIONS

A small sandwich shop is located near large office buildings. The owner has decided that the competitive advantage that the shop has over its main competitors is that all sandwiches are freshly made to order, with quality ingredients, and there is a very quick turnaround time between the order and pick up. Orders can be made over the phone and picked up within 15 minutes.

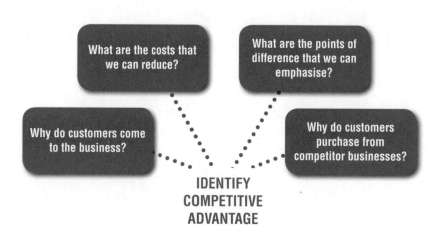

Figure 13.2: Identifying competitive advantage

The marketing mix was introduced in Unit 1, and is one method by which the business can attempt to remain unique and not be copied by competitors. The business owner must develop the four elements of product, price, promotion and place. Three other elements can be added to the marketing mix.

EXTENDED MARKETING MIX

There are three additional elements in the marketing mix, which can be used in conjunction with the '**Four Ps**' outlined previously. This expanded model allows for the fact that the traditional 4 Ps marketing mix model applied more directly to businesses that sell goods. The expanded marketing mix accounts for elements of marketing that are important to service businesses.

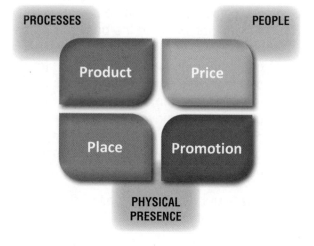

Figure 13.3: The extended marketing mix

People

The '**people**' element of the extended marketing mix requires consideration of the elements of staffing that relate to the market. These include conditions, relevant training and qualifications, development of communication skills, and possessing needed manufacturing and selling skills. The business can define its competitive advantage by focusing on its customers, through ensuring that employees are well trained and competent.

Figure 13.4: The 'people' element of marketing

BUSINESS IN SOCIETY

Jemina owns a small gym that has the target market of women aged over 30. Part of her PEOPLE relationship marketing strategy is to remember her customers' birthdays by sending them a personalised email with a voucher for a free group exercise session.

Relationship marketing: promotional activities that aim to develop and sustain long term connections with customers.

Process

'**Processes**' involve ensuring the business has procedures for correct customer service, provides a great customer experience, always follows up inquiries and provides customer quotes. The business can differentiate itself from the competition by identifying important points where the customer will interact with the business in some way, and by working hard to improve the customer's experience.

Figure13.5: The 'process' element of marketing

BUSINESS IN SOCIETY

Gilbert runs a pool company, where he designs and manufactures backyard swimming pools. As part of the marketing PROCESS of the business, he wants to ensure that customers always have a great customer experience. To achieve this, he always records contact details for new customers, and follows up any queries. He sends quotes out within 24 hours, and his office assistant calls customers to follow up and see if they have any queries about their quote.

Physical

The 'physical presence' of the business encompasses all the elements of business identity that the customer can see. These are aspects of the business such as the design of the shop front, signs, the web site, and employee uniforms. The business defines its competitive advantage through the use of a unique business identity in the marketplace.

Figure 13.5: The 'physical presence' element of marketing

BUSINESS IN SOCIETY

A hamburger shop has created a unique identity through its PHYSICAL and shop front. It has branded itself as being a retro fifties burger bar, and the signage, staff uniforms and packaging all reflect this theme. The burger bar physically stands out from its competitors in a busy street of cafes and restaurants.

THE CONSUMER AND PURCHASING BEHAVIOUR

Understanding **consumer** purchase patterns provides businesses with knowledge of products and services that are in demand in the market. Understanding **customer** patterns also assists in product development as advertising and promotion can be tailored to the habits of the consumer, attracting attention to the product or service.

Consumer: a person, group of people or organisation which uses the products or services of a particular business enterprise.

Customer: someone who regularly makes use of or receives goods or services from the business. A customer is a frequent client who visits a business and who has made it a habit to purchase that business's products.

BUSINESS CONCEPTS

Joseph is a deli owner who specialises in gourmet Italian produce. It is a family owned business and he is the third generation operating the business. The family know every customer by their first name and remember personal preferences. Joseph makes sure his customers' favourite products are in stock. He home delivers to elderly customers if they are unable to get to the shop.

The business owner and employees maintain a positive relationship with the consumer which encourages them to become CUSTOMERS.

Needs and expectations of customers

Customer needs include both everyday needs and long term desires. The level of importance of needs varies depending on cultural values, advertising and marketing, communication with the supplier, and sources such as family or friends. The business owner has many potential options when determining expectations of customers and deciding how to meet their needs, which are outlined here.

Interviews

Interviews involve asking a set of questions of customers in person. Customer responses reveal their needs, expectations and the reasons why they make certain purchases.

BUSINESS CONCEPTS

At a visit to a supermarket Emma meets a sales representative. He talks to her with regard to the product, using a list of detailed questions. Then he makes notes on her comments. This is an example of an informal INTERVIEW where a business is attempting to identify a customer's needs.

Conversations

Conversations are informal methods of gathering information about a customer and their purchasing behaviour. Sole trader businesses use this strategy commonly as they interact with their customer on a one-on-one basis during every sale.

BUSINESS CONCEPTS

The local butcher has made it a habit to have a chat to customers as a means to finding out how satisfied they are with the service, the quality of products as well as to gather their needs. This is an example of a CONVERSATION being used by the business to determine customer expectations.

Statistics

Information gathered by research organisations is a readily available source of information about consumers for business owners. Using statistical information and research data the owner can gather information about the consumers' life style and demands. This is a great source of information to identify a pool of new customers.

BUSINESS CONCEPTS

Referring to INFORMATION sources such as the Bureau of Statistics or local council records would reveal the needs and requirements of a group of customers.

Surveys

Surveys are similar to interview questions, however they are more prescriptive as the questions are pre determined, and can be done online or without an interviewer being present. Surveys assist businesses to identify their customers' changing needs and demands, allowing the business the opportunity to cater for those needs.

BUSINESS CONCEPTS

The local restaurant SURVEYS their customers by offering them the opportunity fill out a simple questionnaire expressing their level of satisfaction and any concerns while the customer is waiting to settle their bill.

Customer survey

The purpose of a customer survey is to collect focused opinions from consumers about a product or service. Surveys are a powerful tool because they allow the makers of the product or service to ask direct questions to the customers. Many online survey tools are available today, allowing a business to quickly and easily distribute a survey to thousands of users at a time.

There are many ways to design a survey. Following are some generally accepted steps for creating an effective customer survey.

SURVEY DESIGN

1. Decide on the aim of the survey.
2. Identify the audience of the survey and how they will relate to the questions asked.
3. Create questions that identify the survey demographic. These are 'qualifying questions'.
4. Design the questions, deciding on the format. Questions can be optional, multiple choice or open ended.
5. Write the survey.
6. Administer a pilot survey with a small sample.
7. Check that the results of the pilot survey are meaningful.
8. Make adjustments based on the results.
9. Publish the survey.
10. Collect results.
11. Analyse results.

Survey demographic: information about the particular survey group, such as income, sex, age, ethnic background.

Pilot survey: a study conducted as a trial to test the effectiveness of the main survey.

Survey results can be analysed with trivial statistics such as averages, maximums and minimums, or more advanced concepts.

CONSUMER DECISION MAKING

When faced with a need or a want the consumer begins their search for a product or service. During this search they find various options and then have to decide which product or service to purchase. The behaviour and thought process that the consumer engages in is called **buyer decision making**.

Buyer decision making: the process of the consumer making a choice of one product from various options.

Due to globalisation and expansion of technology the range of products available to consumers has grown. Consumers are faced with a range of choices. Businesses emphasise providing a range of options for consumers as an attempt to attract them. These options are illustrated in the diagram showing consumer purchase choices.

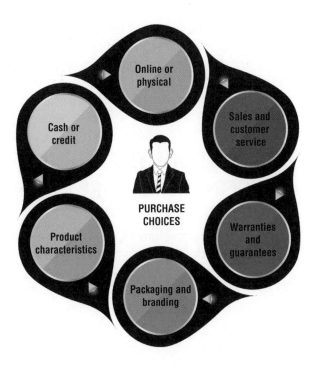

BUSINESS CONCEPTS

Benedict walks into the local deli to pick up some lunch. He needs a substantial meal and a drink. When he looks at the menu on the chalk board, there are many options. He has to decide what to order, a sandwich, roll and so on and in doing so he is undergoing BUYER DECISION MAKING.

Buyer decision process

Buyer decision processes are the decision making processes undertaken by consumers before, during, and after the purchase of a product or service. Common examples include shopping and deciding what to eat. Even a simple decision about what to eat is a type of **decision making**. Once this unconscious decision making takes place, it is followed by a commitment to act on that decision. This action is more visible to the observer than the decision itself.

Decision making: the mental process of selecting a course of action from a range of alternatives.

BUSINESS CONCEPTS

Mark and his mates buy their movie tickets for the 6 pm show. They have lined up at the local food court to order fast food although they are not hungry. Here, the group have unconsciously decided to eat a meal as it is dinner time but the choice of meal is conscious.

Impulse purchasing

An **impulse purchase** is an unplanned or otherwise spontaneous purchase. An **impulse buyer** is a consumer who tends to engage in spontaneous purchase behaviour or impulse buying. Businesses exploit impulses which are tied to a need for **instant gratification**. Impulse buying can also occur when a consumer sees something related to a product that stirs an emotion, for example seeing a certain country's flag on the cover of a magazine.

Impulse purchase: the act of buying due to an urge.

Impulse buyer: the person who gives in to an urge and makes a purchase.

BUSINESS CONCEPTS

A shopper in a supermarket or at a chemist might not specifically be shopping for lollies. However, lollies and mints are prominently displayed at checkout aisles to trigger IMPULSE BUYERS to buy what they might not have otherwise considered purchasing.

Impulse buying disrupts the decision making patterns of the consumer. Instead of analysing, researching available options and evaluating for suitability, the impulse buyer makes the purchase immediately.

This is a moment of human weakness where rational action is replaced with an irrational moment of **self gratification**. Impulse items appeal to the emotional side of consumers. Some items bought on impulse are not considered functional or necessary **post purchase**.

Post purchase: several hours after the purchase.

BUSINESS CONCEPTS

A house keeper walks past a kitchenware store and decides to check out what is on offer as he is in the market for a new frying pan. However, he leaves the shop with an egg separator, feeling good about the purchase. A month or so goes by and he still has not found a use for his impulse purchase.

FACTORS INFLUENCING CONSUMER DECISIONS

Consumers are faced with a challenge due to the range of products (goods and services) available. Many factors influence the way in which consumers make their final choice. The diagram illustrates key drivers that influence a consumers' decision making.

1. Personality and lifestyle

The personality of a person can be defined as their personal characteristics and mannerisms. People behave in different ways in different situations. Two people would behave differently to one another in any given situation as a result of experience.

A person's personality is generally interpreted by others and they also hold a perception of their personality, called **self concept**. This influences the way in which they live, and so lifestyle is shaped by personality. Lifestyle is the way an individual lives through their activities and interests and is often determined by how time and money is spent. This will influence the consumer's purchase choices.

Figure 13.6 Factors influencing consumer purchasing decisions

Individual members of families often serve different roles in decisions that draw on shared family resources. In a family there are **information gatherers** or **information holders**, who seek out information about products. These individuals often have a great deal of power because they selectively pass on information that favours their chosen alternatives.

In a family the decision maker(s) have the power to determine issues such as:

- whether to buy
- which product to buy

BUSINESS IN SOCIETY

Martin is a teenager from a academic family where everyone is generally well informed. Martin sees himself to be the cool trend setter in the family. Therefore he dresses in a manner depicting his self perception, saves his money to buy online music, and goes skate boarding with his mates.

- which brand to buy
- where to buy it
- when to buy.

The **decision maker** is not always the same person as the purchaser. Especially in family situations, the decisions are made at home and one of the adults engages in the purchasing, therefore the purchaser is different from the decision maker. This creates an issue when the purchaser is exposed to **point of purchase (POP)** marketing strategies.

The distinction between the purchaser and decision maker may be blurred as the decision maker may specify the kind of product but not which brand; the purchaser may have to make a substitution if the desired brand is not in stock; and the purchaser may disregard instructions either by error or deliberately. Marketing can deliberately target younger family members, so that they can influence decision through 'pester power.'

2. Peer group factors

People are easily influenced by the social group they belong to and this peer group can be called a **reference group**. The individual uses the group as a reference point or a standard of measure for their consumer decisions.

Peer groups come in three main forms.

- **Aspirational:** a group which an individual would like to compare themselves with; for example, wealthier people.

- **Associative:** a group which represents the individuals current equals; for example, co-workers, neighbours.

- **Dissociative:** a group which one would not like to be part of. For example, young people do not want to dress in the same way as their parents as it is considered to be 'uncool'.

BUSINESS IN SOCIETY

The Charles family is due to upgrade their family car. They are a middle income family with two young children. Ms Charles would prefer to buy a four wheel drive so the family can go on holidays and take the kids to school. Mr Charles would like a cheaper passenger car that is easy to park. The family is exploring their options in the car market.

Their older child, Bratz, is on the net surfing various sites to find information to guide the decision. He stumbles across a motoring advertisement by a car manufacturer, where the four wheel drive is driven by a little child through the city to the beach. Bratz downloads all the information on this car in an attempt to persuade his parents.

BUSINESS CONCEPTS

Stan is in the market to buy a digital camera. He has done his research and decided on the brand, the type of camera and features. As Stan is testing his final choice the shop assistant approaches him and presents him with another camera. Then Stan is informed that the new camera comes with a special offer of a bigger memory card for just for a fraction of the price.

Stan is now tempted to buy the new camera, though he has very limited understanding of its features. The prior research and the decision made at home are now being overridden by the new POINT OF PURCHASE offer that is made.

INNOVATION AND OPERATIONS

The franchise clothing store chain store Gap[1] targets younger people who want to actively DISSOCIATE from parents and other older and 'uncool' people.

---

1   GAP Clothing Company, www.gap.com, accessed 12 February 2007.

3. Psychological factors

There are a range of psychological factors that influence consumer purchase decisions.

Figure 13.7: Psychological factors that influence consumer purchasing decisions

Memory

Consumers notice and remember positive and negative aspects of a business or the service provided. This information is also shared with **reference groups**. The memory of what has happened influences decisions about purchasing from that business.

> **Reference group:** a group of people who are looked to for advice or guidance by the consumer.

BUSINESS IN SOCIETY

George and his friends noticed the friendly service offered to them in a particular café, as opposed to another where they did not even receive a smile when they purchased a coffee. Consumer George will REMEMBER these two experiences and in the future when he wants a coffee he will do business with the café where he was offered pleasant customer service.

Loyalty

Consumers are affected by **rewards**, which can be fixed or variable. A variable reward involves the business giving an opportunity to win a gift. For example, consumers are asked to fill in their details in a coupon and place it in a barrel. There is a possibility of being rewarded for purchase.

> **Rewards:** prize, a payment or an incentive.

Fixed rewards exist where consumers are rewarded for a specific number of purchases. Fixed rewards have a stronger effect on consumer decisions as they are guaranteed the reward. Customers tend to continue repeat purchases to maintain the loyalty status to be rewarded.

BUSINESS CONCEPTS

Many coffee vendors, such as Gloria Jeans[2] have a loyalty card. Every time a coffee is purchased the consumer receives a stamp on their card. As a result, over time, every tenth coffee is free for the consumer. This is a type of FIXED REWARD.

Motivation

The level of motivation influences consumers' decision making. Consumers are generally motivated to make purchases for everyday needs such as meals and personal care; however, they sometimes require extra encouragement to be motivated to use the services of a gymnasium or personal trainer. Motives may be overt or hidden. Consumers may also hold multiple motivations which cause conflicts of interest.

---

2   Gloria Jean's Coffees Australia: www.gloriajeanscoffees.com.au, accessed 12 February 2007.

Perception

There are many factors in consumer perceptions of reality. People are exposed to numerous commercial advertisements or commercial messages while driving on roads: bill boards, radio advertisements, bumper-stickers on cars, and signs and banners placed at shopping centres. These are known as **random** strategies as a person does not seek out these exposures.

> **Random:** action that is accidental or unplanned.

If a consumer is going to make a major purchase they seek out information about the product. For example, when buying a motor vehicle or a new oven, consumers tend to research these before making a purchase. Therefore, random exposure itself is not sufficient to adjust consumer perception and encourage them to purchase. Consumers may completely ignore an advertisement if it is not relevant to their needs. A commercial message will have an impact if factors such as their favourite colour, flavour or brand are apparent.

4. Economic factors

There are a range of economic factors that influence consumer purchase decisions.

Supply, demand and price

The **supply** of and **demand** for a product in the market affects its price. The price range affects the purchasing decision due to affordability. For example, if consumers are wanting more environmentally friendly cars, demand increases and if car manufacturers are incapable of producing cars to keep up with demand, the supply of the car drops. As demand is now greater than supply the price increases, resulting in a limited number of people being able to purchase. Even though everyone may prefer to own an environmentally friendly car not everyone will be able to afford it.

Figure 13.8: Economic factors that influence consumer purchasing decisions

The price of a product affects business profits. Therefore, recognising how demand and supply levels influence the price aids business success. Using this knowledge businesses decide on how many units of a particular item to produce to maintain demand without affecting the price too much.

Supply: available number of products or suppliers for a particular product or service.

Demand: the amount people request or want to buy of a particular product or service.

BUSINESS CONCEPTS

The price of a kilogram of bananas generally ranges from $2-$5 in Australian supermarkets. However, during droughts or after natural disasters when supply decreases, demand from Australian consumers moves the price up.

Economic climate

Several of the drivers of the Australian economic climate include interest rates, commodity prices and petrol prices. **Interest rates** are set by the Reserve Bank of Australia (RBA) and are used in attempts to control spending. At a very simple level, if consumers are spending (buying) so much to the extent that the overall savings are threatened, the RBA increases interest rates to increase the cost of living. This should result in people reducing their purchases.

Commodities include essential food and other goods and services people require to satisfy basic needs, such as bread, milk, transport and healthcare. If the prices of commodities are higher due to a drought or other reasons, consumers may spend less. This is because expensive commodities result in minimal savings or cash, therefore people are unable to spend money on luxuries and comfort items. Consumers will purchase less.

Another important driver of the economic climate is **petrol prices**. Petrol is required by families and industries. The price of petrol therefore dictates the price of the products as well as the level of affordability for families as their expenses are high.

Innovation

The expansion of innovation refers to the introduction of new products, practices or ideas to the market place. When new products or ideas appear they are only adopted by a small group of people initially; later, they expand to other people.

Consumer decisions to purchase are based on the **level of continuation** of the innovation. A continuous innovation includes slight improvements over time. A consumer may continue with

BUSINESS CONCEPTS

In Australia fuel prices have increased due to global influence. As a result the local fuel stations have increased prices. Jollene is a consumer whose cost of fuel, to get to work, has increased. The price of products has increased also, due to transport costs being higher. As a result Jollene's cost of living goes up. However, her pay has not changed. Therefore, she has to pay for the increased costs with the same amount of earnings. Jollene decides she is unable to afford going out for dinner as frequently as she is accustomed.

BUSINESS CONCEPTS

The use of debit and EFTPOS cards increased relatively quickly when they were first introduced. This is partly because the cards were used in public, resulting in others who did not yet hold the cards seeing how convenient they were. Although some people were concerned about security, convenience factors were a decisive factor in persuading consumers to use this new innovation.

their purchase decisions if a product has undergone **dynamically continuous innovation**, which involves some change in technology, even though the product is used much the same way that its predecessors were used. Businesses use this to maintain consumer loyalty, through continuous offers of better features and product improvements to address changing needs.

Consumer decisions are also influenced by **discontinuous innovation**. This is a product that fundamentally changes the way that things are done. Attracting consumers to discontinuous innovations is more difficult as the product is a **novelty** to the consumer. They lack understanding and awareness of the product and there are minimal reference groups.

INNOVATION AND OPERATIONS

When the iPod was first introduced, consumers were unsure about the product. Although consumers are familiar with the concept of portable music, they were wary of this new innovation. Until increased awareness and a strong client base developed, product sales were limited. Today many consumers own an iPod or its equivalent. This is DISCONTINUOUS INNOVATION where the consumer is introduced to a novelty product.

INNOVATION AND OPERATIONS

An office manager who has had Microsoft software installed in his laptop for the last couple of years is contemplating the advantages and disadvantages of upgrading to the latest operating system. Both of similar nature, the products provide software tools to manage office records and communication. However, the later version claims to be full of new features. Though both offer similar service the later is a more effective and advanced version of the prior. This is DYNAMIC CONTINUOUS INNOVATION of an existing product designed to keep the consumer within the same brand type.

ACTIVITIES

A. CHECK YOUR UNDERSTANDING

Competitive advantage

1. Define competitive advantage.

2. What can occur when a competitor identifies the businesses competitive advantage?

3. Compare the two main types of competitive advantage.

4. How does market research assist the business owner to define their competitive advantage?

5. Summarise four questions which the business owner should answer in order to identify their competitive advantage.

The extended marketing mix

1. Revise the first four elements of the marketing mix.

2. Explain the extended marketing mix.

3. What is the purpose of the expanded marketing mix?

4. Draw a diagram outlining the main elements of each of the following:

    A. People

    B. Processes

    C. Physical presence of the business

Consumer purchasing decisions

1. Define the term 'consumer'.

2. What is meant by 'consumer behaviour'?

3. Distinguish between a consumer and customer.

4. Summarise how to design a customer survey.

5. Summarise four methods that can be used to determine customer expectations.

6. What is impulse buying?

7. What is meant by 'post-purchase'?

8. What factors influence consumer choices?

9. Identify the influencing factors on family decision making.

10. Explain the following peer reference groups:

 A. Aspiration group

 B. Associative group

 C. Dissociative group

11. Outline the main element of the psychological factors that influence consumer purchases:

 A. Loyalty

 B. Memory

 C. Motivation

 D. Perception of business image

12. What economic factors influence decision making? Give an example for each.

B. BUSINESS RESEARCH

1. Access at least two online consumer surveys, such as those presented on the websites of the following companies:

 • Dominos
 • McDonalds
 • Qantas Airline
 • Virgin Blue Airline

 A. In groups of two complete the surveys.

 B. Identify the similarities and the differences between each survey, presenting this information in the form of a table.

 C. Prepare a list of key focus areas for a customer satisfaction survey for either an airline or a fast food group.

 Note: Other survey sites can be chosen and the questions may be modified by your teacher.

2. Use the following website to develop a survey aimed at establishing the purchasing behaviours of someone in your classroom.

 • **www.surveysystem.com/sdesign.htm**

C. RESPONSE

1. Using the information provided regarding ways of determining customer expectations, identify four methods of recognising consumer expectations. Select one and explain how it could be used by a business owner in each of the following industries, to find out more about their customers:

    A. Beauty salon

    B. Tutoring

    C. Agriculture

    D. Dentist

2. Use the information provided regarding designing a survey to create a pilot survey for a new type of ice cream.

3. How does a consumer's need for instant gratification result in impulse purchases?

    A. Explain, using examples, how a business might exploit this.

    B. Illustrate an example of purchase behaviour for a consumer going through the process of buying their first car.

4. How can a business use the elements of 'purchase choices' to influence consumers with respect to each of the following products and services?

    A. Washing machines

    B. Bread

    C. Clothing

    D. Computers

    E. Automotive services

5. Identify how a service business could use the following elements to induce a consumer to make an impulse purchase.

    A. People: communication and service

    B. Process: customer experience

    C. Physical presence: shop front, packaging, uniforms

6. How do personality and lifestyle factors contribute to these individual's purchase decisions/

    A. Mark is a middle-aged man who has a highly paid job and lives in a city centre high rise apartment. He drives a BMW to work and owns four-wheel-drive for the weekend activities.

    B. Jemma is living with her parents and she just started a new job. She uses public transport and is aiming to save for a house.

    C. Jordus is a retired farmer who lives with his wife in the country. They enjoy the quiet life and travel annually to visit grandchildren.

7. Identify the level of influence peer reference group factors have on a teenager's purchase choices. Prepare your response in relation to the following aspects of consumer decision making.

   A. Teen culture

   B. Desire to be viewed as 'cool'

   C. Desire to be 'different'

8. As a teenager you are eager to own your own car as you are learning to drive. You would like to drive either a 'Holden Rodeo Ute' or a 'Ford FPV Ute' personally (depending on whether you are a Holden or Ford fan). However, your family has much to say about your car of choice and they have their own opinion on what car you should drive. Discuss what aspects of the family decision making would affect your choice.

9. How would each of the following psychological factors influence your purchase of a new computer?

   A. Memory

   B. Loyalty

   C. Motivation

   D. Perception

10. You are sixteen years old and work at a local business as a shop assistant on casual basis. You live with your parents who provide for you. However, the family policy is that if you want to buy special items such as music and fashion clothing, you to earn your own money after you are 15 years of age. You already pay for your meals, when you eat out with mates on the weekend and entry fees every month to the local sprint car course to see the races. You have no savings. You are saving to buy a computer.

    A. What economic factors would influence your purchase of a computer?

    B. What effect would each of these economic factors have upon your purchase (discuss the positive and negative aspects).

    C. Present your findings either visually or orally to the class.

11. Case study: Factors influencing consumer purchasing decisions.

    > Often advertising is not about keeping up with the Joneses, but about separating you from them. That's especially true of advertising directed at a particular group, such as adolescents or young adults; it's called 'dog-whistle' advertising because it goes out at frequencies only dogs can hear.

    > (Dr James Twitchell)

    Respond to this statement by preparing answers to these questions. Prepare a presentation on your findings.

    A. What is meant by this statement? (Consider how advertisements specifically target groups.)

    B. List at least 10 examples of advertisements that appeal to you, but not to other target markets or age groups.

    C. What is it that separates these advertisements from those that appeal to other target markets or age groups?

    D. How do these advertisements target the consumer decision making of your age group? Do they then influence how your age group influences the decisions of other consumers?

E.   In Australia, is there a difference between advertisements aimed at decision making by teenage girls, and decision making by teenage boys?

F.   Explain how at least one of the advertisements is aimed at family decision making.

D. GROUP PROJECTS

I.   Select one health food item that could be sold at your school canteen. You are to consider how its image could be revised for the students in your community.

A.   In a group, allocate elements of the expanded Seven Ps of marketing to each group member. Each member is to design that element of your business' marketing plan.

B.   Compile a summary of your marketing proposal, and present this to the class.

C.   The class can vote on the best proposal, to be submitted to your canteen manager.

2.   Select a particular product or service that you are familiar with.

A.   Research the marketing techniques used to attract consumers in relation to influencing factors identified within the chapter.

B.   Develop a set of key questions to probe the consumers of the product or service, to identify what motivates them to purchase that item.

C.   Set up the questions in a survey format.

D.   Carry out the survey with a target consumer group. Evaluate the findings by categorising the responses.

E.   Analyse the findings and prepare an information brochure for businesses on what strategies are effective and what strategies require changes.

3.   Complete a class debate after sufficient time to research your topic. When one topic is being debated the rest of the class is to act as an audience and evaluate their peers and the strength of their arguments.

Debate topics:

- Advertising sets us up to feel dissatisfied, even if we think we have everything we need, ads will still try to convince us that there is something else we need.

- Advertisers show us how much more satisfied, popular, happy, hip, attractive, sexy, fun and in control we would be if we had their product.

- Fashion and trends are always changing so that we must continually spend money to be current.

- Advertising stresses competition and status versus feeling good about being who you are and accepting others for who they are.

CHAPTER 14
Managing Operations

'Management is doing things right; leadership is doing the right things.'
– Peter Drucker –

The owner of a small business must fulfill a number of management roles in that they plan, organise and control the business. Most importantly they lead the business and have the vision and direction to steer it in the right direction. In some circumstances they might be able to identify where their own skills are lacking and employ a manager to work in the business.

The operation of a small to medium business requires the careful assessment of risk and the implementation of risk management strategies. Methods of monitoring activities in an ongoing way enable the business to control progress and have regular reviews of goal achievement.

THE MANAGER'S ROLE

All businesses ultimately rely heavily on the people within them. For this reason, understanding the individuals who make up the business' workforce is of great importance. The **manager** of the workforce needs to have clarity about their own strengths and weaknesses in order to be able to care for the employees they work with. The small business owner has to fulfil many requirements of a manager's role.

A small business relies on the management skills of the owner. Management includes coordinating forward planning and organising administrative issues. When **planning**, a manager is generally considering the strategies and direction of the business. They evaluate and review past results in order to consider future goals and objectives. On the other hand, the **administrative** aspect involves performing day to day duties and implementing decisions that have been made. This means that the manager coordinates the business in order to achieve future goals and objectives.

Manager: the person in charge of directing a group of employees toward achieving specific business goals.

Planning: developing a proposed method for moving toward the attainment of a particular goal.

Administration: managing business operation and coordinating all that occurs in an organisation.

The researcher Mintzberg[1] has developed a list of ten possible roles that a manager can take at different times – these are figurehead, leader, liaison, monitor, disseminator, spokesperson, entrepreneur, disturbance handler, resource allocator and negotiator. These roles have been given a definition and examples in the following table.

Table 14.1: Roles of a manager

ROLE	DEFINITION	EXAMPLES
Figurehead	Holding an important role or title within the organisation and representing the business at important events	Signing documents, greeting important visitors, welcoming other managers or chairperson
Leader	Encouraging and motivating employees and supervisors toward the organisation's goals	Chairing meetings, setting goals
Liaison	Networking with people from external organisations	Meeting with external suppliers and managers, participating in community groups
Monitor	Keeping track of information relevant to the organisation	Reading newspapers and journals, collecting useful details
Disseminator	Distributing knowledge and information to supervisors and employees	Meeting with individuals and groups to share out information, organising training for employees
Spokesperson	Distributing knowledge and information about the business to external organisations	Meeting with community groups, presenting at media conferences
Entrepreneur	Taking risks and developing new innovations for the organisation	Encouraging creative thinking in employees, holding planning meetings
Disturbance handler	Negotiating and rectifying problems	Dealing with problems, assisting with fire drills, responding to marketing crises
Resource allocator	Deciding how to distribute resources	Authorising use of supplies, distributing timeplans, arranging rosters
Negotiator	Conferring and consulting with others on behalf of the organisation	Participating in legal discussions, meeting with union representatives

BUSINESS CONCEPTS

Melinda is a manager who distributes information about her business to the media whenever a major function is being held. She will collate data and produce a media release with photographs attached then organise a media conference for newspaper and television journalists. Melinda is performing her SPOKESPERSON role in these situations.

---

1   Henry Mintzberg, *The nature of managerial work,* 1973.

Skills required of business managers

The discussion of business success and failure in the previous section included skills as an important element determining a business' success. Researcher Katz[2] has suggested that there are three main skill areas needed in people who hold management positions. These are conceptual, human resource and technical skills.

Table 14.2: Skills required for the smooth running of business

SKILL	DEFINITION
Conceptual	Understanding the 'big picture', and being able to be visionary and plan for the future of the business. The manager needs to be able to see how the business works as a whole
Human resource	Being able to coordinate the teams of people who work in the business, solving their concerns and working with individuals and groups
Technical	Experience in using equipment and coordinating resources is vital so that the manager can coordinate the main operating functions of the business

The business owner of a sole trader or small business has to contemplate developing all of these skills. It is useful to consider how proficient the business owner might need to be in each of these different skills. Business owners need to use each type of skill to different extents. In a small business, the owner must be either proficient in all these skills, or they need to employ other people to assist them with any areas of weakness.

BUSINESS CONCEPTS

Sascha is the owner of a small business which produces automobile parts for a car manufacturer. When she is completing her four-year business plan update, she must be visionary and rely on her CONCEPTUAL skills. When she is working on the production line and coordinating the use of equipment to manufacture a specific automobile part her TECHNICAL skills are required.

MANAGEMENT ELEMENTS AND BUSINESS IMPROVEMENTS

A business process is a set of tasks or activities that employees or equipment undertake in order to achieve business goals. Business **process management** aims to improve the business processes of an organisation. In their management role, business owners need to look at the changing external environment that is affecting their business, to look at inefficiencies within the business, and to change the processes so the organisation becomes more effective. The owner is aiming to maintain and improve on processes as they operate the business.

Process management: activities involved in monitoring and reviewing the performance of business processes, with the aim of improving methods and meeting business goals.

Business process: an activity that occurs in an organisation, performed by people or equipment, that is aimed at achieving the mission or goals of the organisation.

---

2   Robert Katz, *Skills of an effective administrator,* 1974.

The management roles performed when operating processes in a business are shown in a circular diagram, because they are not necessarily consecutive stages.

As the business owner, or their delegate, performs each of these roles, they may complete a number of tasks, such as those listed here.

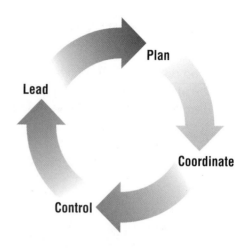

Figure 14.1: Management roles in business process improvement

1. Plan

- Develop objectives
- Set business aims
- Decide how to meet goals and objectives

2. Organise/Coordinate

- Handle resourcing
- Distribute tasks
- Administer the flow of information
- Organise finance

Planning: a management role where the procedures for meeting organisational goals are developed.

3. Control

- Direct employees
- Monitor performance
- Assess results
- Correct problems
- Take action

Organising: management role requiring the distribution of organisational resources.

Controlling: one of the roles performed by managers, where employees are directed, and performance of the organisation is continually assessed.

4. Lead

- Have a vision for the business' future
- Motivate other staff members
- Direct line managers
- Steer employees toward business and personal objectives

The important planning, organising/coordinating and controlling elements required in the management of a small business are examined in detail in the next section.

Leading: arguably the most important management role, requiring the manager to encourage and motivate employees, have a vision for the organisation's future and implement that vision.

BUSINESS CONCEPTS

Serena has decided to move the focus for her locally based children's toy business to have a national selling platform on the internet. She motivates her employees by explaining to them her visions for the future, and discussing their personal goals. This shows her ability to LEAD her business.

Planning business activities

All owners want business to run smoothly. This section will explore how planning will allow them to ensure this happens. Planning is one of the most important parts of the management function of a business. It ensures that there is some coordination between employees, and should minimise any inefficiency from unanticipated events occurring. The owners of a business must ensure that plans are used to guide operations. If there is no planning, then the business will not have any direction and will not know how to prioritise activities.

When managing a small business, three important points should be considered for any plan that is made, no matter how insignificant the plan may be.

> A plan is a proposed method to be used to achieve the organisation's goals and objectives.

> **STEPS IN BUSINESS PLANNING**
> 1. What needs to be achieved?
> 2. How will this happen?
> 3. Who and where will this occur?

Types of planning

There are two main types of business planning. One is in response to a need for goals for the near future, the other is planning for the long term results of the business. Long term business planning tends to be strategic and focused on results. The overall business plan can then be broken down into an Action Plan of short term operational goals.

1. Strategic (Long-term) planning

> **Strategic plan:** a long term plan aimed at setting goals and allocating the resources to achieve these goals.

These are 'big picture' plans, which consider all possible aspects of the entire business. Strategic planning provides a broad picture of the future of the business, and gives a general focus. **Strategic plans** usually define the organisational goals.

2. Action (Short-term) planning

These include specific plans, which pertain to a particular area of the business or a section of the strategic plan. An **action plan** is detailed and provides information about how goals are to be achieved.

Figure 14.2: Breaking down plans and goals into action plans

> **Action plan:** a proposal aimed at achieving a specific result in a short period of time.

INNOVATION AND ENTERPRISE

The Mighty Muffins bakery has developed a strategic plan aimed at 'Improving the position and performance of the business over the next five years'. It has several action plans related to this. One in particular is the food manufacturing plan for 'A five percent increase in production levels within the next six months'.

Coordination of business activities

As part of the initial establishment of the business, and then the ongoing progress, one of the roles of the manager or owner outlined previously is organisation. In completing this management role the business owner has to coordinate many aspects of the business. They will deal with resourcing, the allocation of tasks, daily administration and the supervision of finance.

Business activities are coordinated through various methods such as short and long term planning, the setting up of clear processes to be followed in the business, and having useful systems in place.

STEPS IN BUSINESS COORDINATION

1. Decide what needs to be done, using the business' goals.
2. Group what needs to be done according to who can complete the tasks.
3. Assign work to people in the business.
4. Review the effectiveness of what has been achieved and check that the business' goals have been achieved.

INNOVATION AND OPERATIONS

Patricia owns three newsagencies, and specialises in importing a range of newspapers from overseas. The logistics of completing customs forms, ordering the papers, distributing them to her shops and ensuring that orders are always filled requires her to COORDINATE and ORGANISE business activities.

Control of business activities

Once a business has been established, the owner needs to monitor its progress in an ongoing way. This can be referred to as controlling the business, and requires the owner to examine results and ensure that the business goals are being achieved.

The Business Plan will have identified goals and objectives. Control of the business is a reflective and often active process of questioning whether goals are going to be achieved, and what changes are required to ensure they are achieved.

Internal control in a business is a process of ensuring that assets are protected and any loss from fraud or theft is minimised. In a small business this can be difficult because the duties cannot be split between a number of people and it can be difficult to monitor customers.

INNOVATION AND OPERATIONS

Alex Chong's business Online Latitude Technology3 provides web consulting services for Australian businesses. He has a comprehensive business plan which is reviewed and updated every year. He sees that it is very important to have short and long term goals, and to review the achievement of these on a regular basis. He monitors progress by measuring how his solutions have actually assisted customers. When Alex is reviewing progress and making changes to ensure goals are achieved, he is CONTROLLING business activities.

STEPS IN BUSINESS CONTROL

1. Establish the standard that is to be met, using the business' goals.
2. Monitor how the business performs in this area.
3. Compare the actual performance of the business with the standard.
4. Make any changes required to correct any problems, if the business plan goals have not been met.

---

3   Young Business Network, www.youngbusinessnetwork.com

Business activities that need to be controlled

These include:

- **Stock:** in a merchandising business, the most important asset is inventory and the owner should have methods of ensuring this is being stored, sold and transported correctly. They should have regular stock takes, be aware of slow selling items, and purchase economically viable quantities.

- **Cash:** the owner will need to use their cash budget to monitor the business **liquidity**. Possible indicators of concern include accounts not being repaid on time, the prices of materials or labour increasing,

> **Liquidity:** the ability for the business to pay its short-terms debts on the date they are due.

- **Giving customers credit:** it is useful to be able to extend credit to customers; however, the owner must screen clients carefully. They should check customer credit records, only allow set limits and check the aged debtors on occasion. The business owner can also encourage customers to pay early by offering discounts and must follow up any late payments promptly.

- **Non-financial areas:** the owner should review areas such as employee sick leave, the business occupational health and safety record, **staff turnover**, quality control results and encourage development of new product/service innovations.

> **Staff turnover:** how often the business employs new staff, and loses staff.

RISK MANAGEMENT

Risk management requires the business owner to be cautious and undertake their best efforts to ensure the business is not exposed to negative consequences from decisions made. Risks should be avoided where possible, but it is sometimes not possible to even predict the risks that could occur. The owner would want to ensure business' objectives are not adversely affected by the actions of the staff of the business, as that is an area where they have some level of control. Risk management should result in assets being better protected, employees being more secure, and customers being more confident in the businesses policies and management.

BUSINESS CONCEPTS

Paddy owns a small hardware shop in a rural town. His business is family run and the only shop of its type in the town. Recently a new major competitor has opened a business operating under the name of a popular and well-advertised hardware franchise that is well known for its competitive pricing. In response to this UNPREDICTABLE RISK, Paddy completed market research showing that his business would be well supported if it diversified and offered home maintenance services as well as hardware supplies.

There are broad types of risk, some of which have interchangeable elements.

Table 14.3: Types of risk

TYPE OF RISK	EXPLANATION	EXAMPLES
Unpredictable	Something very disruptive or unforseen, an unexpected event	· Natural disaster such as cyclone · Fire or flood · Unexpected business competitor · Changed government legislation
Financial	Monetary costs that can arise from different decisions	· Exchange rate decline · Share market upsets · Customer bad debts
Opportune	When the business takes up a risky opportunity or conversely, chooses to NOT take up a safe opportunity	· Purchasing new equipment · Expanding a product line · Adding new services to the business · Moving to a new location
Strategic	Protecting intangible assets or items that are difficult to value in dollar terms	· Patent protection · Keeping customer accounts · Responding to new competition
Hazardous	Covered by most Occupational Health and Safety policies, this is where the work environment can be dangerous or potentially harmful	· Poor ergonomics or work place design · Chemicals · Noise, heat and other factors related to the work environment

There are many ways that a small to medium business owner can minimise their risks.

Risk minimisation

Possible ways to minimise risk include the following.

- Have a useful **insurance** policy.
- Ensure that employees are properly **trained** and are the right people for the job.
- Develop and implement a sound OHS plan.
- Make sure all legal requirements to do with the work environment are complied with.
- Develop quality control methods.

BUSINESS CONCEPTS

A small cleaning company that cleans offices has developed a risk management OHS plan for HAZARDS. This includes training staff to be aware of unsafe equipment, ensuring that dangerous environments such as wet floors are signposted, establishing that cleaning chemicals are locked away, and ensuring staff lift heavy objects in the correct manner.

INNOVATION AND OPERATIONS

Sheena owns a small gift centre in the main street of a country town. She has a good location and there is a lot of passing foot traffic. A new shopping centre has just opened up two blocks away, and Sheena has noticed that there does not appear to be as much pedestrian traffic as before. Sales have declined slightly. In order to minimise the UNPREDICTABILITY RISK, she needs to complete a risk management plan that will compare the options of remaining where she is with relocating to the new shopping centre.

Hazard identification

The procedure to be followed in identifying, reporting and implementing occupational health and safety concerns is in the hazard reporting process. This is a simple three-step guide colloquially known as the 'SAM' strategy which stands for 'Spot, Assess and Manage'.

The three steps involve firstly identifying the potential hazard. Secondly, the hazard is assessed to estimate the level of damage or potential damage. Finally, the situation is to be managed by taking the required action to either eliminate the hazard or prevent the hazard from worsening.

Figure 14.3: SAM strategy

More complex hazard identification tools have been developed for specific industries and dangerous working situations, these are available from WorkSafe WA.

There are many potential hazards that could cause serious injury and a range of safe work practices that should be followed to minimise these hazards.

Minor hazards that may cause serious injury

Minor hazards include the following:

- A loose electrical cable may cause tripping and potential spinal injuries.
- A wet floor may cause slipping and head injuries.
- Failure to employ correct equipment, for example a trolley for moving boxes, can result in back injuries.
- Exposure to fumes due to failure to wear masks may cause respiratory problems.
- Use of incorrect sized gloves could result in fingers being caught on machines.

Table 14.4: Safe work practices to minimise hazards

Personal protective equipment	Good footwear, helmets, eye protection and ear protection, high visibility clothing and protective clothing must be used where appropriate
Floors	Keep free of spills and ripped carpets or flooring
Office	Keep corridors and emergency exits clear
Factory	Wear suitable protective clothing
Desk	Position of the chair, computer monitor and keyboard to personally suit the person occupying the station, to avoid strain
Equipment	Follow manufacturers' safety instructions
Work habits	Regular exercise and breaks may assist in protection from occupational overuse syndrome. This is caused by repetitive actions such as typing or staring at a computer screen which results in Repetitive Muscular Injury, commonly known as RMI

Why manage risk?

A business needs to manage risk because a structured approach to risk management will enable it to approach problems in a systematic way. Employees of the business will have confidence that hazards and unpredictable events will be properly dealt with, customers will be confident the product or service they are purchasing has been manufactured to high standards and the long-term viability of the business will be enhanced.

Categories of risk in a business

When producing a risk management plan, the business owner will consider a broad range of categories of risk. It is dependent upon the industry within which the business is located, and the types of tasks that are carried out in the workplace, as to which of these categories will apply to a specific business.

There are several different categories of risk to analyse.

Figure 14.4: Categories of risk

Minimising business risk

There are many controls that a business can use to minimise risks.

INSURANCE POLICIES	· Cover negative impacts of unpredictable events · Unexpected changes
QUALITY PRODUCT OR SERVICE	· Less returns and refunds · Customer safety
STAFF TRAINING	· Ensure staff are safe, responsive, proactive · Quality control
COMPLIANCE	· Legal requirements · Hazard minimisation and OSH plans
REVIEWS	· Ensure hazardous risk minimisation is working · Implement improved procedures

Figure 14.5: Risk minimisation methods

Risk management limitations

Risk management does have limitations. Just because a risk management plan is in place does not mean that the staff of the business will always recognise when it is needed. The owner of the business still has to make difficult daily decisions in response to strategic questions and may not always have all the information they require to make the best decision. Hazards can still exist within a business no matter what precautions are taken and human error is always a factor in safety. Ultimately, unpredictable risks are just that – the business must be prepared for the fact that sometimes adverse consequences might occur in spite of all the precautionary planning that has been undertaken.

Job risk analysis

A job risk analysis is a review of all the potential hazards in the job, and an itemisation of the associated risks. It is carried out in response to the **hazardous** risk type, and categorised as **safety and health**.

1. Prioritise jobs

The risks must first be prioritised. The level of seriousness of each risk needs to be categorised so that critical problems are addressed more urgently. The seriousness of a risk can be established from previous "near misses", known work hazards, the number of employees potentially affected and previous experience with the job and its risks.

Table 14.8: Prioritising job risk

Name of job	The job, eg. forklift operation
Description of job	The job broken into all its components, eg. lifting, rigging and unloading
Seriousness	A scale such as low-moderate-high-extreme.
Explanation of seriousness	Previous 'near misses', known work hazards, the number of employees potentially affected and previous experience, eg. one recent injury to a driver when attaching rigging to load
Priority	Number all job risks in order of priority

2. Analyse risk

Once each job has been prioritised, a job risk analysis is carried out in order to develop methods of minimising risks. The job is broken into all its component tasks and the hazards involved with each task are listed. The frequency with which each task is performed is used to calculate the likelihood of an accident occurring.

3. Reduce risk

Controls to minimise the risk are then reviewed and added and the risk is re-calculated.

BUSINESS IN SOCIETY

Salina has determined there is an urgent need for a job risk analysis of the welding area in her businesses workshops. In her job risk analysis she establishes that the tasks done include welding and soldering. The hazards involved with these tasks include temperature extremes resulting in burns, abrasions and fumes. 50% of the employees of the business are in some way involved in using the welding equipment so there is a high likelihood of an accident occurring. Controls already in place include protective equipment and shielding. Salina determines that the following needs to be reviewed: the size of the welding masks, the ventilation system for the welding bays as a new bay has recently been added, and the ergonomics of bending for long periods of time to complete a new component of a recent addition to the product line.

MONITORING BUSINESS ACTIVITIES

In order to determine whether the business is achieving its goals, the owner must periodically take stock, and consider the progress being made. They will also need to manage potential risks that can occur in the business environment. There are various methods of monitoring the progress of the business in an ongoing way. The owner might choose to use one or all of the following options.

Methods of monitoring

Sales data

The source documents available in the business are used to record purchases and sales. Summaries of the records can be produced using a variety of computing resources such as spreadsheets, graphs and other analyses. These records will allow the business owner to check whether actual results are meeting the targets set in the budgets and objectives of the business.

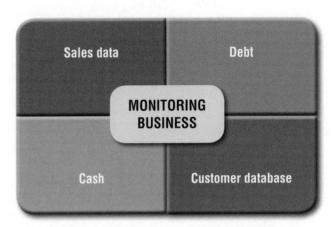

Figure 14.6: Monitoring business activities

Customer data base

By keeping an updated customer database, the owner can gauge how many customers return to the business, how many new customers are attracted and the customer **retention rate** which will indicate how long a customer remains loyal to the business. This information will assist in the development of incentive schemes and loyalty programmes to retain or attract customers.

Retention rate: a measure of how many customers are retained by the business.

Debt

The business owner will use information comparing the levels of external sources of finance (or debt) and internal sources (or equity), which is important because the business will not want to have too great a portion of funding coming from external sources unless interest rates are very low. This is reflected in the gearing calculations. The owner needs to be aware of the level of debt and, if is it increasing, be able to pre-empt any future problems.

Cash

In addition to an awareness of any potential gearing problems, the owner will need to ensure that the business always has enough cash to pay off short term debts, so that a liquidity problem does not arise. They will use the cash flow reports of the business to monitor the cash inflows and outflows.

ACTIVITIES

A. CHECK YOUR UNDERSTANDING

Planning, organising and controlling

1. Define the following terms:
   A. Manager
   B. Planning
   C. Administration

2. Summarise the roles of a manager.

3. Define the three skill areas required of managers.

4. Which skill area from Table 14.2: Skills required for the smooth running of business would a small business owner most often rely on? Under what circumstances?

5. What is process management?

6. Explain the key management roles of planning, organising, leading and controlling.

7. Explain the purpose of setting goals.

8. Compare and contrast strategic planning and action planning.

9. Clearly explain how strategic planning is linked to organisational goal setting.

10. Define the following terms:
    A. Goals
    B. Objectives
    C. Strategic plan
    D. Action plan

11. Summarise the main steps in business organising.

12. Summarise the main steps in business control.

Risk management strategies

1. Explain what workplace hazards are, using examples to illustrate your answer.

2. What benefits will safe work practices bring?

3. What does 'OSH' stand for?

4. What does the acronym SAM represent? Explain how it is applied in a business.

5. List four examples of minor workplace hazards.

6. Give seven safe work practices.

7. What are four potential work hazards in the office environment?

8. Explain the concept of risk management for a business.

9. Define five types of risk. For each one, give an example that would apply to an office workplace.

10. Why does a business owner want to manage risk?

11. Select and define three risk minimisation methods.

12. Why might employees not implement a Risk Management Plan?

13. What are some of the limitations on the use of risk management?

14. Explain the purpose of undertaking a job risk analysis.

Monitoring business activities

1. Why does the business owner need to monitor business activities?

2. Summarise four tools that could be used to monitor business activity.

B. BUSINESS RESEARCH

1. Access the WorkSafe website at **www.commerce.wa.gov.au/WorkSafe** and go to the 'Safety Topics' section. Create a brochure for employees that is focused on a specific area of safety and health. Your brochure should educate employees about the appropriate ways to minimise hazards.

   Safety and health topics:

   - Electricity
   - Forklifts
   - Guarding
   - Hazardous substances
   - Manual handling
   - New and young workers
   - Slips and trips
   - Working at height

2. Complete the student activities on the WA WorkSafe website at **www.worksafe. wa.gov.au**, selecting the 'WorkSafe Smart Move' section.

   Activities:

   i.   Get Creative About Safety and Health
   ii. Act It Out

iii. Investigating an Incident at Work

iv. New to the Job Video – Working Safely

v. On Guard! Do Your Job Safely

vi. Safety and Health Media Watch

vii. ThinkSafe S.A.M. Hazard Assessment in the Workplace

viii. Sign Language

ix. Communication Skills – Talking About Safety and Protecting Yourself At Work

x. Word Scramble

xi. Word Sleuth – Hazards, Risk Assessment and Control

C. RESPONSE

1. Consider the roles of a manager that were outlined in Table 14.1: Roles of a manager. Create a table comparing and contrasting the planning and administrative elements of the management role undertaken by a small business owner. You should classify each of the 10 roles into either planning, administration, or both. Then give an example for each.

2. Explain how the individual in each of the following situations would require a focus on conceptual, human resource or technical management skills, or a combination of these.

   A. An assembly line supervisor in a fruit canning factory

   B. A shift manager at a fast food restaurant

   C. A telephone operator at a call centre

   D. A partner in a law firm

   E. A recreation officer at a leisure centre

3. Write a simple plan for a local or school event that is to occur this year. Set three goals, and then complete a one-page report outlining the following information:

   A. What needs to be achieved?

   B. How will this happen?

   C. Who and where will this occur?

4. Allan is a front line manager for a snack food manufacturer. His role involves the coordination and control of the production lines. Give three goals that Allan might have to achieve, and explain the main type of planning that he will use.

5. Clare is the operations manager of a soft drink manufacturer. Her role involves budgeting and communicating with the line managers for each different type of soft drink. Give three goals that Claire might plan to achieve, and explain the main type of planning that she will use.

6. Explain how each of the following management roles would apply to a small business owner who is wanting to improve an inefficient layout for EITHER a building site OR a kitchen workstation.

   A. Plan
   B. Organise
   C. Direct
   D. Lead

7. Use Table 14.4: Steps in business coordination to produce a basic business activities plan for your choice of a well-known local business in your geographic area.

8. Use Table 14.5: Steps in business control to produce a basic plan for the control of stock, cash or creditors for your choice of a well-known local business in your geographic area.

9. Using Table 14.7: Safe work practices to minimise hazards identify how the employer in each of the following businesses can provide a safe working environment:

   A. Bicycle repair workshop
   B. Hotel kitchen
   C. Chemist
   D. Building site
   E. Roof tiler
   F. Accountancy firm.

10. Referring to 'Table 14.6: Types of risk', identify the risk category of each of the following situations and explain how an employer can minimise the risk for either the business, customers, employees and/or other stakeholders.

   A. Flooding from a burst water main
   B. Storage of cleaning chemicals
   C. Extending credit to customers who then do not pay their debts
   D. Purchasing a new 'all-in-one' photocopier and fax machine in order to print advertising brochures
   E. Developing an innovative new product
   F. Using inexpensive office furniture and equipment that is not tailored to each individual employee
   G. Roof damage from a storm

D. GROUP PROJECTS

I. My management style

Complete the following appraisal about management methods:

Consider how you act in a specific area of life (at work, school or home) when answering all the questions. Choose the answer that most represents you. Remember that everyone has different methods of managing in different situations, and all have both good and bad characteristics. This is about understanding yourself in a particular situation.

1. When someone I care about is aggressive toward me, I will usually:
    A. Be aggressive in response
    B. Listen to them in a thoughtful manner
    C. Ask them what is wrong and try to be friendly
    D. Move away from them

2. When someone I do not know very well is aggressive toward me, I will usually:
    A. Be aggressive in response
    B. Listen to them in a thoughtful manner
    C. Ask them what is wrong and try to be friendly
    D. Move away from them

3. When I am in charge and a job needs to be completed, I will generally:
    A. Make sure that everyone involved knows how the work should be completed
    B. Want the best outcome for everyone involved
    C. Consult everyone involved and ask their opinions
    D. Go along with everyone and provide assistance

4. If the person in charge of a job is being too 'pushy', I will generally:
    A. Tell them why I dislike their management style
    B. Subtly let them know that I am not happy, by dropping hints
    C. Ask them to discuss the problem in order to find a solution to my concerns
    D. Not say anything and put up with it

5. I believe that disagreements help people by:
    A. Helping them to see the reality of a situation
    B. Airing different viewpoints so that everyone can compromise
    C. Ensuring relationships are improved and people understand one another
    D. They do not help people and should be avoided

6. If one person in my group is disagreeing about how the group should work together, and no-one agrees with them at all, I will most often:
    A. Argue back and tell them to either fall in line with the group or leave
    B. Ask the person to communicate their opinion calmly
    C. Ask the group to negotiate and discuss the problem with the person
    D. Not get involved at all or change the subject

7. If I am unhappy about a situation, I will most often:
   A. Make some jokes at the expense of other people
   B. Try to use humour to relax everyone else
   C. Use humour about myself and how I am coping
   D. Not feel relaxed enough to laugh or joke around

8. If I am able to choose a person to work with on a project, I will find someone who:
   A. Supports my opinions and always does what I say
   B. Wants to include most of my opinions as well as the ideas of other people
   C. Considers all opinions, works out which will be most effective, and finds solutions to any problems that come up
   D. Is precise and gets the work done without worrying about what anyone thinks

9. If I something happens that makes me angry, I will most often:
   A. Fly into a rage and say exactly what I think
   B. Try to relax and make a joke
   C. Calmly express my concerns and discuss the situation
   D. Leave and forget about the problem

10. I believe that miscommunication between individuals occurs because:
    A. Often people don't say what they really think
    B. People try to copy their peer group, instead of stating the truth
    C. It is too difficult for some people to cooperate
    D. People can't be bothered to find out what others really need

Score yourself as follows:

one point for every A	
two for every B	
three for every C	
four for every D answer	
TOTAL SCORE	

SCORE BETWEEN	YOUR MANAGEMENT METHOD	DESCRIPTION
10-17	Authoritarian or controlling	You like to make all decisions yourself, without consulting others. Your focus is your own goals, not others. You dominate decisions, set all the goals and communicate 'downwards' to others.
18-25	Compromising	You like to make your own decisions; however, you often try to make decisions that will support others as well as you. You communicate with other people by clarifying details and trying to ensure their needs are being met. You try to find the "middle ground" in any dispute.

SCORE BETWEEN	YOUR MANAGEMENT METHOD	DESCRIPTION
26-33	Democratic or autonomous	You involve other people in decision making, and aim to benefit both yourself and others as a result of the decisions that are made. Communication occurs between everyone involved and you are collaborative.
34-40	Accommodating or laissez-faire	You avoid making decisions, and leave this up to other people. There is very little communication involved in this management method, and you allow people to manage their own goals.

Reflect on your management style:

- Summarise your management style. Remember that this is your style now, at this point in your life. How might your management style change in the future?

- Compare your style with other people in the class.

- Compile a summary of the management styles of all class members.

Set your personal goals:

- Summarise the planning methods that you currently use in your personal life, considering the areas of study, leisure and work.

- Set personal goals for each of these areas.

- Compare your 'work' related goals with others in the class, and classify the goals into strategic plan and action plan categories.

CHAPTER 15
Financial Records

'Profit is not the legitimate purpose of business.
The legitimate purpose of business is to provide a product or service
that people need and do it so well that it's profitable.'
– James Rouse –

Simple records are important to the small business owner as a way of keeping track of finances. Keeping accurate records, and understanding the relevance of source documents, is useful to be able to enter accounting information correctly.

To establish whether the business is profitable the owner needs to calculate the profit or loss. In addition, the operations of business should always include planning for the expected income and expenses. In this regard, the ability to perform a break even analysis is very important.

RECORDS FOR SMALL BUSINESS

A small to medium business enterprise will need to keep careful records and to develop useful documentation. Most small businesses are run on a cash basis, and money is recognised as being earnt or spent at the time cash is paid or received.

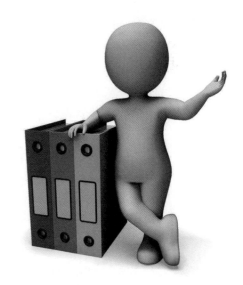

Accurate financial record keeping is vital, as it ensures that the owners and managers can be fully informed of the current state of profitability and liquidity. Good financial records show how efficient the business is, assist when approaching external organisations such as financial institutions and the taxation department, and allow planning for the future to occur. Basic record keeping requires the business to keep a particular set of information and data. These can be written manually or through the use of computerised management and accounting packages which is more common. Following is an explanation of the basic records that would need to be kept by any small business.

Documents and records

This section will focus on external business communication using standard forms to communicate information to other businesses. Standard forms might include common business documents such as order forms, invoices, credit notes, statements, receipts, deposit slips and reconciliation statements.

Table 15.1: Common business documents

Invoice	When a sale or purchase has been made, this shows the amount owing. It also includes the date, quantity, price, any GST, discounts, address and terms of sale. It must state that it is a Tax Invoice.
Receipt	A record that the amount owing on an invoice has been paid. This should include the date, details and amount. These can be paper, electronic, or EFTPOS.
Order form	Used to request a sale or purchase. Contains details such as the date, quantity, price, any discounts and address information. Can be paper or electronic.
Bank deposit slip	Shows a sum of money that has been banked.
Credit note	If a product is returned for any reason, a credit note records the credit the customer or supplier has been given for the return.
Statement	Used to provide a summary of the customer's or supplier's account. Includes amounts outstanding, amount that have been paid and all other details such as dates, address and products.
Bank reconciliation	Used to compare the cash payments and receipts of the business with the records held by the bank.

1. Invoice

An invoice is issued when products are sold to a customer on credit. It contains details of the business name and Australian Business Number (ABN), the date of issue, the invoice number, details of the customer purchasing the product and a unit description of each good or service supplied, plus a breakdown of the GST applied to each part.

The Australian Taxation Office (ATO) requires tax invoices to include:

- the business name and Australian Business Number (ABN) of the supplier or seller
- the date of issue and the words 'Tax Invoice' at the top, on the right hand side
- an invoice number next to 'Tax Invoice'
- the purchaser's name, address and ABN for goods or services costing $1000 or more

BUSINESS OPERATIONS

A small business using a paper-based system would write out an Order Form when the customer requests a product. They would be Invoiced, and when payment has been made the business will provide the customer with a Receipt. If the product is returned because it is faulty the business generates a Credit Note. The customer would also receive a monthly Statement detailing any overdue money.

- a unit description of each good or service supplied, including quantities
- an indication of which goods or services do not include Goods and Services Tax (GST) by showing a zero in the GST amount column and an indication of which goods or services include GST by showing the GST amount
- the GST exclusive price, the GST amount and the GST inclusive price for each item, together with the totals.

Example 15.1: Invoice layout

TOM'S GARDEN PLANNING PTY LTD
ABN: 123 456 789

✉ PO Box 88 Carramar 6666   ☎ (80) 9999 7777   ✏ ADMIN@TOMSGARDEN.COM.AU

TAX INVOICE NO: 7654

DATE: 1 May 2016

TERMS: 2/5, n/30

TO: Customer name
Customer address

DESCRIPTION	QUANTITY	UNIT PRICE (EXCL GST)	SUB TOTAL (EXCL GST)	GST AMOUNT	AMOUNT PAYABLE (INCL GST)
Totals					
TOTAL (excl GST)					
TOTAL GST AMOUNT PAYABLE					
TOTAL AMOUNT PAYABLE (incl GST)					

2. Receipts

The ATO requires cash register receipts to include:

- the business name and the ABN of the supplier
- the date of issue and the words 'Tax Invoice' at the top, on the right hand side
- an indication of which goods or services are taxable by showing an asterisk * with a note at the bottom advising what the * indicates
- the final amount payable, GST inclusive
- the amount of GST which is payable stated as follows: 'Total includes GST of $.....'

Example 15.2: Cash register receipt layout

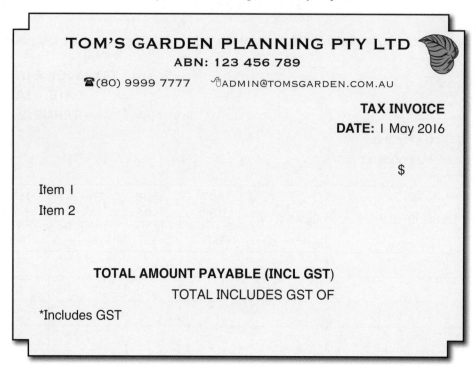

TOM'S GARDEN PLANNING PTY LTD

ABN: 123 456 789

☎(80) 9999 7777   ✉ADMIN@TOMSGARDEN.COM.AU

TAX INVOICE

DATE: 1 May 2016

$

Item 1

Item 2

TOTAL AMOUNT PAYABLE (INCL GST)

TOTAL INCLUDES GST OF

*Includes GST

Example 15.3: EFTPOS receipt

EFTPOS receipt

To pay for a purchase without using cash or a cheque, most businesses have EFTPOS available. This acronym stands for **Electronic Funds Transfer at Point of Sale**. A PIN (Personal Identification Number) is required for the customer to purchase goods in this manner. Providing there are enough funds in the account and the set daily withdrawal limit has not been exceeded, transactions for the customer will be approved and a receipt similar to the one here will be issued by the business.

BANK OF WA Pty Ltd
MOUNT CLAREMONT WA

CARD NO:	67890
EXPIRY DATE	19/21
SAVINGS	875.50
PURCH	50.00
TOTAL	AUD 50.00

| 06/08/16 | 15:20:05 |
| KEYCARD | |

APPROVED

Electronic receipt

Electronic banking also allows simple funds transfer using the Internet for either a direct deposit between accounts or for using BPay. When the customer pays for items using BPay, the business will email an electronic receipt with details of the payments, the biller code and the receipt reference number.

Example 15.4: Electronic receipt

TOM'S GARDEN PLANNING PTY LTD
ABN: 123 456 789

☎ (80) 9999 7777   ✎ ADMIN@TOMSGARDEN.COM.AU

TAX INVOICE/RECEIPT
DATE: 1 May 2016

$

Item A
Item B

TOTAL AMOUNT PAYABLE (INCL GST)
TOTAL INCLUDES GST OF

Biller code   123123
Reference number   992288374613

Internet banking allows the user to log on to their accounts to see current balances, view transactions or statements, transfer funds between accounts, pay bills and change any personal details requiring updates. A receipt is printed as evidence of the transaction.

3. Order form

An order form can look very different depending on the business that is using it. Every business has different products or services that they will sell, and so they will record orders differently. For example, the difference between the order form used in a restaurant, a furniture shop and an abseiling adventure business will be massive.

The basic sections of any order form would be the businesses information, customer information, a description of each item being ordered and their cost.

Example 15.5: Order form

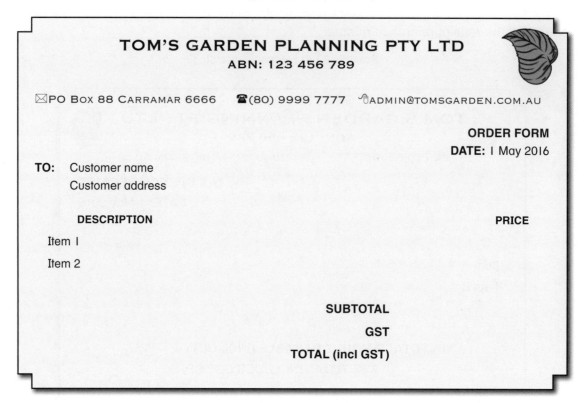

4. Bank deposit slip

This is a receipt issued by the bank when the business sends a staff member to the bank to bank the cash collected in the business. It contains details such as the account that the money is to be paid into, the date and the amount. The business then uses this basic information to enter more detail.

Example 15.6: Bank deposit slip

BANK OF WA Pty Ltd
MOUNT CLAREMONT WA

Date: _____

Payee: _____

Account number: _____

Amount: _____

5. Petty cash

A petty cash system is established because it is too difficult to have all payments being made from the business using a cheque. If small items of expenditure are needed, cash, a business credit card or direct transfer can be used. This section discusses how the use of cash for business payments can occur using a petty cash system.

Ensuring the business has good internal control processes means that instead of just taking some cash from the cash register, the business has a separate amount of cash allocated for small cash payments by employees of the business. The business sets up this system by writing out a cheque for cash, and then keeping this amount of cash safely in the business, with an employee in charge as the petty cashier. If a staff member needs to pay for a taxi fare, postage, morning tea or other small amount, they fill out a voucher requesting the cash, then use this for the purchase and give the petty cashier their receipt as evidence of the transaction. On regular occasions, the business writes out another cheque for cash to bring the balance of the petty cash fund back up to the initial amount.

Example 15.7: Petty cash voucher

```
PETTY CASH VOUCHER                          NO........

Date: ..................

Issued to: ...........................      For: ............................

Amount: ...........................         Charged to: ...........................

Signed ...........................

Authorised by ...........................
```

As money is taken from the petty cash total, the staff member in charge of petty cash will record the amount and the account that the cost is to be charged to. They will also record the reimbursements of the fund through regular cash cheques.

Example 15.8: Petty cash book

DATE	DETAILS	VOUCHER	AMOUNT IN	AMOUNT OUT	OFFICE	STAFF	OTHER
1 Jan	Advance	-	200.00				
2	Pens	15		5.00	5.00		
3	M. Tea	16		23.00		23.00	
5	Taxi	17		37.00			37.00
7	Stamps	18		20.00	20.00		
10	Flowers	19		25.00		25.00	
11	Milk	20		5.00	5.00		
	Balance			85.00			
	Reimbur.	Chq 43	115.00				
12	Balance			200.00			

DOCUMENTATION FOR INTERNAL CONTROL

Control of cash

Cash control requires keeping clear records of transactions using source documents, correct petty cash and banking procedures, and control procedures within the business to ensure that cash is not misplaced, stolen or unaccounted for.

- Bank cash on a regular basis and do not keep large amounts of cash on the premises.
- Have cheques signed by two people when the cheque amount is over a certain limit.
- Count the cash in a secure location away from customers.
- Regularly empty the cash register so that there is never a large amount of cash contained in a register.
- Ensure a receipt is written out or printed for every transaction, including petty cash.
- Investigate any cash shortages or irregularities with cash register totals.
- Do not borrow money from cash registers but use a petty cash system.
- Complete regular bank reconciliations.

A **bank reconciliation** is a check that the payments and receipts of cash and cheques for the business have been processed through the bank account. Every month, the business will receive or download a bank statement which is a summary of all payments and receipts that have gone through the businesses bank account. The business should tick off every item by checking it against the records that are kept in the accounting system. There will be some unpresented cheques and some deposits not recognised yet, and these should be further investigated, or reconciled. There may also be direct debits that the business has not yet entered into the accounts and these can also be reconciled.

Debtors and creditors

The business needs to keep careful track of the credit sales and credit purchases that are made. It will also need to work out when debts are due, in order to be sure that the cash flow of the business stays positive. If there is a large amount owed to accounts payable but the accounts receivable are not due until weeks later, then the business will have a serious problem. An example of the **debtor's statement** document is shown on the following page.

Debtor's statement: a summary of the amount owing from a customer.

Example 15.9: Sample debtor's statement

Moran's Garden Supplies and Services
Making your exterior life perfect

✉ PO Box 99 Carramar 6777   ☎ (80) 9999 7777   ✆ MORAN@GARDEN.COM.AU

DEBTOR'S STATEMENT

Period ending: 31 May 2009
Customer name: B. Hamburg   **Customer number:** W435

BPAY Biller code: 1234567   **BPAY Reference:** W435030609

Date	Details	Amount	Outstanding	Total owing
2016	Brought forward		$100.00	$100.00
1 April	Mowing	$50.00	$50.00	$150.00
	Payment, thank you	$50.00	$100.00	$100.00
15 April	Garden bag	$30.00	$30.00	$130.00

Your account is now overdue.

Inventory record

A business that manufactures or sells a product needs to use **stock cards** to keep track of the inventory at various stages of completion, as well as stock levels and reordering requirements. Stock cards are automatically kept in a computerised accounting system where the cash register is connected to a bar code scanner. An example of a Stock Card document is shown below.

Example 15.10: Sample stock card

STOCK CARD

Stock item: Candles   **Code:** LGERED   **Style/size:** Large, Red   **Reorder at:** 20

DATE	IN	OUT	BALANCE
7 June	40		40
10 June		3	37
13 June		2	35
14 June		5	30

Asset register

As the business is likely to own several key assets, it will record all the details of these assets in a register. Each asset has information such as purchase price, upgrade details, depreciation rate, storage requirements, serial numbers, insurance and so on, contained on its register card. An example of an Asset Register document is shown below.

Example 15.11: Sample asset register

ASSET REGISTER

Asset: Subaru motor vehicle **Location:** Main office **Identification code:** 345 ACT

DESCRIPTION
Make: Impresa **Model:** QP **Serial number:** 492817484 **Supplier:** Sal's Secondhands

INSURANCE
Provider: HBF **Policy:** Extra special for cars

Date	Details	Amount	Accumulated depreciation	Written down value
2/09/16	Purchase	10 000	0	10 000
1/07/17	Annual depreciation	1 000	1 000	9 000
1/07/16	Annual depreciation	1 000	2 000	8 000
6/11/17	Disposal	(6 555)		

UNDERSTANDING BUSINESS

The average small business in Australia is likely to have a computerised accounting system which can keep records of transactions, amounts paid and owing, inventory and assets all in the one records management system. These computerised packages will also allow the business to easily complete and send in required taxation information to the government.

CALCULATION OF PROFIT

Income and expenses

Income and expenses are most relevant to the budgeting function of resource allocation. A business will show income and expenses in the form of an Income Statement, also called a Profit and Loss Statement or a Statement of Financial Performance. This statement gives important information about the profit or loss that the business has earned, and shows the financial performance over a period of time.

An Income Statement is composed of two main elements: income and expenses. A simplified definition of each is given here.

The Income Statement is used to calculate whether the business has made a profit or a loss for a period of time. If total income is greater than total expenses, then the business has made a **profit**. If expenses are greater, then the business will record a **loss**.

Money received by the business, eg. sales, fees, interest.   **INCOME**

EXPENSES   Payments or costs incurred by the business, eg. cost of sales, rent, wages, Internet, water

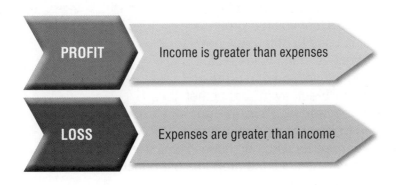

| PROFIT | Income is greater than expenses |
| LOSS | Expenses are greater than income |

Examples: Simple calculation of profit or loss

Clara runs a lawn mowing business. In the last financial year, she took in $26 000 in fees. Her costs for the year were as follows: Advertising $2000; Repairs $3000; Petrol $4 000; Fertiliser $3500.

An example of the Income Statement for a **service business** such as Clara's is shown here.

Clara has made a profit of $13 500 for this financial year.

Clara's Lawn Mowing Income Statement

	$
Fees	26 000
Less: Expenses	
Advertising	2 000
Repairs	3 000
Petrol	4 000
Fertiliser	3 500
PROFIT	**$ 13 500**

Sam owns a cake shop. In the last financial year, the business sold $66 000 worth of cakes. His costs for the year included: Rent $22,000; Telephone Bill $6000; Cost of Sales $21,000; Wages $16,000; Consumables $5500. An example of the Income Statement for a **retail/trading business** such as Sam's is shown here.

Sam made a gross profit of $45 000 for this financial year, however his final result was a loss of $4 500.

Sam's Cakes
Income Statement

	$
Sales	66 000
Less: Cost of Sales	21 000
Gross Profit	45 000
Less: Expenses	
Rent	22 000
Telephone	6 000
Wages	16 000
Consumables	5 500
LOSS	**($ 4 500)**

A loss is shown in the Income Statement using brackets ( ) to indicate that it is a negative number.

BREAK EVEN ANALYSIS

Business owners must make decisions about the setting of prices in order to obtain a profit. Cost-volume-profit analysis, or **break even analysis**, is used to determine how costs and profits are affected by changes in the volume of production. A business will calculate the volume of a product that must be sold at a specific price to 'break even', or in other words to completely cover costs of the product. **Percentage mark up** is the difference between the cost of a product and its selling price. A business may be a retailer who purchases items from a wholesaler, or a manufacturer who purchases raw materials and prepares a product for sale. For both types of business there is a similar process to be undergone in order to decide on the percentage mark up. The business owner must decide how much each item costs and add the percentage mark up on to decide the sale price of the item.

> **Break even analysis:** a method used to calculate how profits are affected by changes in sales and costs.

> **Percentage mark up:** sales price less costs.

> **Mark up = Cost price + Percentage**

Break even point

Selling price can depend on the number of items that can be manufactured or sold. To work out the number of items required in order to cover costs, or in order to make a particular profit, a business can calculate the break even point.

> **Break even point is the number of sales, or the dollar amount of income, where all expenses are covered and neither a profit or a loss will be made.**

Types of costs

Fixed costs = Expenses that do not change, no matter how many units of sales are made or how the volume of activity changes; for example wages/salaries, rent, advertising, bank charges and government charges.

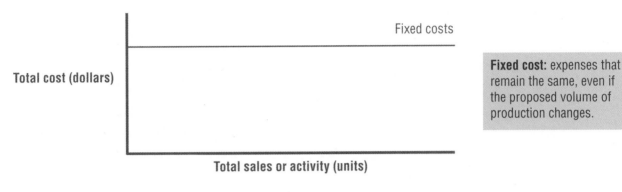

Figure 15.1: Graph of fixed costs

Fixed cost: expenses that remain the same, even if the proposed volume of production changes.

Variable costs = Expenses that change, dependent on the amount of sales or the volume of activity; for example wages/salaries, sales commission, product related promotions, raw materials and product packaging.

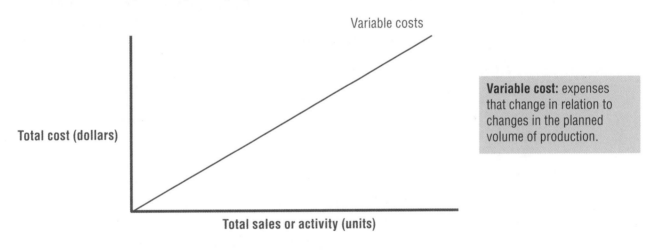

Figure 15.2: Graph of variable costs

Variable cost: expenses that change in relation to changes in the planned volume of production.

Mixed costs = Expenses that can be both fixed and variable; for example wages/salaries, electricity and lights.

Some costs are partly fixed, and partly variable. For example, some lights in a business must be kept on at all times for security purposes, however other lights will only be used when production is in process. Thus, increased production levels will increase lighting costs because the use of lighting is dependent upon the units of production required, or the changing volume of activity that comes with changing sales amounts.

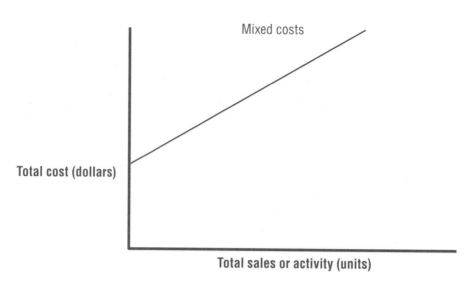

Figure 15.3: Graph of mixed costs

CONTRIBUTION MARGIN

The contribution margin is the difference between income and variable expenses for an item of product. It is the amount of income that each product 'contributes' to the overall result of the business. Fixed expenses do not change as the volume of sale or activity increases, however the variable costs do alter.

> **Contribution margin = Selling price – Variable costs.**

Break even

Break even analysis involves calculating how many sales of the product are required in order to completely cover all the costs of producing that product. At the 'break even point', the business will make neither a profit or a loss.

There are two main methods of calculating a business' break even point: mathematical or graphic.

1. Mathematical calculation

The number of units required for **breakeven** =

$$\frac{\text{Fixed costs}}{\text{Contribution margin}}$$

The number of units required to make a **specific profit** =

$$\frac{\text{Fixed costs + Profit}}{\text{Contribution margin}}$$

EXAMPLE: Break even analysis

Meg runs a fruit juice store. The cost of making one fruit juice is $3, which she plans to sell for $6 each, giving a contribution margin of $3 per juice. Her weekly costs are $400 rent, $600 wages and $50 electricity and phone.

Breakeven point $\quad = \quad \dfrac{\$1050}{\$(6-3)} = \quad$ 350 fruit juices a week.

This means that if her shop is open 5 days a week, she needs to sell 70 juices a day, just to break even.

Meg can rerun her break even analysis for different selling prices, or see if she can adjust the fixed and variable costs. To calculate break even mathematically, a business owner must try several different selling prices. If Meg conducts a market survey and decides that she can only sell 50 juices a day, then she will need to reconsider her selling price or see if she can adjust the fixed and variable costs.

What selling price is needed if only 50 juices can be sold daily?

Selling price $\quad = \quad \dfrac{\$1050}{(\text{Selling price} - \$3)} \quad = \quad$ 250 juices a week

At the lower expected sales, Meg needs to sell her juices for $7.20 in order to break even. If customers will not pay this price Meg will definitely reconsider costs.

2. Graph

This shows the relationship between expenses (costs, number of products [volume]) and profit for all possible expenses. It is often called a **Cost-Volume-Profit** graph. The graph is developed by determining total expenses and total income for differing volumes of sales.

Meg's fixed costs are graphed as follows:

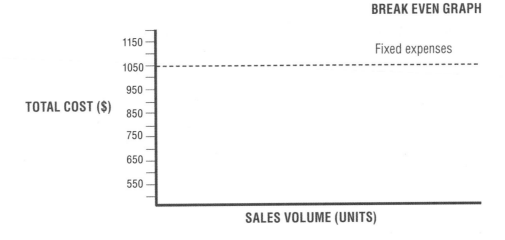

Figure 15.4: Example graph of fixed costs

Variable costs are graphed as follows:

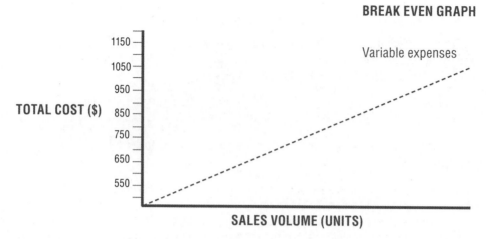

Figure 15.5: Example graph of variable costs

To show total costs and their change in relation to total products (or units) sold, add them together:

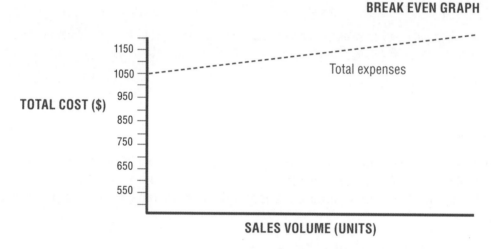

Figure 15.6: Example graph of total costs

The same graph can be used to show sales income at all possible selling prices. Firstly assuming a selling price of $6, the graph is as follows:

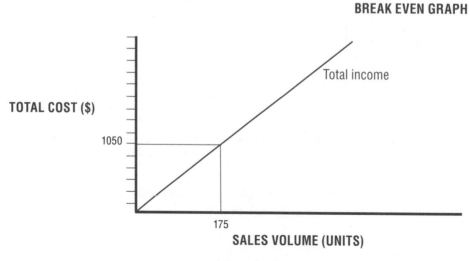

Figure 15.7: Example graph showing income

Put these two lines together on the same Cost-Volume-Profit break even graph:

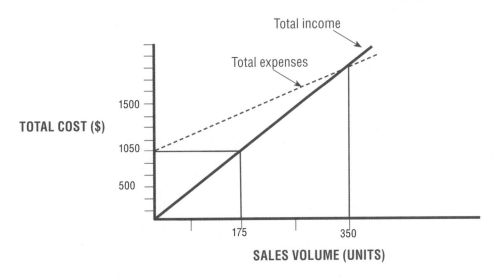

BREAK EVEN GRAPH

Figure 15.8: Sample graph of break even analysis

The two lines cross over at the break even point of 350 fruit juices (units) or total sales income of $2100. If any changes to the costs or the selling price need to be made, the break even point will change.

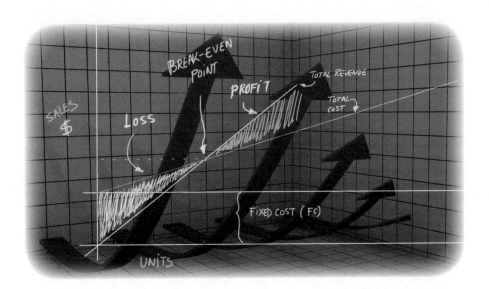

ACTIVITIES

A. CHECK YOUR UNDERSTANDING

Simple cash records

1. Summarise the basic records management requirements of a small business.

2. Explain the purpose of the following cash records:
   A. Bank deposit slip
   B. Bank reconciliation
   C. Receipt

3. What is a transaction?

4. Why would a small business owner keep an asset register?

5. Outline why a bank reconciliation is prepared.

Source documents

1. What is a source document? Explain the purpose of each of the following source documents:
   A. Tax invoice
   B. Order form

2. What is the difference between an EFTPOS payment and an internet payment?

3. Why are cheques now rare as a form of payment?

4. What is the relationship between an invoice and an order form?

5. Why is petty cash used in the workplace?

6. Explain how the use of a petty cash system assists with internal control.

7. What internal control procedures should be in place to ensure that banking of workplace funds is not subject to fraud or theft?

Calculation of profit

1. Define income and expense, using examples.

2. Explain the meaning of a profit and a loss.

3. Why is an Income Statement prepared for a business?

4. Outline the purpose of break even analysis.

5. Define the following terms:
   A. Fixed costs
   B. Variable costs
   C. Mixed costs
   D. Contribution margin

B. BUSINESS RESEARCH

I. Find samples of the following source documents, using real local businesses and Internet sample forms.

   A. Receipts
   B. Bank deposit slips
   C. Invoices
   D. Order form
   E. Credit note

Using these samples, create a set of source documents for a small business of your choice.

C. RESPONSE

I. Draw a flow chart showing how each of the documents in this chapter would be used when a customer orders a set of dining room furniture, returns one chair a week later, and pays 50% of the invoice price one month after the sale.

2. Define each of the following types of records, and explain why each is important in a small business:
   A. Debtors statement
   B. Receipt
   C. Bank deposit slip
   D. Order form
   E. Tax invoice
   F. Stock card
   G. Asset register

3. Explain how each of the following financial records would be used at each stage of the financial transaction outlined in the scenario.

   • Order form
   • Invoice
   • EFTPOS receipt

   SCENARIO: a customer enters the shop, orders a product (of your choice), returns later to pick up and pay for the product using EFTPOS and then comes back again to return one part of the order and be given credit.

4. Explain the meaning of each transaction in the Debtor's Statement shown here.

Neenad's Car Supplies

Debtor's Statement

Period ending: 31 December 2016 **Customer:** Nooni's Repairs and service

Date	Details	Amount ($)	Paid/Unpaid ($)	Total owing ($)
01/12/16	Brought F/W			300.00
04/12/16	Brakes and liners	400.00	U	700.00
10/12/16	Spark plugs and electrical	808.00	U	1 508.00
15/12/16	Payment received	(1 508.00)	P	0
24/12/16	Gaskets	556.00	U	556.00

Thank you for your prompt payment.

5. Label each part of the Asset Register card below, and complete the final column.

Tessa's Builders

ASSET REGISTER CARD

Asset: Ute **Location:** Warehouse **Identification code:** SSS WA1

Make: Holden **Model:** SS **Serial number:** SS9879871 **Supplier:** Cashed Up Cars

Insurance: Cars for Cars Insurance Co, Premium level. **Expiry date:** 1 Nov 2016

Date	Details	Amount	Acc. Depr.	WDV
01/11/15	Purchase	50 000	0	
30/06/16	Annual depreciation	8 000	8 000	
30/06/17	Annual depreciation	12 000	20 000	
30/06/18	Annual depreciation	12 000	32 000	
31/07/18	Disposal	(15 000)	33 000	

6. Draw a flow chart showing the business record keeping procedures that should be followed for the following internet transaction. You will need to decide on the items and their prices.

   SCENARIO: A customer orders three items online and these are dispatched by the business using Australia Post packs. They are emailed their invoice and the customer pays for the items using BPay. The receipt and warranty information are then sent.

7. For each of the following businesses, calculate the percentage mark-up (ignore GST):

   A. Business X selling flowers with a cost price of $3.00 for $6.00

   B. Business Y which purchases magazines for $5.50 and sells them for $8.30

   C. Business Z requires inventory valued at $0.50 to manufacture a cup of coffee that sells for $3.80

8. For each of the following businesses, calculate the contribution margin (ignore GST):

   A. Business P selling flowers with variable costs of $3.70 for $6.00

   B. Business Q which sells and packages magazines with a variable cost of $6.50 and sells them for $8.30

   C. Business R requires inventory valued at $0.50, wages of $1.00 and a takeaway mug costing $0.30 to manufacture a cup of coffee that sells for $3.80

9. Complete a break even analysis for a kebab shop. The cost of making one kebab is $3.70, which is sold for $8.90 each. Other weekly costs are $500 rent, $40 maintenance and cleaning, $1000 wages, $10 internet phone and $20 electricity.

   A. What is the break even point?

   B. When you have calculated the break even point, determine the level of sales required for weekly profits of $100, $400 or $700.

   C. Complete an Income Statement for one week of business.

   D. Complete a Break Even Analysis graph.

10. Jimeone has just started a weekly market stall selling pasta. He produces three main varieties and he sells at two local markets in the suburbs. Jimeone sells 100 packets of pasta a week for $8 each. Weekly costs include $50 petrol, $30 advertising, $400 ingredients and $150 packaging.

    A. What is Jimeone's weekly profit or loss?

    B. Complete an Income Statement for his first year of business.

D. GROUP PROJECTS

1. In groups of three, budget the profit that would be earned from setting up your own business. Assume that the business is going to sell a maximum of five different products, and use information from prices on the Internet to estimate the income, as well as the expenses. Calculate the break even point for each product. Ask your teacher for assistance with approximate mark ups.

MANAGEMENT CROSSWORD

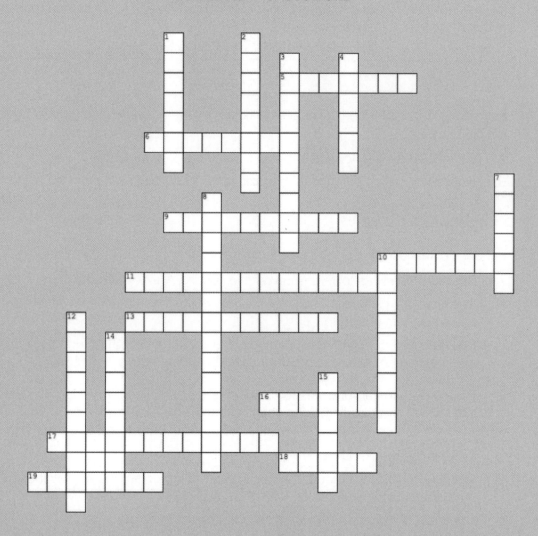

Across

5. A record of the amount paid
6. An individual who uses the products or services of a particular business enterprise
9. The social group to which someone belongs
10. A source document that shows the amount owing
11. Managing business operations and coordinating all that occurs in an organisation
13. A record of returned product
16. Buying on .... due to an urge to purchase
17. A group to which some belongs
18. A study conducted as a trial to test the effectiveness of the main survey
19. The person in charge of directing a group of employees toward achieving specific business goals

Down

1. One of the roles performed by managers, where employees are directed and performance of the organisation is assessed
2. A frequent client who visits a business and has made it a habit to purchase that business' products
3. Paperwork used to request a purchase
4. A role where employees are encouraged and motivated to achieve the business vision and goals
7. Using pre-determined questions to gain customer feedback
8. A check that payments and receipts have been processed through the bank account
10. Asking market research questions of customer in person
12. Management role requiring the distribution of organisational resource
14. A management role where the procedures for meeting organisational goals are developed
15. Available number of products or suppliers for a particular product or service

UNIT 2
SECTION C: PEOPLE

CHAPTER 16
Teamwork

'Unity is strength …
when there is teamwork and collaboration, wonderful things can be achieved.'
– Mattie Stepanek –

Humans are beings who require affection, acknowledgement and companionship to feel satisfied in their day to day lives. This also applies to people's expectations, approach to work and how they measure satisfaction, and it influences their level of willingness to contribute at work. Most people perform better in nurturing and caring team environments. This chapter gives an overview on what teams are and their operation.

This human need for companionship entails openness, honesty, acceptance and support which validate the vital role of teams in the workplace. Therefore, we explore collaborative teams, team building and key traits of teamwork. Finally the chapter aims to identify how the above aspects of teams foster creativity and innovation in the workplace.

TEAMS

In small business environments there is generally one team or a small number of teams that operate together to achieve business goals. A **team** comprises any group of people linked in a common purpose. Teams play a key role in small business and assist it achieve targets and goals. Teams can be very useful for conducting tasks that are complex and have many interdependent tasks. This section provides an overview on teams under the headings contained in Figure 16.1.

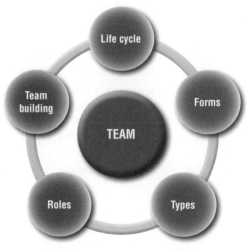

Figure 16.1: Overview of teams

Life cycle of a team

All teams go through a life-cycle and the five stages[1] include **forming, storming, norming, performing** and **adjourning**. These stages are defined in relation to how the small business owner could influence each of them to maximise the efficiency and effectiveness. In a small business context it's common for the business owner to assume the role of **team leader**. Stages of a team's life cycle are not always clearly distinguishable and may seem blurred due to the length of time the teams work together.

Figure 16.2: Life cycle of a team

TABLE 16.1: Life stages of a team in small business

Team life stage	Role of small business owner
Forming The stage prior to a team being formally established. At this point, people are still working as individuals and the first signs of a team are emerging in their approach to the task or goals.	• Introduce and assist the new employee to become part of the existing team • Clarify the new employee's duties and responsibilities, having clear procedures • Discuss concerns and provide nurturing feedback to grow in the job
Storming The team is facing conflict and developing an understanding of each other. During this stage the team becomes more aggressive and challenges previously agreed or taken-for-granted rules and restrictions, allowing the individuals within the team to reveal their true values and motives.	• Acknowledge employee's sense of vulnerability and act with care and promote trust • Use an empathetic approach with constructive feedback acknowledging the employee's point of view to encourage them to be honest and open • Manage conflict between employees (ie. within teams) by being fair and firm • Facilitate a transparent approach towards business goals where employees contribute fully due to team cohesiveness

---

1   Model of group development first proposed by Bruce Tuckman in 1965.

Team life stage	Role of small business owner
Norming The consolidating phase. The team plans for the use of resources to meet goals. In this stage individual strengths, weaknesses and personality traits are identified, resulting in better understanding of the team's own strengths and weaknesses. 	• Facilitate constructive discussion • Ensure decisions are made with mutual agreement or at least everyone feels their opinion is valued and listened to • Create opportunities for each employee to grasp a clear understanding of the business's goals and approach to achieving them as well as their role in that journey • Promote harmony and respect
Performing The most optimal stage. The team works effectively and efficiently at this stage. It strives to be even better by concentrating on the development of the team, individuals and achievement of the goal in hand.	• Assess the effectiveness of individual employees' contribution to the business • Assess the overall employee group dynamics that contribute towards it • Reward individuals, while acknowledging team contributions • Manage rewards and beware of inducing unhealthy competition and hostility • Provide feedback where it's due and reward the whole team rather than individual employees to lift overall employee morale and develop a positive sense of team
Adjourning The final stage where the team either disbands or reforms itself. Individuals move on to other responsibilities following either the achievement of the team's goals or failure to achieve. If goals are not achieved, teams tend to re-evaluate and restructure, thereby reinstating the 'forming' stage.	• Look beyond day-to-day processes • Review the progress of the business and the employees' contributions on a periodic basis • Identify how efficiently business goals are being achieved • Identify the direction the business is taking • Provide regular feedback and reassess the employee team's approach and redirect where necessary • Celebrate achieved goals which all contribute to team harmony for strength

Forms of teams

The form of a team is how that team is structured and operates. There are many forms of teams and this text explores two key forms that affect small business. An **interdependent team** meets regularly and all members rely heavily on each other, whereas an **independent team** is more job focused and members operate with more autonomy. The best way to start improving the functioning of an independent team is to assist everyone to enhance their workplace performance.

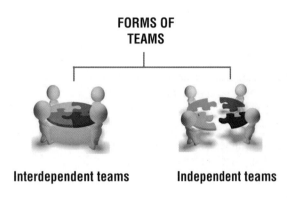

FORMS OF TEAMS

Interdependent teams   **Independent teams**

Figure 16.3: Forms of teams

BUSINESS CONCEPTS

A football team is an INTERDEPENDENT TEAM, no significant task can be accomplished without the help of essentially all team members. Team members specialise in different tasks such as carrying the ball, kicking the ball, blocking opposing members, and the success of every individual is bound to the success of the whole team.

A tennis team is an INDEPENDENT TEAM, matches are played and won by individuals, every person performs basically the same actions, and whether one member wins or loses has no direct affect on the performance of the next. The end result for the overarching team is affected by the collective impact. If all team members each perform the same basic tasks, it is an independent team. They may be able to help each other but each individual's success is primarily due to each individual's own efforts.

Types of teams

Teams in the workplace vary based on their role and where and how they operate as well as their purpose within the business. Figure 16.4 depicts four types of teams commonly found in small business structures.

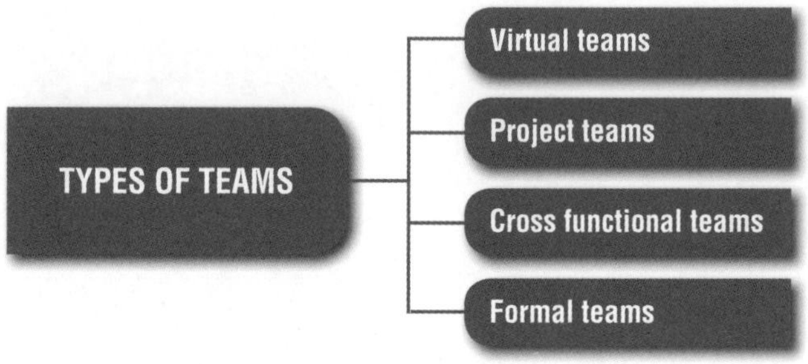

TYPES OF TEAMS
- Virtual teams
- Project teams
- Cross functional teams
- Formal teams

Figure 16.4: Types of teams

1. Virtual teams

Even small businesses hire employees to work from home for the business, especially in administrative roles or in small businesses that sell services. A virtual team consists of members joined together electronically, with nominal in-person contact. Virtual teaming is made possible with technology tools, especially the Internet. This allows teams to be formed with employees who might be otherwise unavailable.

A virtual team can allow the small business to operate without having to provide physical office space for certain job roles. Research can be performed using input from the best minds around the world. Work projects can be completed by spreading the workload among long-distance employees. Many businesses build their competitive edge on the capabilities and efficiencies of virtual teams.

INNOVATION AND ENTERPRISE

Administrative job roles such as accounts payable officer or clerical services are performed by employees who work remotely from their homes, rather than reporting to the physical business location on a daily basis.

2. Project teams

A team used only for a defined period of time and for a separate, concretely definable purpose often becomes known as a project team. Businesses commonly label groups of people as a *team* based on having a common function.

Members of these teams might belong to different groups but receive tasks for the same project, and so are viewed as a single unit. In this way, setting up a team facilitates the creation, tracking and assignment of a group of people based on the project in hand.

3. Cross functional team

A **cross-functional team** consists of a group of people working toward a common goal and made up of people with different functional expertise. It could include people from finance, marketing, operations, and human resources. It also includes employees from all levels of a business, or from outside the business.

Cross-functional teams are often **self-directed teams** and have broad objectives, but not specific directives. Decision making may depend on consensus, but often is led by a team leader.

These teams allow information to flow in multiple directions within the small business. They require a wide range of information and might work on the full range of goals including strategic, tactical, and operational decisions. These teams allow for unstructured techniques and revolutionary idea generation as they allow increased interactivity and flexibility.

4. Formal groups in a Small Business

Work teams are formal groups responsible for achieving a set of goals.

Figure 16.5: Reasons for teams in the workplace

Roles within a team

Small business teams are often put together on the basis of the availability and skills of employees. These teams are able to perform well and achieve business goals if they are managed and led properly. A business owner who is able to relate to employees, and able to inspire and motivate them, is able to get the best out of the people they have available.

A team is made up of a set of individuals. Therefore it is vital that the small business owner takes in to account the personal attributes of these individuals that influence their behaviours, along with their professional skills and knowledge when dealing with the team. This assists the business owner in assigning suitable team roles or duties for employees.

A team role is the contribution an individual makes towards the overall team performance. There are six key roles within a team. Each of these roles is described in Table 16.2.

BUSINESS CONCEPTS

Vancouver Café[2] in Albany employs disabled members of the community to fulfil various roles within the business. Most business owners tend to assume that due a certain disability an individual may not be able to perform a task fully. Under the nurturing guidance of Alison Teede, the business owner, each and every member has risen to their potential and excelled at customer satisfaction at every level, resulting in Vancouver Café becoming a well patronised business within the Albany local community and among its international[3] visitors.

Figure 16.6: Roles within a team

---

2 Vancouver Café – Albany, https://www.facebook.com/VancouverCafeAlbany, accessed 07 June 2014.

3 Tourism site promoting Vancouver Café, http://www.tripadvisor.com.au/Restaurant_Review-g261671-d1223894-Reviews-Vancouver_Cafe_Store-Albany_Western_Australia.html, accessed 07 June 2014.

TABLE 16.2: Team roles explained

	Team leader	Responsible for the team result. Guides and motivates the team to achieve goals. He or she creates the working environment for the team.
	Team facilitator	Responsible for keeping all team members on track and focused on the task at hand. They manage and assist the decision making process by refocusing the team to minimise time wastage. He or she takes charge when necessary and encourages everyone to have input while maintaining team harmony.
	Recorder	Responsible for maintaining records such as notes, and documenting decisions made by the team. They need to be prepared and organised at all times.
	Time keeper	Monitors the time consumed by the team in completing tasks and keeps the team informed of time restrictions. He or she works closely with the team leader to ensure efficiency.
	Team member	Contributes towards team goals with their knowledge and skill. They need to be motivated, honest, reliable and committed to the success of the team.
	Critic or reviewer	Review the performance of the team and provide feedback on progress. He or she ensures the team is continuing to achieve its goals.

Team building

The success or failure of a small business is the result of how the people within the business work together, not just the result of market forces such as customers, demand or suppliers. The development of a team of employees is a major challenge that small business owners face, because they must enable individuals to work together efficiently.

There is no 'I' in Team

Team building is the process of establishing and developing collaboration and trust between team members. It refers generally to the selection and motivation of teams, or specifically to group self-assessment and reflection. When a team starts a process of self-assessment to gauge its own effectiveness and improve performance, it is team building. To assess itself, a team seeks feedback to find out its current strengths and current weaknesses. They can do this through interactive exercises, team assessments and group discussion.

> **Team building:** the process which forms a team that operates effectively together.

> **Interactive exercises**: activities that require members of a team to communicate with each other.

Individual influence in teams

Bringing individuals together into a team can be risky and unpredictable. However, it can be beneficial, especially if the small business owner considers the influence that each individual might have on the whole group.

> **INNOVATION AND ENTERPRISE**
>
> Staff at Lime303 restaurant, travelled to the nearby town of Denmark and engaged in a day of socialising and bonding with each other over meals. This is an example of team building where the employees who work together as a team were given an opportunity to strengthen their team cohesion.

REASONS TO COMBINE INDIVIDUALS INTO A TEAM

✓ Encourages the exchange of ideas

✓ Enhances motivation and job satisfaction

✓ Fosters peer learning and extend individual roles

✓ Promotes creativity

✓ Improvez productivity, quality and customer focus

✓ Encourages employees to be more flexible and can improve the ability of the business to respond to fast-changing environments

These benefits are vital to all small businesses. Therefore, it is important that employees understand their role within the team and identify how their social interactions affect the team.

Table 16.3: Social skills needed for teamwork

	Each employee needs the following social skills for successful teamwork
Listening	It is important to listen to other people's ideas. When people are allowed to freely express their ideas, these will produce other ideas.
Questioning	It is important to ask questions, interact, and discuss the objectives of the team.
Persuading	Exchange, defend and then ultimately rethink ideas.
Respecting	Treat others with respect and support their ideas.
Helping	Help one's co-workers, this is the theme of teamwork.
Sharing	Communicate with the team to create a positive environment.
Participating	All members of the team are encouraged to contribute to the team.

Characteristics of effective teams

The characteristics of an effective team include the following:

- **Clear goals:** achievable, worthwhile and everyone knows what is expected.

- **Relevant skills:** group members have the necessary skills and abilities to achieve the task.

- **Mutual trust:** trust is fragile and needs to be built and maintained. Trust is more likely to exist in an organisation where the culture is characterised by openness, honesty, collaboration, employee involvement and **autonomy**.

- **Unified commitment:** loyalty and dedication to the team.

> **Autonomy:** practicing self-management or control through a set of personal rules and values.

COLLABORATION

Collaboration refers to processes where people work together. This applies to both the work of individuals as well as larger collectives and societies, including business. **Collaboration** involves working together on a project. When individuals work together, for example in an academic setting, *collaboration* includes being jointly credited for work completed.

The vital importance of collaborative work practices is explored here. Other, similar but different aspects, such as coordination, cooperation, and teamwork, are discussed in relation to collaboration. Furthermore, the barriers to collaboration and strategies to enhance work place collaboration within teams and groups are analysed.

Figure 16.7: Overview of collaborative teamwork

Table 16.4: Definition and differentiation of coordination, cooperation, collaboration and teamwork

	DEFINITION	REQUIREMENTS	EXAMPLES
Coordination	The organisation of different individuals or groups to reach a common goal	• Shared objectives. This is the need for more than one person to be involved and the ability to understanding of who needs to do what by when • Effective problem solving. To deal with differences	Harmonising simple tasks, roles and schedules

	DEFINITION	REQUIREMENTS	EXAMPLES
Cooperation	Mutual assistance, with gains and losses on the part of each individual or group	• More than one person to be involved • Mutual trust and respect • Acknowledgment of mutual benefit of working together • Frequent consultation and knowledge sharing	Solving problems in complicated environments
Collaboration	Working together and building consensus to reach a decision or create a product, the result of which benefits all	• Relationship must continue beyond the accomplishment of the task • Sense of belonging • Open communication • Mutual trust and respect	Achieving collective results which cannot be achieved in isolation
Teamwork	An interdependent group Collaborative groups are teams, coordinated groups are not, and cooperative groups may or may not be	• Mutual trust • Open to ideas • Flexibility	Sporting teams

BUSINESS OPERATIONS

Members of the Albany Community Foundation[5] could not come up with a theme for their major annual fundraiser. Brainstorming, however, resulted in many ideas being placed on the table and together ,in COLLABORATION, the group developed ideas and modified them to find the ultimate fundraising campaign.

Collaboration in teams

The business owner must understand the concept of collaboration to be able to build teams and ensure positive **teamwork** results. Positive attributes of team collaboration include openness, supportiveness, a positive outlook, a sense of equality, confidence, active listening and effective communication. These are vital in developing team relationships both within the business and externally.

> **Teamwork:** ensuring that employees who are members of a team work together cooperatively.

---

5   Albany Community Foundation, www.acfwa.com.au, accessed 20 May 2014.

Positive teamwork outcomes are a result of the individual employee's social and **self-management skills** as well as the business owner's ability to understand and manage group dynamics. Key attributes that contribute towards this are highlighted in Figure 16.8.

Self-management skills: a set of skills used by employers to formally identify organisational and planning skills that contribute towards job performance in their employees.

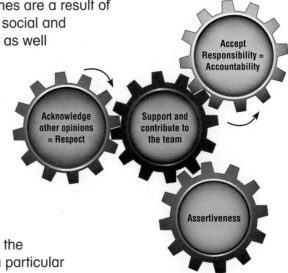

Figure 16.8: Requirements for collaboration in teams

Accepts responsibility

In team environments **responsibility** is shared within the individuals of the team, rather than being isolated to a particular individual. However, each employee within the team needs to assume ownership of their own duties or role within the team and contribute what is expected of them to ensure success. Accepting responsibility results in **accountability.**

Accountability

Responsibility: an aspect of the business that an employee is relied on to take charge of and executes.

Accountability is the responsibility of an individual to act upon duties and fully accept the consequences of their actions. In team situations, when holding an individual as accountable or responsible, it is vital to note that their responsibility ends at their duty role within the team. It is essential that all members of the team realise that the end result or the outcome is the responsibility of the whole team.

A good team shares its winnings together as well as its losses. They praise great contributions towards the success. They also support and encourage strugglers as well as having in place penalties for those who fail to contribute, in a compassionate and empathetic manner.

Figure 16.9: Strategies for attaining accountability

Support and contribute to team effort

Contributions of every member of the team are crucial to business success. Lack of contribution by one or over-contribution by another could lead to conflict or unhealthy competition within the team.

Therefore managing team member contributions by the business owner is vital. Effective team members work **cooperatively**, contributing to the team, while supporting and encouraging others do to the same.

> **Cooperation:** is the act of working with others and acting together to accomplish a job.

Good team members, despite differences they may have with other members concerning strategy and methodology, figure out ways to work together to solve problems and get work done. They respond to requests for assistance and take the initiative to offer help.

Promoting contributions to the team

Small business owners should be able to motivate and promote the contributions the employees of their team make towards the business goals. Team members would have prejudices, assumptions, attitudes and values that influence the team's direction. These are influenced by their prior experiences and knowledge. Therefore, the business owner must guide and redirect the team when their prejudices tend to influence the business performance.

Figure 16.10: Qualities of a supportive team effort

> **FACTORS TO CONSIDER WHEN PROMOTING CONTRIBUTIONS**
> ✓ How well do the allocated tasks fit the person's preferred role?
> ✓ Who has the skills and experience to handle a particular task competently and efficiently?
> ✓ Who will find the task useful for their development?
> ✓ What further training, development or support might an individual need?
> ✓ What are the factors that are influencing individual's behaviour?

Acknowledge other points of view

Teams function best when they are harmonious. Therefore, respect is vital. Team members who treat fellow members with courtesy and consideration promote trust and openness. Demonstrating empathy by showing understanding of other view points promotes respect. Good team members also have a sense of humour and know how to have fun, but not at someone else's expense. Effective team members deal with each other in a professional manner.

Team members with commitment look beyond their own piece of the work and care about the team's overall work. In the end, their commitment is about achieving team goals and knowing they have contributed to this success. Winning as a team is one of the great motivators of employee performance. Good team members have and show this motivation.

Respect

When team members accept each other for who they are, a sense of mutual respect results. This requires **empathy** for others, as well as tolerance. A workplace with open communication nurtures **respect**.

Empathy: compassion or sympathy.

Tolerance: ability or willingness to endure opinions or behaviours of others that one may not agree with themselves.

Assertiveness

Assertiveness is a skill that can be learnt and an important communication skill. **Assertiveness** is the quality of being self-assured and confident without being aggressive. It is different to both aggression and passivity. Passive communicators do not defend their own personal boundaries and allow aggressive people to harm or unduly influence them. An assertive communicator, in contrast, interacts with confidence, speaks their mind while respecting others' points of view and they defend their own point of view.

Barriers to collaboration

While collaboration is natural in some societies, and is generally natural in pre-existing teams, collaboration is often perceived as unnatural in new groups and some societies. Some of the perceived barriers to collaboration are:

- **Stranger danger:** which can be expressed as a reluctance to share with unknown others.

- **Finding assistance:** people believe that others may have already solved the businesses problem but cannot be found.

- **Hoarding:** where employees do not want to share knowledge because they see accumulating ideas as a source of power.

- **Not here:** avoiding previous knowledge not originally developed within the business.

BUSINESS OPERATIONS

When a new member of staff joins a team, the other members tend to be more cautious in their responses and behaviour towards the new member. This is an example of the STRANGER DANGER BARRIER.

Facilitating collaboration

As teams grow larger or diversify as the business expands or changes direction, the skills and methods business owners must use to create or maintain teamwork change as well. The intimacy of a small group is lost, and the opportunity for misinformation grows. Owners find that communication methods need to change.

**GUIDELINES A SMALL BUSINESS OWNER MUST
ABIDE BY TO MAINTAIN COLLABORATION**

✓ Clearly communicate the goals of the team to each team member.

✓ Ensure those goals are clearly understood and accepted by each team member.

✓ Ensure everyone is clear about their own responsibilities and role.

✓ Encourage trust between team members.

✓ Utilise team building activities to encourage an honest environment where everyone is comfortable with their capabilities.

✓ Involve the team in decision making to generate belonging.

✓ Maintain clear and open communication lines.

✓ Ensure everyone is well informed.

**INNOVATION AND
ENTERPRISE**

An employee does not know what is happening with the business and their day to day duties. This could be a result of the individual lacking the motivation to be informed as result of feeling isolated from the rest of the team.

CREATIVITY AND INNOVATION IN TEAMS

Creativity and **innovation** are seen as the keys to business longevity and success. The key traits of teamwork that facilitate both creativity and innovation are explored in this section of the chapter.

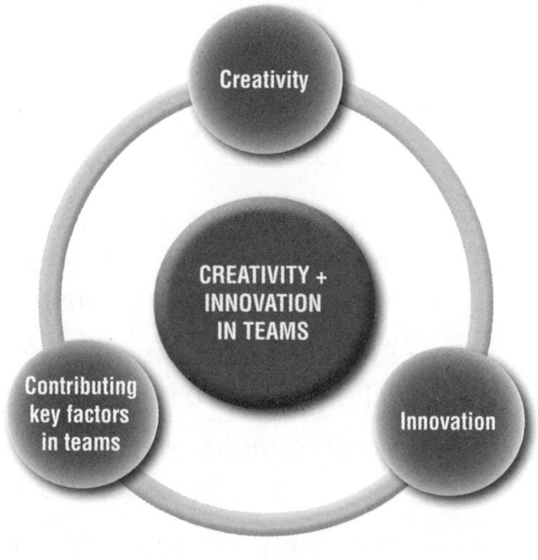

Creativity

Creativity is the realisation of a new idea or concept into an actual product or service. Creativity is characterised by an ability to perceive the world in new ways, to find hidden patterns, to make connections and to generate solutions. Simply having a new idea does not result in creativity; the idea needs to be tested and a final outcome produced.

Figure 16.11: Overview of creativity and innovation in teams

Innovation generally refers to renewing, changing or creating more effective processes, products or services. For a small business this means implementing new ideas, renewing products or improving existing services. To be innovative a small business owner requires team members who are able to adapt to the evolving needs of the business.

Creativity: the act of turning new and imaginative ideas into reality.

Creativity and innovation can enable a small business to grow and adapt in the marketplace. Therefore, fostering creativity and innovation is beneficial for business. This can be done by encouraging openness and honesty, valuing ideas and learning from unsuccessful ideas.

Openness and honesty

Openness demands team communication that creates a sense of security and belonging. If employees trust each other they will be transparent in their communications with one another. This results in **honest** discussions, especially with regard to personal interests and expectations.

Openness: sincerity or directness

Honesty: level of truthfulness or integrity.

Trust requires employees to be transparent and honest with one another. Honesty should minimise doubt, uncertainty and anxiety in the workplace, and foster a motivating, nurturing and enterprising environment where innovative teams thrive. If the small business owner demonstrates trustworthy behaviour and operates in an honest manner, this will influence employees within the team.

Business owners should promote openness and honesty by involving team members in setting team and individual goals and by giving team members the necessary autonomy to carry out tasks without undue interference. This enables employees to be creative and innovative without being fearful that they might need to hide any errors or mistakes.

CREATIVITY + INNOVATION

Figure 16.12: Key traits of teamwork that facilitate creativity and innovation

Valuing ideas and contributions

Creativity is a result of human thoughts, which rely on emotions and a person's state of mind. Creative and innovative people are usually happy and content individuals who are able to see a problem then develop a solution for it. Therefore, members of a team who feel that their contributions and ideas are valued and respected are inspired to be innovative.

The business owner can ensure that ideas are valued by setting clear team goals and conducting regular reviews. This provides the team with a framework to work within and measure their output. The allocation of tasks, responsibilities and priorities of individual team members should be done through discussion and negotiations. When goals are achieved it is important to reward the whole team and also recognise the individual contributions. If this is done well, it promotes an atmosphere of value and recognition.

Teams in small businesses are ad hoc groupings that do not always contain the ideal mix of individuals. It is the responsibility of the business owner to promote respect and empathy, and include all team members in discussions. This will foster a creative team environment that values the contribution of all members.

Learning from unsuccessful ideas

Having clearly set out guidelines on team goals and how to measure achievement could provide a clear view of the team's performance. Teams do not always succeed in their journey to achieving a goal, nor is it expected of them. When faced with failure, the key is to own the mistakes, learn from them and review what can be improved in the future.

Figure 16.13: Stages of learning from failure

1. Own the mistake

Mistakes are unavoidable. No individual or team can predict the exact outcome of their efforts, only the *anticipated* outcome can be predicted, as no one is able to look in to the future. However, acknowledging mistakes are inevitable allows the team to continue to strive regardless of some failures or unsuccessful ideas.

If the team is bound by trust, honesty, openness, respect and accountability the individuals who are part of that team will operate with ease. They will acknowledge those aspects of ideas and decisions that led to the failure. Acceptance of failure without pointing blame would encourage further commitment to improve in the future.

2. Review and learn from the mistake

Failed ideas and decisions provide a fantastic learning opportunity to a team. They could use this particular scenario and discuss various possible other avenues that may has been taken. Mistakes could make the team smarter and stronger.

What went wrong?
What were the influencing factors?
What did we not do right?

They could review the outcome in relation to the other influencing factors and analyse how the failed outcome came about. This would provide an in-depth insight to the problem. This in turn would strengthen the team's future processes of idea generation or decision making processes.

3. Devise new strategies

Once the mistake has been reviewed and analysed the team has a clear view of the factors that led to the failed outcome. With these revelations the team could start to rebuild. It must begin by implementing corrective measures to eliminate the same mistake occurring again in the future. It is necessary to review the team dynamics and attend to any conflicts or factors that have a negative influence on the team. Mistakes are an opportunity for the team to rebuild and rise even stronger.

Mistakes are a common occurrence in business, however if the same mistake is reoccurring, the business is in dire need of assistance. This is because mistakes may be small but when they are repeated their impact is huge. This starts to threaten the business' viability. Therefore ignoring an even minute mistake and letting it reoccur is not a risk a small business owner can afford.

REASONS FOR ATTENDING TO MISTAKES[6]

✓ The size of the mistake itself, which is usually small

✓ The size of the consequences if the mistake is not found and corrected, which can be huge

✓ The size of the time and cost it will take to fix the mistake

✓ The size of the causes of the mistake

✓ The size of the effort to prevent the mistake from happening again

✓ The size of the benefits from ensuring the mistake doesn't happen again

---

6   Learn From Your Mistakes, published on 24 September 2009
    http://www.entrepreneur.com/article/203498, accessed 12 June 2014.

ACTIVITIES

A. CHECK YOUR UNDERSTANDING

Teams

1. Define 'a team' in business.

2. What is meant by 'life stages' of a team?

3. List and define the stages of a team life cycle.

4. Name and explain the two forms of team that exist in business.

5. Define and give example of the following:

   A.   A virtual team

   B.   A project team

   C.   A cross-functional team

6. Why are formal teams a benefit to small business?

7. Identify the six roles within a team and define each of them.

8. What is team building?

9. What are the social skills necessary in a team member?

10. What are the four characteristics of an effective team?

Collaboration

1. Define collaboration in teams.

2. Define coordination.

3. Define cooperation.

4. What are the four common barriers to collaboration?

5. Define self-management.

6. What are four essential factors for collaboration in teams?

7. List five ways to promote collaboration in teams.

Creativity and innovation in teams

1. Define creativity.

2. Define innovation.

3. What are the two process of creativity?

4. List three factors within a team that induce creativity and innovation.

5. Define openness and honesty.

6. What are the three steps to learning from bad decisions or failures?

7. Give six reasons why it's important to attend to mistakes and take ownership.

B. BUSINESS RESEARCH

1. Visit the *SlideShare* site: **www.slideshare.net** and view the slideshow on the topic 'teamwork'. There is a large range; your teacher will guide you on which power point is most suitable for your activity.

   Select 7 quotes from the selection available. Clearly outline how each of those quotes applies to a small business concept. Present your response in the form of a slide presentation.

2. Conduct an online image search (**www.pinterest.com** or **www.google.com**) for the following key words:

   - Team
   - Team building
   - Collaboration
   - Mistakes

   Select a quote for each word that appeals to you most. Design a postcard for the quote, image or words you've selected. Within the postcard include a note describing why this quote appeals to you in communicating the true sense of those key words in small business teams.

3. Access the website **www.teampedia.net** for a range of practical activities and information on team building and collaboration.

   With teacher guidance form small teams of 4-6 members and complete the following:

   A. Research the topics 'Teamwork' and 'Ice Breaker Activities'.
   B. Trial at least five activities. Discuss how these activities are effective in making your team work together well. Analyse any problems with the activities.
   C. Present your findings to the class in the form of a group presentation. You may choose to have visual aids.
   D. Complete a written reflection on your role as a team member.

C. RESPONSE

1. A team consists of a group of individuals with a range of skills, knowledge and experiences working together to achieve the same goal. In this process each member of the team holds roles and responsibilities. These roles are assigned or undertaken based on each person's skills, knowledge and experiences. In pairs, respond to the following questions with reference to team roles and their requirements.

    A. Identify the six major roles that exist within a team and define them.

    B. For each of those roles, identify three skills and two aspects of knowledge or prior experience that would support the role.

    C. Now look around your classroom and assign a colleague to each of those roles and justify your reasons for assigning that role to them. Your justification must include what skills, knowledge or experiences they have that would assist them in performing that role effectively. Be positive and respectful in your remarks.

2. You are setting up a team to promote a youth event in your home town. You have decided to invite your role model, may it be a sportsperson, musician, politician, business person, anyone you choose, to become the ambassador for the event. You also want them to hold an office in the team and contribute.

    This is a two-part activity.

    Part A – To be completed in pairs or groups.

    Prepare a report as to how you plan to set out this team. In your report include the following:

    A. What form of team would you require for this project, an independent or interdependent team? In your response draw links to the definitions of those forms of teams and their structures.

    B. Referring to the six stages of a team's life cycle, make assumptions as to what jobs or duties the team could be undertaking during each of those stages. Identify what challenges the team will be facing during those stages. Present your response in the form of an oral presentation. Provide supporting notes.

    NOTE: Your teacher may choose to insist on written notes as evidence of planning to provide you with a grade.

    Part B – to be completed individually

    A. Research your role model of yours and identify their strengths, weaknesses, skills, knowledge and experiences. List these.

    B. Now decide which team role you would assign to them.

    C. Validate your reasons within a two-page report with supporting evidence from your research and ream roles description from the text.

3. Your local council has reached out to the youth of your town, calling for tenders for a proposal for a Youth Activity/Entertainment Centre. Previously, teams have come together to try and prepare this proposal but have been in conflict. A cohesive team needs to tender for this project which is a great opportunity for the town.

    In groups of 3 respond to the following and present your findings in a formal report.

A. What are the possible factors leading to conflict among teams in the past?

B. What personal and social skills could assist these teams to function effectively in the future and why?

C. Analyse and identify how these teams can enhance collaboration. Support your response with evidence from the text and give reasons why your suggested strategies would be effective.

D. How can employing the creativity and innovation aspects of teamwork benefit this type of team? Justify your responses.

E. How could these teams have learnt from their mistakes? Explore the possibilities and present a recommendation.

D. GROUP PROJECTS

I. Cooperative games are a great way to help young people learn crucial teambuilding skills. Read the following team building games, that aim to foster critical thinking, teamwork and communication skills.

In groups, complete these team building games. Discuss how you applied teamwork to the task at hand, why teamwork helped you complete the tasks, and tactics you used that did or didn't work.

GAMES:

• **Fingertip hula hoop**

In this game, students stand in a circle and raise their arms, then extend their index fingers. The group supervisor places a hula hoop so that it rests on the tips of the students' fingers. Students are told that they must maintain a fingertip on the hula hoop at all times, but are not allowed to hook their finger around it or otherwise hold the hoop; the hoop must simply rest on the tips of their fingers. The challenge is for the students to lower the hoop to the ground without dropping it. To make this more challenging, you can place communication constraints on the students – no talking or limited talking, for example.

• **Don't wake the dragon**

This game has a fun element of pretend. The premise is that the students are villagers in a town under siege by a fire-breathing dragon. The only way to save their village is to line up in order of height. But, they can't talk to each other, or they'll wake the dragon! Once the students feel they have lined up correctly, they should simultaneously say 'Boo!' to scare away the dragon.

• **Group jump rope**

This simple game encourages teamwork while incorporating healthy movement and coordination. Two adults hold the ends of a large jump rope and swing it, with the students standing in the middle. All the students must jump together at the same time or it won't work. You could break the students into groups to compete and see which group can land the most successful jumps in a row.

• **Minefield**

In this game, students learn cooperation. It also segues nicely into a discussion about diversity. To play, first set up an obstacle course. Students play the game in pairs. One child is blindfolded and the other child attempts to verbally navigate their partner through the obstacles. Be sure to reconfigure the course between each team; that way the students watching their peers play won't know what to expect when it's their turn to be blindfolded.

- **Human knot**

  Human Knot is a simple game that can be played without props both indoors and outdoors. This game teaches both problem solving and teamwork skills. Students stand in a closed circle, facing inward, and place their hands and arms in the center of the circle. At random, students hold on to the hand or wrist of their peers. The challenge is now for the students to disentangle themselves. This game works best with small to medium sized groups. To make the task more challenging, try having the students complete the activity without talking.

- **Cross the river**

  In this game, students must collaboratively cross a 'river'. You can create a river by making two parallel lines on the ground. Try using sidewalk chalk if you are outside or masking tape if you are inside. Each team of students is given six square cardboard 'rafts' to use in crossing the river. Impose rules on the rafts to encourage the teams to apply critical thinking skills. For example, if a raft is left unattended, it will float away; or if a raft has more than two feet and one hand on it, it will sink. A monitor is required to remove the rafts that are out of play. Break students into smaller groups and have them compete to see who can cross the river fast enough for an added challenge.

- **Stranded!**

  This game requires students to be resourceful and work together to save their 'stranded' peers. As in Cross the River, you will need to cordon off a body of water. Designate two or more students to play the part of the stranded islanders. The students on the main shore must use what they can find to fashion a life line to pull their stranded friends to safety. They may use their shoelaces, clothing or other items they can find in the classroom.

- **Circle sit**

  This simple but effective activity is fun for students and adults. It teaches teamwork as well as a little bit of physics. First, have everyone stand in a circle facing inward. Then, each person rotates a quarter turn in the same direction. If everyone is standing close enough together, they can sit on the lap of the person behind them, all at the same time, and remain supported.

See more at: **http://online.brescia.edu/social-work-2/team-building-exercises/#sthash.bXg4tUht.dpuf**

or **www.huddle.com/blog/team-building-exercises/**

CHAPTER 17
Entrepreneurship

'Highly successful people have three things in common:
motivation, ability, and opportunity.'

– A Grant –

Successful business men and women who have a good understanding of their capabilities and weaknesses are those who show emotionally intelligent traits or habits in their behaviour day in and day out. They are known as enterprising people and entrepreneurs. They have very effective self-management skills, and a range of both inherited and learnt skills, attitudes, traits and characteristics, which they utilise in their approach to business and life. They are able to adopt skills they lack, or employ them through others who are rich in those skills and abilities.

This chapter explores who is an enterprising person; what their traits, skills and attributes are; and how those traits influence their small business and their team. Entrepreneurial characteristics are outlined to identify how they have an impact on success for an enterprising business owner.

BEING ENTERPRISING

An enterprising business owner is a confident person with the initiative and self–determination to pursue and conquer personal and professional challenges. They demonstrate internal drive to realise a dream, consider failure as a learning opportunity, strive for positive change and improve strategies. They demonstrate a range of **enterprising skills** in their day-to-day approach to business and life. These skills can be attained as result of life experiences or can be learned.

Enterprising skills: abilities that may be gained through experience and developed through practice.

Enterprising individuals succeed and their traits are worthy of adapting. Enterprising individuals have balance in their life. They know what it is to have work-life balance.

Very successful small business owners tend to be enterprising individuals. Such enterprising individuals demonstrate certain **traits** that distinguish them.

Trait: a distinguishing characteristic or quality, especially of one's personal nature.

A list of common and influential enterprising traits are presented in Figure 17.1. These characteristics are evident in the entrepreneurial practices of successful business women and men.

Figure 17.1: Enterpising traits

Risk taking

Risk taking is the unknown or unpredictable element about a particular project and its outcome. The key difference between the risk taking behaviours of an enterprising individual versus a less enterprising person, is their approach and attitude towards the project.

A less enterprising person would perceive the risk as a threat and either be less interested or seek alternative projects. An enterprising person would perceive the risk as challenge, explore the level of risk involved and type of challenges it presents, and evaluate the risk prior to making a decision.

Entrepreneurs in particular get excited over challenges and risk based projects and thrive on them.

Optimism

Optimism is a sense of hopefulness and confidence about the future success of a project. Optimism allows enterprising individuals to view the world with a positive outlook and downplay the challenges ahead. This promotes positive thinking, induces creative thought and assists with persevering with the chosen approach to fulfil a goal or project.

An optimistic attitude is valuable to an entrepreneur, as long as this does not crowd out reality. Enterprising individuals tend to influence others and, as a result, promote a positive and forward thinking business culture.

Creativity

Creativity involves developing new concepts or new connections between existing concepts. Creative thought results in originality and is the act of making something new. When an enterprising individual is presented with a challenge or problem they instinctively start to develop ideas and strategies to overcome it. They are not afraid to use their intuition and take the risks needed to solve a problem. They are creative thinkers with infectious optimism who develop great ideas. This ability provides them an edge as they are able to generate ideas to maintain a unique and innovative approach to their business.

Perseverance

Perseverance is continuing on the chosen path regardless of opposition or challenges. Perseverance is a result of commitment and optimism, giving a sense of confidence in the chosen approach.

To facilitate perseverance in their approach, enterprising individuals seek knowledge and experience regarding their project, they analyse and evaluate the threats ahead, they plan and develop strategies, and move forward with an optimistic attitude.

Figure 17.2: Attributes of a persevering individual

Autonomy

Enterprising individuals have a strong sense of personal autonomy. Autonomy is when an individual is in control of themselves and their direction in life. An autonomous person tends to demonstrate behaviours where they are able to control their environment. They want to choose their own way, to create their own path. They believe in their destiny.

Autonomy is a result of other characteristics such as self-confidence and optimism. Enterprising individuals are confident individuals who are self-assured and believe in their abilities. They know their strengths and build on them. They know their weaknesses and compensate for them. This deep knowledge provides them with a sense of autonomy.

INNOVATION AND OPERATIONS

Three young mothers who James Dyson[2] is a British industrialist whose claim to fame is the Dual Cyclone bagless vacuum cleaner. Dyson's invention helped revolutionise the vacuum cleaners along with other appliances in the world. His perseverance at finding an innovative solution resulted in his invention becoming the most successful in this industry, making him a fortune.

Other enterprising skills, attributes and attitudes

Enterprising individuals demonstrate many features that lead to their success. Most of these factors overlap from one to the other and influence one another. Figure 17.3 distinguishes between the skills, attributes and attitudes of an enterprising individual.

---

2   James Dyson, www.dyson.com.au, accessed 10 June 2014.

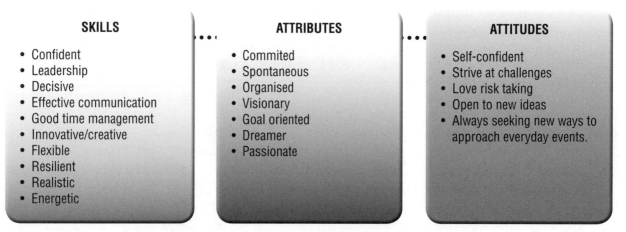

Figure 17.3: Skills, attributes and attitudes of an enterprising person

Being enterprising may not be perceived as a naturally inherited trait; however, a person's upbringing, life experience, inspirations and motivation together with 'learned skills' could lead to the development of an enterprising person. Successful people are enterprising individuals who promote change, design creative ideas to resolve problems, and lead with confidence. The manner in which enterprising individuals pursue their goals sets them apart from others and allows them to make their mark.

ENTREPRENEUR

Entrepreneurs are self-motivated individuals who demonstrate initiative and optimism and who take calculated risks. They look for opportunities and act after careful analysis of alternative courses of action.

Business oriented entrepreneurs may effortlessly become business leaders, due to their highly developed intrapersonal skills. They can develop efficient and committed business teams and inspire their team to succeed.

Elements of entrepreneurship in small business

Some individuals, businessmen and women in particular, demonstrate elements of entrepreneurship in their approach to business. The entrepreneurial approach benefits both the business owner and employees as it promotes a positive work environment with high morale and commitment. Figure 17.4 lists commonly demonstrated entrepreneurial elements in small business owners.

Entrepreneur: a person who undertakes planning, management and control of a reasonably risky business operation.

INNOVATION AND OPERATIONS

An individual such as Andrew Forrest 'Twiggy'[3] displays immense levels of enterprising behaviour. He has undertaken high risk projects from the early days of his business ventures. He has faced many failures and drastic challenges. However, he never gave up but continued to be motivated through his failures and employed innovative and talented people in his business operations in search of success.

---

3   Andrew 'Twiggy' Forrest, www.fmgl.com.au, accessed 10 June 2014.

ENTREPRENEURIAL ELEMENTS OF SMALL BUSINESS OWNERS

✓ Have a clear understanding of the purpose and vision of their business venture.

✓ Inspire and continuously motivate.

✓ Reward, develop and train employees.

✓ Employ new technologies to ensure efficiency.

✓ Strive to maintain an effective and harmonious working environment; for example, by organising many social outings and events to bond as a team.

✓ Promote ethical business practices and human relationships.

✓ Control and manage with a system that is mutually understood and respected by all members of the team.

Figure 17.4: Entrepreneurial elements of small business owners

Entrepreneurial characteristics

Entrepreneurs are individuals with passion, drive and devotion. An entrepreneur's motivation for their work is infectious and addictive. Yet with all the success and challenges an entrepreneur can be humble. An entrepreneurial business owner possesses certain **characteristics**. These are vital elements of their success. Figure 17.5 explores some common characteristics, which are outlined in detail in this chapter.

Characteristic: a distinguishing feature or quality that helps identify, tell apart or describe recognisably.

INNOVATION AND OPERATIONS

Muzz Buzz is an West Australian-owned and operated drive-through coffee franchise chain, originating in Perth. Established in the metropolitan suburb of Belmont, Western Australia in 2001, Muzz Buzz has seen rapid expansion in recent years. Franchising of the brand commenced in 2004, with individual outlets closely resembling the original design and ethos, a 'carbon-copy' franchise model.

Muzz Buzz was formed in response to growing Australian tastes for premium coffee which was, at the time, not commonly available within the Perth metropolitan area in drive-through form.

Most individuals would have considered opening another coffee sales business to be limited in profitability. However, the entrepreneurial traits of the creator of Muzz Buzz combined with an unwavering desire to succeed has made this business a success.

Muzz Buzz locations can be found in over 35 locations within the Perth metropolitan area, and there are 10 stores in Victoria, two in QLD, two in SA and two in New Zealand.

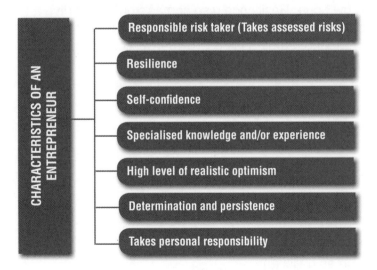

Figure 17.5: Characteristics of an entrepreneur

INNOVATION AND OPERATIONS

Timothy Goodman[4], a creative designer, decided to change his life by giving up his day job as the in-house designer at Apple[5] to find a career following his passion for design. His unique approach to establishing this combined with his entrepreneurial characteristics has resulted in it becoming a reality with his own design studio and top-listed clients. His top rated client list includes J.Crew, MoMA and the New York Times. He lives by the motto 'never give up on what you really want to do. The person with big dreams is more powerful than one with all the facts'

H.Jackson Brown J

---

4   Thomas Goodman, tgoodman.com, accessed 10 June 2014.
5   Apple Computers, www.apple.com, accessed 10 June 2014.

Responsible risk taker (takes assessed risks)

Risk is an essential part of success, and assessing risk is the underlying key. Success is a result of seizing a good opportunity at the right time. Various levels of risk are associated with business opportunities. To be able to unpack a business opportunity to identify its true potential, a small business owner requires knowledge to fully explore the risk of the business venture.

An entrepreneur would seek the necessary information to assess whether the risks are worth the potential success. The key difference between an ordinary business owner and an entrepreneur is that the entrepreneur seeks the necessary information regarding a business venture, then assesses the risks and make an informed decision whether or not to take the opportunity.

Examples of business risks include:

- current and future demand for the product or service
- production, marketing and sales costs of the product or service
- anticipating the threats associated with the venture
- current and future market trends of the potential market
- finance requirements for initial set-up and operating.

Resilience

Entrepreneurial resilience is a distinguishing characteristic. Resilience is the ability to continue functioning effectively while faced with stress, anxiety and challenge.

Resilience is developed through life experiences, where an individual may improve their thinking, self-management and knowledge. Resilience also comes from supportive relationships with parents and peers, and other factors such as cultural beliefs and traditions. These all assist the entrepreneurial small business owner to cope with the challenges faced in their business life.

Factors that contribute to resilience include:

- close relationships with family and friends
- a positive view of self
- self confidence
- the ability to manage strong feelings and impulses
- good problem solving and communication skills
- feeling in control
- a willingness to seek help when necessary
- seeing oneself as resilient (rather than as a victim)
- coping with stress in healthy ways and avoiding harmful coping strategies
- helping others
- finding positive meaning despite difficult or traumatic events.

Challenges faced by entrepreneurs

Entrepreneurs face many challenges in the current business environment. Some of these examples are outlined the figure below. Successful entrepreneurs, however, manage these demands on themselves and their personal life effectively. These individuals live a very active life style, both mentally and physically. They are highly organised and committed. These entrepreneurs have very good self-management skills and cognitive skills. They recruit the services and skills of others who are able to assist them to be organised and healthy so they can deal with the stresses presented by their businesses. These facilitate resilience in these successful individuals.

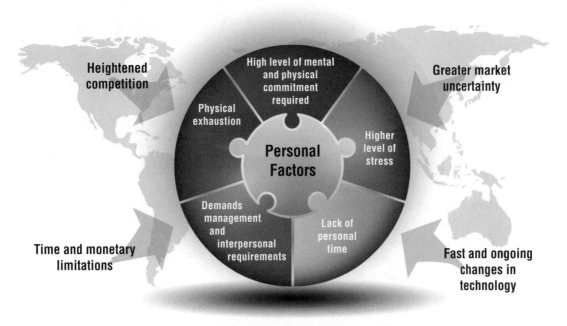

Figure 17.6: Challenges faced by entrepreneurs

Self-confidence

Self-confidence is a character trait that needs nurturing. It is highly influenced by an individual's life experiences and how they have learned to view themselves in different circumstances.

Ways to promote self confidence include the following:

- Be honest and respectful.
- Acknowledge self-doubt and attend to fear.
- Be informed of the world.
- Surround yourself with trustworthy reliable people.
- Assess challenging situations fully with an open mind.
- Attempt new and challenging experiences or business ventures.
- Ask questions and develop knowledge.

Entrepreneurs have a firm belief in their self-worth, their skills and abilities as well as their chances of success. Self-confidence together with a sense of self-worth allows entrepreneurs to perceive that they are a gift for the venture and gives them sense of authority. This in turn promotes an innate drive for facing challenges head-on to strive for success.

The most significant factor about self-confidence in entrepreneurs is that their confidence is never shattered in the face of failure. They learn from their failures, acquire new skills and knowledge, thrive on challenges and their self-worth keeps them focused on the big picture, allowing self-confidence to strengthen.

Specialised knowledge and/or experience

In-depth knowledge about a product that a business is marketing is vital to small business success. Business owners are sometimes undertaking business ventures due to their probortunity. Therefore, they may not be a specialist in that business. Entrepreneurs, however, tackle this obstacle by investing both time and resources to attain knowledge about the business venture. Entrepreneurs are aware of the importance of knowledge in making the new business venture a success.

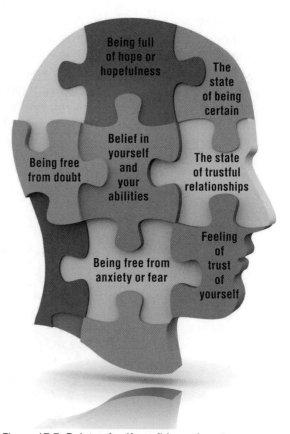

Figure 17.7: Points of self-confidence in entrepreneurs

Ways to generate and gather specialised knowledge include the following:

- Undertake research and learning.
- Employ individuals who specialise in the field of interest.
- Research market information.
- Access product or service information.
- Access business environment reports and media releases.
- Become personally involved in the processes involved within the business.

Entrepreneurs are constant learners, they learn from their day to business activities and experiences, from other professionals, and from the general public. They take special interest in fields of knowledge that contribute to their business ventures.

INNOVATION AND OPERATIONS

Sir Philip Green[6], a billionaire, who made his fortune in garments retailing, claims that the cornerstone of his success is his knowledge of the 'rag trade'. He, presumably, can price a fabric simply by rubbing it between his fingers. Just by looking at a rack of coats he can predict which ones won't sell next season. That's the kind of knowledge required in order to become successful in entrepreneurship.

---

6   Sir Phillip Green: CEO Arcadia Group, http://www.arcadiagroup.co.uk, accessed 10 June 2014.

Realistic optimism

Realism is a person's willingness or ability to accept a particular situation as it is and deal with it in a realistic sense. **Optimism** is a sense of hopefulness and confidence about the future success of a venture.

Optimism alone could lead a business owner to make non-viable business decisions; however, combined with realism they are protected against unrealistic optimism. Entrepreneurs have a positive outlook due to their self-confidence, ability to assess risks effectively, and their access to specialised knowledge, which makes it possible for them to be optimistic. This provides them with a realistic view of the situation or the business venture, allowing them to make good decisions. This enhances their optimism for a business project.

Determination and persistence

Entrepreneurs are faced with demanding hours of work, they need to be firm and assertive, and they need to make unpopular but necessary decisions. All these make them somewhat unpopular, which could lead to uncertainty and loss of confidence. However, successful entrepreneurs have a strong sense of determination to achieve their goals and persist for the success of the business venture.

Determination is a characteristic of being firm and committed. Persistence is the ability to continue to follow a project regardless of the opposition or challenges faced. Therefore these two characteristics combined provide the ability for an entrepreneur to face obstacles in the business environment as driven by their commitment, desire to progress and ability to tackle challenges,

The passion the entrepreneur has for the business venture is the inspiration for this level of determination and persistence; a distinguishing fact between an entrepreneur and mere business owner. A successful entrepreneur will persist regardless of failure with amendments to the their approach; however, they also know when to stop a business venture. Instead of being disheartened over the failed effort, they take responsibility for their actions and learn from their mistakes.

Taking personal responsibility

Taking responsibility has two parts. It involves taking responsibility for the direction of the business, and taking ownership of actions and outcomes.

When taking responsibility for the direction of their business, entrepreneurs recognise that if a problem or a challenge exists and requires change, it needs a response. They act upon the required change and lead the change as they recognise that change for the good starts with self. Instead of complaining about a problem they seek out a solution, they become the solution. This leads to efficiency and promotes positive action within the business that is led by the entrepreneur.

As leader of the business and the key decision maker the business owner is ultimately responsible for the impact of decisions on the business. This is particularly important when the decisions made result in undesirable outcomes. When the entrepreneur recognises that they have made a mistake, they acknowledge the reason.

Figure 17.8: Ways to take responsibility

Entrepreneurs engage in this, taking responsibility and sharing responsibility for both success and failures, because they are aware of the benefits.

The benefits of taking responsibility for failures include the following:

- It demonstrates leadership, humility, strength and vulnerability.
- It allows the entrepreneur to build strong and trustworthy relationships with teams.
- It promotes commitment and team coherence.
- It eliminates a 'blame culture' inducing a sense of safety for team members.

Entrepreneurs also share their wins with their business teams, promoting a sense of belonging and ownership. They recognise the effort of every member regardless of how minute the contribution may be. This enhances overall staff morale leading to business success.

ACTIVITIES

A. CHECK YOUR UNDERSTANDING

Being enterprising

1. What does being enterprising mean?

2. Define the terms 'enterprising skill' and 'trait'.

3. List five enterprising traits.

4. What is risk taking?

5. Define optimism.

6. How is creativity considered an enterprising trait?

7. What is the role of perseverance in being enterprising?

8. List five attributes of a persevering individual.

9. Define autonomy in relation to enterprising skills.

10. Make a list of other enterprising attitudes, attributes and skills.

Entrepreneur

1. Who is an entrepreneur?

2. List seven elements of entrepreneurship evident in enterprising small business owners.

3. What is an entrepreneurial characteristic?

4. List six entrepreneurial characteristics.

5. What is responsible risk taking?

6. Define the terms 'resilience', 'realistic', 'optimism', 'determination' and 'persistence'.

7. List five factors that contribute to resilience in a person.

8. What are internal and external challenges faced by entrepreneurs?

9. List four aspects that lead to self-confidence in an entrepreneur.

10. How do entrepreneurs attain 'specialised knowledge' and/or 'experience'?

B. BUSINESS RESEARCH

I. Undertake the personality test on **www.123test.com/personality-test** to identify what enterprising traits are dominant in you and identify what personality category you are in. Share your findings with your fellow class mates.

Following the above activity complete the career quiz on **www.carecareers.com.au**. You will be required to select the drop down menus: *careers* and *quiz*.

2. Engage in a class discussion with your teacher's guidance about the following:

   • Did you get allocated the career option you hoped you would or is it different?
   • Why do you think this is? Give reasons.

3. The following site is designed and influenced by successful entrepreneurs. Visit the site and engage in the interactive activities and quizzes.

   • **www.enterprising-women.org**

4. Visit the **www.lifehack.org** website. This has an article on the topic of '21-entrepreneurship-websites-worth-checking-out'. Explore the sites available in this article and identify how the current entrepreneurs have facilitated opportunities for future up and coming entrepreneurs to make their first business start-up a reality.

Write a short report on your findings.

5. Visit the following sites and see how you could establish a 'Young Entrepreneurs' program at your school.

   • **www.hubaustralia.com/spark/**
   • **www.youngentrepreneur.ie**

C. RESPONSE

1. Research at least four young up and coming entrepreneurs and prepare responses to the following questions. Select one entrepreneur and complete a written report summarising your findings.

   A. What are the motivations behind their business start-ups?
   B. What are the common enterprising traits evident?
   C. What key entrepreneurial characteristics have they demonstrated?
   D. What is their attitude towards risk and how have they dealt with it?
   E. Who is your favourite entrepreneur? Justify your response with evidence relating to their personality and entrepreneurial traits.

2. Explore the success stories of two entrepreneurs who are Perth based with both state and national markets.

Examples:

- Dome Coffee – Patria Jaffries and Phil May
- The Jungle Body – Tara Simich
- Muzz Buzz Coffee – Warren Reynolds
- Naked Bean Coffee – Pat McSweeney

Prepare a report explaining how creativity and innovation are evident in their approach to their particular business venture. Outline evidence of these two attributes in the the planning, establishment, operational and expansion stages of their businesses.

3. Research the stories of three successful and well established entrepreneurs. Focus on their 'start-up days' and the challenges and failures they faced at the early stages of establishing themselves.

Prepare a presentation covering the following:

- What failures did they endure?
- What impact did failure have on them?
- How did they rebuild themselves?
- What was their attitude and approach to failure and challenges?
- What lessons did they learn?
- What are the common traits of 'entrepreneurship' that are evident in all of them?

D. GROUP PROJECTS

1. Research the success story of one of the young Australian entrepreneurs listed below or select one that has inspired you.

- Bradley 'Brad' Smith: 2010 Young Australian of the Year for Tasmania Australian Young Entrepreneur of the year.
- Janine Allis: Boost Juice founder and owner.
- Adam Boyle: Pegasus CEO.
- Naomi Simson: Internet marketing guru web-based business owner of Redballoon.

Prepare a case study revealing their inspirations, motivations, challenges, failures and the personal and professional attributes that contributed to their success. Share their success story with your class via a presentation on your selected young entrepreneur.

CHAPTER 18
Mind Matters

'Logic will get you from A to B. Imagination will take you everywhere.'
– Albert Einstein –

Creativity combined with critical thinking generates unique and novel business concepts and approaches to business operations. Creativity is both a natural trait and can be generated through the use of critical and creative thinking tools. This chapter gives insight into creativity and critical thinking in the workplace. Creative and critical thinking tools are explored. Harmonious working environments that facilitate improved performance, innovation and creativity and an 'edge' over competitors are outlined.

For small businesses to thrive in today's competitive global market, the business owner needs to be a shrewd decision maker and take opportunities as they arise. Differentiating between a successful venture and one that is not, is crucial to success as well as to securing future viability. Tested and proven business decision making tools are explored within this chapter to enhance understanding of how these could be used in small business.

CREATIVE THINKING

Creativity in business is the process of developing marketable ideas that can be implemented in daily business practices or marketed as a product (good or service). It involves developing new concepts, or new connections between existing concepts. Creative thought produces both **originality** and appropriateness and is the act of making something new.

Creativity: imagination or inspiration of new ideas or thought.

Originality: novelty or uniqueness.

Creativity is a natural gift for some and others acquire it through life experiences, education, training and development. In the small business context, creativity could occur in the form of either a product or service.

There are five main stages in the creative process and the process can be commenced at any point in the cycle.

 Firstly the small business owner recognises that there is a problem that needs resolving or an individual identifies a business opportunity that is yet to be taken up.

 Secondly, this person becomes engaged by immersing themself in the opportunity or the problem.

 Thirdly, the business owner invests both time and resources to research the problem, resulting in increased understanding of the situation.

4 Fourthly, analysing the scenario with regard to possible solutions or strategies to move forward provide the business owner with choices.

5 Finally after assessing all options and potential outcomes the business owner is able to settle on a final solution or strategy.

The solution or strategy is implemented and assessed for its viability over a period of time. If effective, the strategy and solution would continue to evolve with the business' needs. If the solution fails to eliminate the problem or realise opportunities, the business owner will re-engage in this creative process to identify new alternatives.

Creativity in small businesses

Small businesses are **creative industries** that generate business and wealth through creation and utilising employee knowledge and capabilities. These types of businesses provide unique products (goods or services) to the market place or they deliver an existing product in a unique manner.

INNOVATION AND OPERATIONS

The concept of Viber is an example of thinking creatively by its creators. Viber is a mobile application that allows you to make phone calls and send text messages to all other Viber users for free! Viber is available over WiFi or 3G. "Our sound quality is much better than a regular call. Once you and your friends install Viber, you can use it to talk and message as much as you want. Viber lets everyone in the world connect. Freely." Claim the creators and marketers of Viber. Millions of Viber users call, text, and send photos to each other, worldwide- for free.

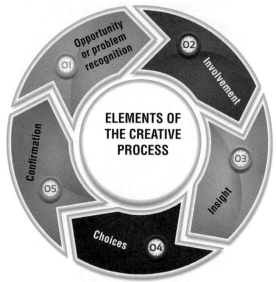

Figure 18.1: Elements of the creative process

Creative industries: businesses which operate using new concepts or by being innovative in their business approach.

INNOVATION AND OPERATIONS

Raphael Lawrence is a young artist with a knack for designing trendy business wear for young women. Raphael's dream was to become an international label; not in 20 years but in the next two years. He achieved this aim by taking his designs to online forums and advertising on popular sites. Soon he was shipping his clothes to all ends of the earth by setting up partnership with a Chinese clothing manufacturer that would design the clothes for the customer orders and Raphael's design specifications.

Emotion: a feeling or a sensation.

To be effective in a creative business, it is vital to develop and foster creativity and **emotion** over logical and analytical thought.

Creativity techniques are strategies and practices which facilitate or induce creativity within a person or group. They include:

- providing an environment that fosters creativity
- providing training and development to fster creativity
- valuing emotional input.

Table 18.I identifies the conditions a small business owner must facilitate if he or she wishes to foster creativity within their team of employees. Attending to these internal and external factors would induce creative thinking and a creative approach to work duties.

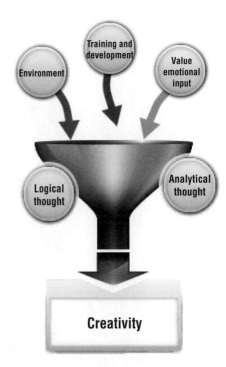

Figure 18.2: Fostering creativity

TABLE 18.1: Conditions for fostering creativity

INTERNALLY	EXTERNALLY
• Ability • Level of task enjoyment • Creative thinking activities	• A need or problem must be present • Encouragement • Respect and value ideas

Creativity strategies

Design thinking: a process for the practical, creative resolution of problems or issues.

Small business owners can use a range of strategies to induce and enhance creativity with employees. When using creativity tools it is sensible to engage in **creative thought processes** such as **design thinking** to enhance effectiveness.

Two of the well proven strategies are the SCAMPER technique and Six Thinking Hats. A range of other common creative strategies are shown in Figure 18.3 on the following page.

Figure 18.3: Creative thought processes – generating innovative ideas

Design thinking

Design thinking is one example of a creative strategy. It is based on the building up of ideas. There are no judgements in design thinking; eliminating the fear of failure and encouraging maximum input and participation.

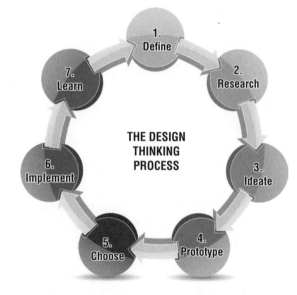

Figure 18.4: The design thinking process

Design thinking is developed around the concept that 'wild' ideas are welcome, since these often lead to the most creative solutions.

Ideate: to visualise or create a mental picture of something.

Prototype: a mock-up or model of a real product.

The design thinking process is illustrated in Figure 18.4. The stages of the **design thinking process** allow a business to frame a problem, ask questions, develop ideas and alternative solutions, and select the best outcome. These stages are not linear, and can occur simultaneously or be repeated.

Lateral thinking

Lateral thinking defines thinking as being methods of thinking that are concerned with changing **concepts** and **perception**. Lateral thinking is about reasoning that is not immediately obvious and ideas that may not be obtainable using traditional logic.

Concepts: ideas, beliefs and thoughts.

Perception: a feeling or view associated with a product or service.

INNOVATION AND OPERATIONS

Initially Farmers Market was a concept where people think of something that you can access if you live near that particular market, physically. With the emergence of online business systems, online forums such as FaceBook, Twitter, Instagram and improved delivery systems the Farmers Market concept has had a face-lift, Adelaide Farmers Market is a great example of this. Using these services together a group of creative thinking famers were able to set up a system where local producers and buyers who are interested in home grown produce meet virtually and have their produce delivered to the clients.

Techniques that apply lateral thinking to problems are characterised by shifting thinking patterns away from predictable thinking to new or unexpected ideas. A new idea that is the result of lateral thinking is not always a helpful one, but when a good idea is discovered in this way it is usually obvious in hindsight.

INNOVATION AND OPERATIONS

American business tycoon Donald Trump resolved a problem of choosing a suitable apprentice for his business management skills. Mr. Trump decided his applicants were to face a set of challenges set by him and that he would select the apprentice based on their performance and approach to dealing with the challenge.

Lateral thinking and problem solving

The concept of **problem solving** implies that there is a problem to respond to that can be resolved. That eliminates situations where there is no problem or a problem exists that cannot be resolved. It is logical to think about making a **good situation** that has no problems, into a better situation. Sometimes removing its cause cannot solve a problem. Lateral thinking can be used to solve problems and more.

EXAMPLE OF LATERAL THINKING

It took two hours for two people to dig a hole five metres deep. How deep would it have been if ten people had dug the hole for two hours?

The answer appears to be 25 metres deep. This answer assumes that the thinker has followed a simple mathematical relationship suggested by the description, but they can generate some lateral thinking ideas about the size of the hole which may lead to different answers:

- A hole may need to be of a certain size or shape so digging might stop early.
- The deeper a hole is, the more effort is required to dig it, since waste soil needs to be lifted higher to the ground level. There is a limit to how deep a hole can be dug without use of ladders or hoists for soil removal, and 25 metres is beyond this limit.
- Deeper soil layers may be harder to dig out, or the diggers may hit bedrock or the water table.
- Are we digging in soil? Clay? Sand? Each presents its own special considerations.
- Holes required to be dug beyond a certain depth may require structural reinforcement to prevent collapse of the hole.

- Digging in a forest becomes easier once you have cut through the first several feet of roots.
- Each person digging needs space to use a shovel.
- It is possible that with more people working on a project, each person may become less efficient due to increased opportunity for distraction and so on.
- More people could work in shifts to dig faster for longer.
- There are more people but are there more shovels?
- The two hours dug by ten people may be under different weather conditions than the two hours dug by two.
- Rain could flood the hole.
- Would we rather have 5 holes each 5 feet deep?
- The two people may be an engineering crew with digging machinery.
- What if one person in each group is a manager who will not actually dig?
- The extra eight might not be strong enough to dig, or much stronger than the first two.

The most useful ideas listed are outside the simple mathematics implied by the question.

Lateral thinking puzzles

When using lateral thinking puzzles it is important to check **assumptions**. The individual completing the puzzle needs to be open-minded, flexible and creative in questioning and able to put lots of different clues and pieces of information together. Once a viable solution is reached, keep going in order to refine it or replace it with a better solution.

> **Assumption:** a theory, belief or an idea about something.

THINKING OUTSIDE THE BOX

Thinking outside the box is a catchphrase used to refer to looking at a problem from a new perspective without preconceptions. This is also a process of lateral thought.

The nine dots puzzle: The challenge is to connect these dots by drawing four straight, continuous lines, and never lifting the pencil from the paper. The puzzle is easily solved, but only if you draw the lines outside of the confines of the square area defined by the nine dots themselves. Thus, the phrase 'thinking outside the box' was born.

- A hole may need to be of a certain size or shape so digging might stop early.
- The deeper a hole is, the more effort is required to dig it, since waste soil needs to be lifted higher to the ground level. There is a limit to how deep a hole can be dug without use of ladders or hoists for soil removal, and 25 metres is beyond this limit.
- Deeper soil layers may be harder to dig out, or the diggers may hit bedrock or the water table.
- Are we digging in soil? Clay? Sand? Each presents its own special considerations.
- Holes required to be dug beyond a certain depth may require structural reinforcement to prevent collapse of the hole.

One of many solutions to the puzzle:

SCAMPER strategy

SCAMPER was developed by Bob Eberle. Here, employees are given a particular set of questions, posed in order to develop new ideas or creative thought. This technique uses an approach where an individual is attempting to answer unusual questions that induce a particular thought pattern.

The aim of this technique is to encourage creative thought while the employee is attempting to find solutions to the questions.

The acronym SCAMPER, as outlined in Table 18.2, stands for seven different types of questions. For the strategy to be effective at least one question should be asked for each word in the acronym.

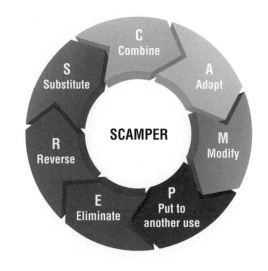

Probortunity: a term combined to state the words, problem and opportunity.

TABLE 18.2: SCAMPER acronym

S	Substitute	In the process of seeking a new product or process, new ideas are generated by thinking about substituting part of the product or process for something else.	*What can I substitute to make an improvement? What if I swap this for that and see what happens? How can I substitute the place, time, materials or people?*
C	Combine	Thinking about combining two or more parts of the probortunity to achieve a different product or process.	*What materials, features, processes, people, products or components can I combine? Where can I build synergy?*
A	Adapt	Think about which parts of the product/process could be adapted to remove the probortunity or how the nature of the product/process could be changed.	*What part of the product/ process could I change? And in exchange for what? What if I were to change the characteristics of a component?*

→

M	Modify/ Distort	Think about changing part of the current situation or distort it in an unusual way. This may create an alternative product or process.	*What happens if I warp or exaggerate a feature or component? What will happen if I modify the process in some way?*
P	Put to other use	Think of how the current product/process could be put to other uses, or think of what could be reused from somewhere else. Think of another way of solving the probortunity or finding another target market.	*What other market could I use this product in? Who or what else might be able to use it?*
E	Eliminate	Think of what might happen if various parts of the product/process/probortunity are eliminated and consider what would be done about that. This often leads to different ways of tackling the probortunity.	*What would happen if I removed a component or part of it? How else would I achieve the solution without the normal way of doing it?*
R	Reverse/ Rearrange	Think of possible outcomes if part of the product/ process/probortunity worked in reverse or was done in a different order. What would be the result if it would happen in reverse? See the probortunity from different angles and come up with new ideas.	*What if I did it the other around? What if I reverse the order it is done or the way it is used? How would I achieve the opposite effect?*

INNOVATION AND ENTERPRISE

A manufacturer of small nuts and bolts, is looking for new products. SCAMPER would assist in the following ways.

- Substitute – use of high versatility products for niche markets – eg. carbon fibre, plastics, non-reactive material
- Combine – integrate nuts and bolts? Bolt and washer? Bolt and spanner?
- Adapt – put an Allen key or Star head on bolt? Countersink head?
- Modify – produce bolts for watches or bridges? Produce different shaped bolts (eg. screw in plugs)? Pre-painted bolts?
- Put to another use – bolts as hinge pins? As axels?
- Eliminate – which item to eliminate; nuts, washers, heads, thread?
- Reverse – make dyes as well as bolts, make bolts that cut threads for themselves in material.

Six thinking hats

This technique was created by Edward de Bono[1]. It assists the business owner to engage in creative thought, developing new or changed business ideas. It gets individuals viewing a problem from a range of perspectives. This forces employees to adopt a **thinking outside the box** strategy.

> **Thinking outside the box:** a thinking pattern that is different from the norm.

The **Six Thinking Hats** strategy uses colour to differentiate 'hats' and each colour is associated with a different thinking style. The business owner can use this strategy personally or involve their employees. Figure 18.5 explains each of the six hats with their corresponding thinking style.

The main purpose for using the strategy of six thinking hats in the small business context is to promote creativity and critical thinking among the team of employees.

Other underlying benefits to using this strategy are to:

- focus on the problem at hand
- improve the thinking and problem solving process
- encourage creative, **parallel** and **lateral thinking**
- speed up decision making
- avoid debate.

> ○ **White hat (Blank sheet):** information, reports, facts and figures (objective)
> ● **Red hat (Fire):** intuition, opinion, emotion, feelings (subjective)
> ○ **Yellow hat (Sun):** praise, positive aspects, why it will work (objective)
> ● **Black hat (Judge's robe):** criticism, judgment, negative elements (objective)
> ● **Green hat (Plant):** alternatives, new approach, idea generation, provocation (speculative/creative)
> ● **Blue hat (Sky):** big picture, metapicture, thinking about thinking, (overview)

Figure 18.5: Thinking styles corresponding to the six thinking hats.

> **Parallel thinking:** a thinking pattern where similar to or corresponding patterns are used.

> **Lateral thinking:** imaginative or logical thinking pattern.

SIX THINKING HATS EXPLAINED

Gets the individual to focus on the data available.
- Look at the information available and see what can be learned.
- Look for gaps in knowledge and try to fill them or take account of them.
- Analyse past trends.
- **Extrapolate** from historical data.

Gets the individual to look at problems using intuition.
- Use gut reactions and emotion.
- Think how others will react emotionally.
- Understand the responses of people who do not fully know the reasoning.

---

1   Edward de Bono, www.debonothinkingsystems.com, accessed 19 December 2007.

Gets the individual thinking about the bad points of the decision.

- Look cautiously and defensively.
- Try to see why it might not work.
- Highlight weak points in a plan before implementing it.
- Eliminate, alter or prepare contingency plans.
- Make plans and strategies tough and more **resilient**.

Gets the individual to think positively.

- Adopt an optimistic viewpoint
- See all the benefits and the value.
- Keep going when everything looks difficult.

Gets the individual to be creative.

- Develop creative solutions.
- Think freely with no criticism.

Gets the individual to be aware of process control.

- Chair meetings.
- Point other individuals toward the use of each hat.
- When **contingency** plans are needed, ask for Black Hat thinking and so on.

DECISION MAKING

Decision making is an everyday activity that people engage in at work every day. Decision making in relation to conscious and unconscious decisions will be outlined here. Elements of decision making reveal the underlying factors that influence the work place. From a small business point of view, some effective decision making process are explored along with suggestions on how to improve decision making.

Decision making is the **cognitive process** leading to the selection of a course of action among alternatives. Every **decision making process** produces a final choice which can be an action or an opinion, which initially requires careful interpretation of the problem, and analysis and evaluation of alternatives, prior to making the final choice. The small business environment is so competitive that one simple move could make or break the viability of the business.

INNOVATION AND OPERATIONS

Lydia enters a café with the intention to buy a milkshake. The owner asks her what flavour. Then, Lydia orders a strawberry flavoured milkshake over a chocolate flavoured one. Here, Lydia is unconsciously engaging in decision making. She has made a decision based on the two options available.

Cognitive process: process of thinking or using the brain.

The factors that influence decision making in small business, and effective decision making processes, are important in business, as are suggestions on how to improve decision making. Figure 18.6 outlines the decision making process from a business context.

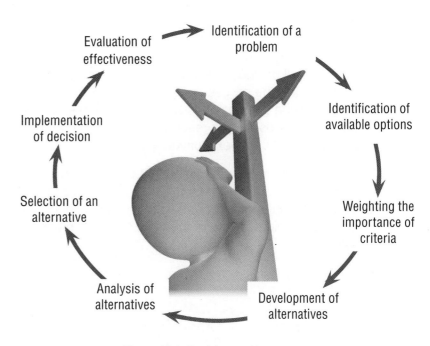

Figure 18.6: Decision making process

The decision making process firstly involves the identification of the problem elements. When elements are identified the problem may be clearly understood. Secondly, each factor is prioritised. Thirdly, alternatives should be set. This can be done through brainstorming possible options, then available options should be analysed to ensure their degree of effectiveness in resolving the problem. Following **analysis**, a single alternative has to be chosen. Then that particular solution or strategy is implemented. The decision making process does not end here. The most crucial step is the evaluation stage, through close monitoring of outcomes. Then review to see whether the problem is solved. If the problem is not resolved the decision maker or makers have to engage in the same process again until the situation is resolved.

Analysis: study or an investigation of someone or something.

Types of decision making

If a person is aware they must make a choice, they engage in exploring options and make an informed decision. However, in life people are not always given this opportunity. There are many occasions where they have to make decisions without enough information, leading to two decision types.

1. **Programmed decisions** are made in advance as the situation was foreseen, or because of a desire to change direction.

2. **Un-programmed decisions** occur when the individual is unable to make a decision until the situation arises.

Decision making tools

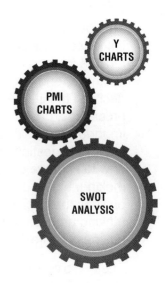

When small businesses engage in decision making, they should ideally follow the process outlined here. Two important factors when making business decisions are related to managing people, such as human resource decisions, or to managing operations, such as executive decisions.

Small business owners can benefit greatly from employing decision making tools in their everyday business practices. There are range of tools and techniques available, and this segment explores three of the most common decision making tools.

TABLE 18.3: Decision making tools defined

PMI charts	Weighing the pros and cons of a decision.
Y charts	Grouping of thoughts and ideas on a problem.
SWOT analysis	Evaluation by individual or organisation of strengths, weaknesses, opportunities & threats.

PMI charts

A PMI chart is a tool used to weigh up the advantages and disadvantages of a particular decision. PMI is an acronym for **Plus, Minus** and **Interesting**.

Elements of a PMI chart

Reviewing the points written down in the chart provides an overview to the business owner of whether it is sensible to act on the decision or if alternative strategies should be developed. To assist, the design maker can allocate negative or positive scores to each element (plus, minus and interesting). Then they add up the scores to calculate the final result. A high score indicates the decision is a good one. In contrast a negative score indicates that the decision is not a good one.

An example of a PMI chart is presented in Figure 18.7 on the following page.

Plus	Score	Minus	Score	Interesting (+ or -)	Score
TOTAL Plus		TOTAL Minus		TOTAL Interesting	
FINAL DECISION:					

Figure 18.7: Example of a PMI chart

INNOVATION AND OPERATIONS

Marco is a manager at a trucking business that has many branches throughout WA's north. The company owner, Mr Hall, has unexpectedly offered Marco a promotion. Marco is excited about the opportunity, but he knows that there are several downsides to leaving his current team of office staff and drivers to take on a new role in a new town. He decides to weigh the pros and cons of the decision using the PMI tool.

Plus	Minus	Interesting
Higher income (+4)	Much more responsibility (-2)	Challenge myself professionally? (+4)
Get to meet new people (+3)	Likely to be more stress (-4)	Will be living in a new area (+3)
Self-Confidence improves (+5)	Have to sell house and move (-5)	
	Must learn how to manage others (-2)	
+12	-13	+7

Marco scores the table as 12 (Plus) – 13 (Minus) + 7 (Interesting) = +6

For him, the promotion will be worth the stress and inconvenience that comes with the new role.

Y charts

A Y-Chart is a three part graphical grouping of ideas, thoughts and feelings about a topic. The three perspectives it aims to reveal are: **Looks like**, **Feels like** and **Sounds like**. This provides a framework for consideration.

A Y chart is an ideal strategy to involve employees in in-depth thinking on any business scenario. It encourages them to move from **concrete** descriptions, such as looks like positive body language to **abstract** descriptors, such as looks like determined, visionary. Before beginning any team work, a Y chart could be developed on effective team work; thus setting the scene for the expectations of cooperation and teamwork whilst working in groups to resolve a problem in the business or make a decision on an issue the business is face with.

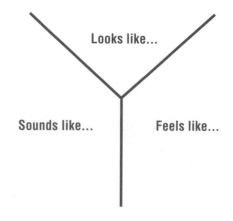

Figure 18.8: Y chart example

Elements of a Y chart

There are three elements to the Y chart and they are:

- **Looks like:** obvious aspects, as well as implied.
- **Feels like:** tactile, as well as emotional, spiritual feelings.
- **Sounds like:** encourages employees to think of the type of conversations that may be heard, as well as the obvious sounds heard.

The Y-Charts can be used in different formats as shown below.

Using Y charts

Y charts can be developed for a variety of purposes, not only for attitudinal or behavioural outcomes, but also for exploring the development of a product or design. The real value of the Y chart is that it provides a higher range of responses by which a better product or business concept can be achieved. This could be very versatile when exploring and defining the task at hand.

The guidelines in Figure 18.10 on the following page can assist a user of a Y chart to use this decision making tool.

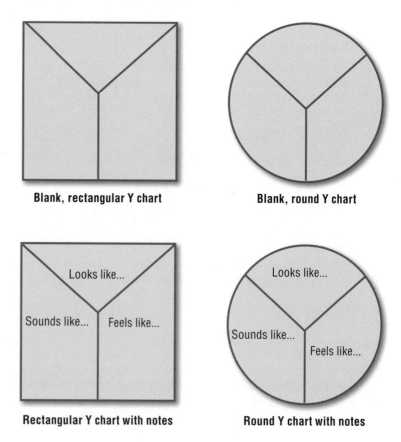

Figure 18.9: Various forms of Y-Charts

USING Y-CHARTS

- Decide on the topic to explore with employees.

- Divide employees into small groups, allocating tasks to each group member such as **recorder**, **reporter**, **time-keeper**, **organiser**.

- Hand out blank Y charts.

- Have employees brainstorm as many possibilities as they can within a time limit.

- Each group reports back.

- Discuss and clarify the topic.

Recorder: a person within a team who keeps written record of discussions.

Reporter: a person within a team who reports on their findings.

Time-keeper: a person within a team who keeps the team informed of time restrictions.

Organiser: a person within a team who controls and manages the team.

Figure 18.10: Using Y charts with employees

SWOT analysis

Small business owners are the key decision makers for their business. However, their decisions are influenced by a range of factors that are clearly identifiable using a decision making tool such as the SWOT analysis.

A SWOT analysis is a tool used to categorise and gather information about a particular situation or scenario. SWOT is the acronym for **Strengths, Weaknesses, Opportunities** and **Threats**. See Figure 18.11 on the following page.

Strengths and weakness are seen as **internal environment** factors, whereas opportunities and threats are considered **external environment** factors.

The SWOT analysis is a planning tool that is effective at evaluating the current state of a business. It explores the business' internal and external elements, comparing those which are favourable and unfavourable, and showing its position in relation to achieving the business goals. If a clear target has been identified, SWOT analysis can be used to help in the pursuit of the business mission.

INNOVATION AND OPERATIONS

Drovers Meat & Poultry[3] business owner decided to analyse his staff and their capabilities. He used a SWOT analysis and these are the results he found.

Strengths: Enthusiastic, Energetic, Imaginative, Friendly.

Weaknesses: Struggles to deal with multiple tasks at once, Requires directions, Struggles to express opinions.

Opportunities: More training, Continue on routine tasks

Treats: Other businesses looking for staff, Limited skills available locally.

INNOVATION AND OPERATIONS

When setting up Chocolate Buds[2], a unique gift hamper business as a home business, the Colalillo Family had to decide whether to sell the products from home, have market stalls, set up a shop in an arcade or use the internet. The mother and daughter team evaluated the benefits (Strengths and Opportunities) and the losses (Weaknesses and Threats) associated with each of the above locations.

---

2 Chocolate Buds – Chocolate bouquets, www.facebook.com/BabyLuvNappyCakes, accessed 10 June 2014.
3 Drovers Meat & Poultry, http://www.droversmarketplace.net.au, accessed 13 July 2014.

Figure 18.11: Elements of a SWOT analysis defined

Examples of both internal and external attributes and conditions are shown in Table 18.4.

TABLE 18.4: Examples of SWOT attributes and conditions

INTERNAL ENVIRONMENT	EXTERNAL ENVIRONMENT
Strengths and Weaknesses	Opportunities and Threats
• Financial resources	• **Takeovers** or mergers
• **Intellectual resources**	• Economic conditions
• Location	• **Joint ventures**
• Staff	• Technology
• Reputation, brand, logo	• Public expectations
• Cost advantages from business knowledge	• Competitors
• Ability to develop new products and services	• Markets
• **Intangible assets**	• Regulations and laws
• Competitive abilities	• Criticism (Media or word of mouth)
• Quality of product or service	• Environment

Intellectual resources: levels of employees' mental capability.

Intangible assets: an asset with no physical existence, such as a patent.

Joint venture: when two or more businesses combine resources on a project.

Takeover: when one business buys another business.

Using SWOT analysis

SWOT Analysis can be used in the small business context to analyse business goals or to analyse future business strategies. This tool assists the business owner/s in determining whether the chosen approach or the existing strategy or goals are viable. As the SWOT analysis provides an insight into **strengths, weaknesses, opportunities** and **threats**, the business owner has the ability to review the situation and utilise the strengths and opportunities to benefit the business while developing ways to minimise the damaging influence of weaknesses and threats.

Figure 18.12 shows examples of common uses of SWOT analysis by small business owners.

INNOVATION AND OPERATIONS

Mary, a final year accounting student is employed as a receptionist at a small financial planning business. Her employer recognises her skills in the field of accounting and the potential benefits of picking a new graduate and moulding that employee to the business. Therefore, he offers her a job position within the business at the end of her education, on a probationary period.

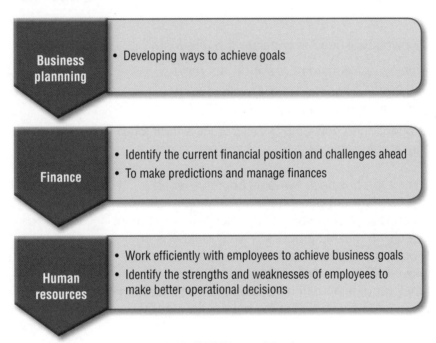

Business plannning
- Developing ways to achieve goals

Finance
- Identify the current financial position and challenges ahead
- To make predictions and manage finances

Human resources
- Work efficiently with employees to achieve business goals
- Identify the strengths and weaknesses of employees to make better operational decisions

Figure 18.12: SWOT in small business

Team decision making in the workplace

When a team of employees gathers together to make decisions, the business owner can use the techniques and decision making tools discussed above together with effective team management strategies discussed in previous chapters of this text, to efficiently address concerns and resolve problems. They should facilitate cooperation, encourage collaboration and give a voice to the opinion of all individuals affected by the decision.

GROUP DECISION MAKING

Advantages:

✓ More complete information due to brainstorming

✓ Generate more alternatives due to the range of ideas shared

✓ Increased solution acceptance due to the ability to share options

✓ Increase legitimacy

Disadvantages:

✗ Time consuming

✗ Minority opinion might dominate

✗ Pressure to conform to group members

✗ Ambiguous responsibility

The business owner will need to consider the following.

- Realise employees react to **perception** not reality.
- Understand that individuals make decisions based on what they perceive, not what is really there.
- Pay close attention to how employees perceive their jobs and management practices.

It is essential that the business owner is cautious when making decisions. Furthermore, where a business is allowing employees to engage in some decision making, it is essential to guide the decision making process. This should ensure that the final outcome will be pleasant for both the business and the employees. This is where decision making tools are versatile as they require input from employees and provide a sense of engagement with and ownership of the decision making process.

Effective decision making is an essential skill in both individual business environments and in team environments. Where people are required to work with others it is essential that everyone feels included in decision making. Therefore cooperative group decision making is an important element of any successful business.

However, the decision making process does not always flow smoothly. In group decision making, there are many ideas and strategies that are highly valued by the individuals that present them and there is a certain level of **stigma** and personal emotion attached. Each employee considers their idea to be the best; however, only a limited number of ideas will be chosen and implemented. Successful business owners are able to manage these situations effectively with good leadership skills.

Perception: a feeling or view associated with a product or service.

INNOVATION AND OPERATIONS

Local coffee shop owner, Jeffrey, decided to change his customer service approach. He discussed his ideas with his staff. Then he listened to the ideas staff had. Following further discussion and analysing the possible outcomes of their preferences, as a team they made some decisions on changes to implement.

Implementing some of these changes were not easy as they required changing staff working hours and their customer service approach. However, as Jeffrey consulted his staff he had the full support of this team. They were willing to change their ways to improve the business as they felt valued. This is an example of BEST PRACTICE in decision making.

Stigma: association of a sense of shame or disgrace with an idea.

ACTIVITIES

A. CHECK YOUR UNDERSTANDING

Creative thinking

1. Define creativity.

2. Define originality.

3. List five elements of the 'creative process' and explain them.

4. What is meant by the term 'creative industries'?

5. Define emotion.

6. List the three elements required to foster creativity.

7. What are the internal and external environmental conditions that need to be facilitated to foster creativity?

Design thinking

1. Define design thinking.

2. List eight thought processes that induce creativity.

3. List and explain the seven stages of the design thinking process.

4. Define the terms 'ideate' and 'prototype'.

Lateral thinking

1. Define lateral thinking.

2. Define the terms 'concept', 'perception' and 'assumption'.

3. List two lateral thinking/creativity tools listed within the chapter.

SCAMPER

1. What does the acronym of SCAMPER stand for?.

2. Explain the SCAMPER strategy.

3. Explain how the SCAMPER thinking tool allows a small business owner to be creative in their thinking.

4. For each of the seven types of questions in the SCAMPER strategy create a possible question you could pose to an employee.

5. Define the term 'probortunity'.

Six thinking hats

1. Define the phrase 'thinking outside the box'.

2. How does the strategy of 'six thinking hats' work?

3. What is the aim of the 'six thinking hats' strategy?

4. What are the six types of thinking hats mentioned in this strategy and what type of thinking do they promote?

5. List 5 benefits of using this strategy in Small Business.

Decision making

1. What is decision making?

2. Define cognitive process.

3. What are the elements of the decision making process?

4. List and explain the two types of decisions.

5. What are decision making tools?

6. List three decision making tools mentioned within the text and give a brief outline of what they do.

PMI charts

1. What does the acronym PMI stand for?

2. How does the PMI work?

3. What do each of the elements of PMI mean?

Y charts

1. What is a Y Chart?

2. What are the three components of this chart?

3. How does the Y chart work in decision making?

4. Draw and respond to the Y chart components, based on your current classroom environment.

5. Give five examples of how a small business owner could utilise a Y chart for decision making.

SWOT analysis

1. What is a SWOT analysis?

2. What does the acronym SWOT stand for?

3. Which components of SWOT are internal and which are external factors?

4. Give three examples for each of the internal and external attributes and conditions.

5. Why is SWOT analysis beneficial to small business?

6. What does each attribute of this strategy mean?

7. Define the following terms:
   - intellectual resources
   - intangible assets
   - takeover
   - joint venture

8. Give six examples of how SWOT can be used in small business

9. List four advantages and disadvantages of team decision making.

10. What are some aspects the small business owner must take into consideration when engaging in team decision making?

B. BUSINESS RESEARCH

1. Visit the **www.mindtools.com** and select the drop menu 'Tool Kit' then select 'Creativity Techniques'.

   A. Identify and explain how the DO IT creativity tool works and promotes creativity.

   B. Summarise this strategy into four simple steps.

   C. Explore and research how this site presents the SCAMPER theory and prepare a presentation with support notes on this theory.

      i. In your presentation you must explain the theory.
      ii. State how the theory works.
      iii. State why this is an effective strategy for creativity.

2. Visit the **www.mindtools.com** and select the drop menu 'Tool Kit' then select 'Creativity Techniques' and select the 'How Creative Are You' and take the quiz. Then calculate your score and interpret your score. Share your findings with the class.

   Your teacher may facilitate a brief in-class sharing activity.

3. Visit the **www.lateralpuzzles.com** or **www.folj.com** (select 'lateral') and attempt a few of the puzzles, under your teacher's guidance and according to the time allowed.

4. Working with your teacher, generate three example scenarios of a business owner faced with decision making. Respond to each of the scenarios using a different decision making tool (PMI, Y-Chart, SWOT) to analyse and reach a decision.

   You can select a suitable decision making tool from this chapter, or from **www.enchantedlearning.com**.

5. Visit the **www.mindtools.com** and select the drop menu 'Tool Kit' then select 'Decision Making Techniques'.

   A. Identify what other decision making tools and resources are available.

   B. State how to make effective decisions and how to ensure business decisions are sound decisions.

   C. List a few steps to improving decision making, as recommended by this site.

C. RESPONSE

1. Maale` runs a small business by the sea selling coffees and snacks for beachgoers. He also retails local craft products. Maale` has three employees helping with the day to day operations of the business. He feels it is time for some improvements in the business and its overall appeal. He intends to involve his team. As Maale`'s business analyst, you are to assist him in utilising the SCAMPER strategy to change and improve his business.

   A. Identify the seven types of questions in the SCAMPER strategy.

   B. Explain in simple terms the purpose of each question in inducing creative thought or critical thinking.

   C. Develop a list of at least three questions Maale` could pose his employees for each type of SCAMPER strategy.

   D. Anticipate the responses to each of the above questions and present this in a suitable format.

2. A group of small business owners operating businesses in the dairy industry have met together to discuss the impact of new mobile technologies and their development in the dairy industry. The business owners would like to identify methods to use and implement these new mobile technologies in their businesses. This encompasses farming, product retailing and the dairy industry generally.

   You are a business adviser specialising in critical and creative thinking. Respond to the following questions in groups or individually, depending on your teacher's instructions. Present your response in the form of a formal business report, to the small business owners.

   A. Identify and explain the aims of the six thinking hats strategy.

   B. Justify why the six thinking hats strategy could assist the dairy industry small business owners to identify new ways to use technology in their business operations.

   C. Identify each of the hats within this strategy and describe what they do for each type of thinking.

   D. Prepare a question sheet with at least three questions and possible responses for those questions, within each coloured hat, in relation to the above scenario.

3. The owner of a local fruit and veg mart is selling his business. As a potential buyer of this business you must convince the bank that it is a viable business and a good investment, if they are to assist with your finances to make the purchase. To make your claim to the bank you are preparing a SWOT analysis.

   A. What are the strong points of this business?

   B. What aspects of this business do you view to be its weakness?

   C. Are there any growth opportunities for this business and if so what are they?

   D. What threats or challenges do you foresee for this business venture in the next five years?

4. Your school's senior ball is coming up. You are one of the organisers of the ball and a keen admirer of this annual event.

   A. Using the template for a PMI chart in pairs analyse the PMIs of your school ball.

   B. Complete a Y chart for your ball and share your thoughts with your classmates via an oral presentation.

D. GROUP PROJECT

Research a case study on mothers who have set up businesses or entered the workforce while remaining to be the primary carer for their children. Use one of the following sitesfor your research or select your own with guidance from your teacher. This activity can be completed in groups of 3-4 students.

- **www.businessmums.com**
- **www.theentrepreneurialmother.com.au**
- **www.100mums.com.au**

These are case studies of Australian and international parents who have turned their business inspirations in to real business opportunities. Prepare responses to the following based on the case study and present your findings in a portfolio.

A. Prepare a brochure on your selected business providing an overview of the business, its services, customers, how it operates and so on.

B. Using the creativity process identify each of the stages of this process the business owner has engaged in her business. You may be required to make some assumptions.

C. For the selected business's product or service conduct SCAMPER and report your choices.

D. Complete a SWOT analysis for the business if it were to expand its market and employ new staff. Finally justify your decision as to whether or not to expand based on the findings.

E. Use a PMI chart to analyse the question: Should this business decrease the selling price of its main product or service?

PEOPLE CROSSWORD

Across

1. Generating solutions and ideas
5. Guides and motivates others
11. A group of people sharing ideas and solutions
13. Ending
14. Consolidating
15. A distinguishing characteristic
18. A feeling or sensation that is experienced
19. Ability to carry on when faced with stress and challenges

Down

2. Reliant on each other
3. A problem solving method that uses questions to induce creativity and solutions
4. Number of people working together
6. Reaching an agreement
7. Working together
8. A new idea being realised
9. Successful self-motivated business people with many positive traits
10. The setting up of something new
12. Time span from start to finish
13. A theory of prediction
16. A way of reaching a solution outside the traditional methods
17. Sense of positive outlook